Garlic Capital of the World

PAULINE ADEMA

UNIVERSITY PRESS OF MISSISSIPPI / JACKSON

Garlic Capital of the World

GILROY,
GARLIC,
AND THE
MAKING
OF A
FESTIVE
FOODSCAPE

www.upress.state.ms.us

The University Press of Mississippi is a member of
the Association of American University Presses.

First printing 2009

∞

Library of Congress Cataloging-in-Publication Data

Adema, Pauline.
Garlic capital of the world : Gilroy, garlic, and the making
of a festive foodscape / Pauline Adema.
p. cm.
Includes bibliographical references and index.
ISBN 978-1-60473-120-0 (cloth : alk. paper)
— ISBN 978-1-60473-121-7 (pbk. : alk. paper)
1. Food habits—California—Gilroy.
2. Garlic—Social aspects—California—Gilroy. 3. Folk festivals—
California—Gilroy. 4. Gilroy (Calif.)—Social life and customs.
I. Title.
GT2853.U5A34 2009
394.1'20979473—dc22   2008018532

British Library Cataloging-in-Publication Data available

CONTENTS

CONTENTS

PREFACE

For those with sufficient food and economic resources, food is not merely a means for survival; it is encoded with symbolic significance and is a vehicle for communication. Episodes abound throughout American history that exemplify the symbolic capacity of food. Consider, for example: the Boston Tea Party, which was not about tea but taxes; a roast turkey served in late November, meant to embody the first communal celebration between Pilgrims and Native Americans; enduring images of apple sellers and bread lines, symbolic of the rampant hunger and deprivation of the Great Depression; and Wonderbread® and Swanson TV Dinners, emblematic of 1950s food technology and changing domestic patterns.

Just as food can come to symbolize historical moments, food and place can become inscribed upon each other. Over time, through film, literature, advertising, and other media, food-place associations become ingrained in the popular imagination. Consider, for example, the widely accepted association of beef cattle and Texas, lobster and Maine, or gumbo and southern Louisiana. These associations embody complex histories, including forces of industrialization, immigration, commerce, natural resources, tourism, and the changing American sociocultural landscape. In such associations, however, the forces informing the food symbolization are condensed, and often completely abstracted: the historic, ethnic, and/or geographic sources of the association are blurred or obviated. Nevertheless, particular foods become iconic of specific places.

In the pages that follow, I scrutinize the deliberate signification of food as iconic of localities' communal identities, with particular attention to Gilroy, California, and Coppell, Texas. These two examples are emblematic of what seems to be a ubiquity of food-themed local identities across America. This investigation reveals the processes by which community leaders in these two towns choose to represent their locality—to themselves and to others— through selection of a particular food item grown or produced in the area, how this relationship is commemorated, and how the chosen identification symbol is, as a tourist attraction, iconized and becomes a defining element of the localities' identity. I consider the creation of food-themed community identities, the image makers that inform them, and how the collective, mediated identities are promoted. While most attention is directed toward image makers and the food-focused identities they advance, implicated in these discussions are the voices and experiences of those who are not part of identity formation.[1]

This study regards food not as alimentary sustenance, but as a medium for the creation of community identity. Eating is implicated in this work because eating is a primary pursuit at food festivals; privileged here, however, are the creation, festivalization, and consumption of food-themed places and communal identities. This project is not about the festival experience, per se, but about more generalized experiences of branding and consuming identity, consumption that is both literal, as festival goers eat garlic-laden foods, and ideological, as tourists plan a visit to Gilroy because of its reputation as the Garlic Capital of the World. In particular, this work considers local initiatives to differentiate place, both as a strategy to generate a sense of place among residents and as a strategy to create a sense of place that appeals to tourism and commerce.

Several questions guided this investigation of food-place symbolization. Why do some community leaders select a food item around which to build and maintain a collective identity? What is the process by which food becomes iconic and emblematic of community identity? How do the historic uses and symbolism of the iconized food shape acceptance of and responses to that food item as a marker of identity? How are place and identity realized through an association with a single food item? How do residents and visitors partake in the invention and subsequent consumption of a food-themed place? How do claims of "world capital" contribute to or detract from communal identity? Such questions of food-themed identity lead to other concerns visible on the American cultural landscape, notably the apparent desires to be part of a community and have a connection to place. This project considers one manifestation of how some planners and merchandisers use specific foods to address ongoing uncertainties about community and place. Consideration of the construction of food-themed, place-specific communal identities—one example of what I call foodscapes—builds on the literature of community studies, folklore, place marketing, and cultural anthropology and geography to offer a multidisciplinary approach to the study of creating distinction, an approach that recognizes the mutual push and pull of culture, geography, and food.

As with any study that considers the dynamics of place, food, and identity, this study also has to do with the experience of community and place. *Community* as a concept and a social reality is nebulous, multidimensional, and extremely important. As a theoretical construct and rhetorical descriptor, *community* takes on a multitude of meanings depending on its use and users. The term is loosely applied to geographically as well as non-geographically situated groups, further muddling its meaning. *Community* implies some degree of collectivity: community center, a community college, speech communities, a gated community, the international community, a couple's community property, community service, or the European Economic Community. In most instances, *community* has come to convey positive nuances and associations.

A community, a collective of individuals who share something in common and whose participants perceive a bond, is presumed to have an identity of its own. Although intangible, regional identity, ethnic identity, and national identity readily are conceived of as intrinsic. Places generally are regarded as having an identity as well, an intrinsic and perceptible essence. A neighborhood or suburb, for example, can be perceived as having a distinct identity of its own, a subcategory of the metropolitan area's identity.

For most people, " 'Community' feels good because of the meanings the word 'community' conveys—all of them promising pleasures, and more often than not, the kinds of pleasures we would like to experience but seem to miss" (Bauman 2001, 1). The sentiment that lingers in the popular imagination is that *community*, whatever it is, is assumed to have existed previously, is desirable, and can be orchestrated when or where it does not already exist.

To conceive of community as constructed, as something that can be invented, may seem oxymoronic, yet the invention of community is analogous to the "invention of ethnicity" (e.g., Conzen et al. 1992, Sollors 1986, 1989, Yancey et al. 1976). As emergent phenomena, ethnicity and community are negotiated and renegotiated, defined and redefined. The threads of change—through the processes of assimilation, accommodation, compromise, conflict, resistance, or manipulation—woven into conceptions of ethnicity appear as well in the tapestries of community.

Communities exist to the degree that people recognize affiliation or, as Benedict Anderson (1983) calls it, an imagined comradeship. Accordingly, what constitutes community is a matter of perception and interpretation by members of the group of affiliated individuals.

The nature and forms of community are affected by the forces of globalization, as are all aspects of social and economic life.[2] The concept of community has transformed from locality-oriented to non-geographically fixed expressions for which a geographical "place" is absent.[3] A paradigmatic shift in how landscape is envisaged accepts that the trope of landscape is not necessarily geographically situated. Media such as radio, television, and the Internet can function as social contexts and centers of meaning, thus creating communities not confined by traditional political or geographic boundaries. A reconception of the physical spaces so long presumed to contain communities results in new spatial renderings of those communities, and involves a similar re-envisaging of the contexts, landscapes, or –scapes that foster community. Through and within various geographic landscapes and non-geographically situated –scapes, including the foodscapes explored in this book, information and ideas flow in various directions, informing identities and other cultural realities.

Just as modern forces impact concepts and manifestations of community, they also affect the concept of and attitudes toward place. Amid the time-space compressed global market economy, there seems to be an increased value in the situatedness of place. Place, Yi-Fu Tuan observes, "supports the human need to belong to a meaningful and reasonably stable world. . . . Place helps us forget our separateness and the world's indifference" (1992, 44). The sentimental value of place is analogous to nostalgic attitudes toward community. Both are part of what Marshall Berman calls the paradox of modernity: "Our desire to be rooted in a stable and coherent personal and social past, and our insatiable desire for growth—not merely for economic growth but for growth of experience, in pleasure, in knowledge, in sensibility— growth that destroys both the physical and social landscapes of the past, and our emotional links with those lost worlds . . ." (1982, 35).

Contemporary interest in place in both the public and academic sectors is a manifestation of the paradox that the exhilaration of modern possibility is deflated by senses of loss and longing (Oakes 1997). This ambivalence results in a generalized nostalgia for what place and community connote, which effects an increased valuation of the experiential sense of place and sense of community. One consequence of these sentiments is the commodification of community and place.

The fact that town leaders perceive a sense of community as something important that can be cultivated is significant. This suggests that sense of community is identifiable, noticeable by its absence, perceived as desirable, and something that can be manufactured. Recognizing the community-building capacity of communal events, towns and cities across the country often have event coordinators within their administration. Deliberate efforts to fabricate and promote this experiential essence indicate that its role in the market economy has shifted: it has entered the realm of commodity.

One noteworthy example of the trend to market a sense of community is New Urbanism. New Urbanism is an urban design movement that gained popularity through the 1980s and 1990s, intended to retard the spread of dehumanizing suburban sprawl. The movement focuses on "the revival of our lost art of *place-making*, and is essentially a re-ordering of the built environment into the form of complete cities, towns, villages, and neighborhoods—the way *communities have been built* for centuries around the world" (New Urbanism [2005]). Although an oversimplification of the movement's principles, the aspect most relevant to this discussion can be summarized as follows: by adhering to the public policy principles and design guidelines of New Urbanism, including creating mixed-use neighborhoods that are pedestrian friendly, town planners and developers can reduce negative impact on the environment and facilitate a sense of community among residents, thereby improving their quality of life. According to its proponents, New Urbanism facilitates a quantifiable sense of community (Duany et al. 2000, Kim and Kaplan 2004). Implicit in the doctrine of New Urbanism is an understanding that sense of community is positive and desirable, and that it can be created.⁴ As testament to the planning movement's success, the organization boasts that "there are over 500 New Urbanist projects planned or under construction in the United States alone."⁵

Related to the commodification of community is the emergence of a field called place branding. Place branding, a public relations and advertising subfield of brand management, manipulates "place" through marketing and is contingent on incorporation and use of "what it considers real, authentic places" (Pedersen 2004, 77). A branded place exists vis-à-vis its acceptance by those to whom the place brand is marketed. Place branding aims to facilitate what Søren Buhl Pedersen (2004, 78) calls the "legibility of a location," something assumed by ethnographers and cultural geographers who, for generations, have "read" landscape. Through marketing, place branding aspires to create a viable collective identity, an identity that will be accepted by locals and believed by nonlocals. Although Gilroy's identity as a foodscape explored in this book was not generated by professional place branders, the rhetoric of that field parallels the processes civic-minded image makers employed in the service of community building.

The example of Gilroy is emblematic of the seemingly ubiquitous phenomenon of towns, cities, even regions, becoming associated with particular foods. Regional foodways become markers of regional identity, much as built structures come to symbolize cities in or near which they stand, for example, Times Square for New York City, or the Golden Gate Bridge for San Francisco. Such symbolic markers are necessarily selective and are therefore limited representations of the complex sites they represent. Nevertheless, they are tenacious symbols of place, the meanings of which are reinforced by visual and rhetorical representations in media, popular culture, and commercial travel literature. While the association of Gilroy and garlic may seem organic, it is not; the process of its realization is a superb study in place branding through iconizing food.

· ◆ ·

Over the years of working on this project, I have talked with many people about my interest in food and community identity, especially as articulated through place-specific food festivals. Inevitably, the persons with whom I was speaking told me of other similar festivals throughout the country that I *must* include, from the Poteet (Texas) Strawberry Festival to the Olathe (Colorado) Sweet Corn Festival to the Barnsville (Minnesota) Potato Festival. Although I've had the pleasure of attending many such festivals, there are even more that I have yet to experience. As important, fun, and exhausting as it could be to visit all the food festivals in the country for comparative research, practical constraints kept me from doing that. Through detailed consideration of two festivals—the Gilroy Garlic Festival and the Coppell PigFest—I explore the invention and subsequent consumption of food-themed place and communal identities or foodscapes. These festivals articulate the theme of cultural productions as collective self-inscriptions. Accordingly, they are read as locality-specific, food-themed place making narratives.

Place-specific food festivals involve the theming of place as well as the theming of identity. The end result of successful food-themed place branding is a mediated foodscape that is at the heart—and the stomach—of an ongoing campaign for selling place and identity. In Gilroy, California, and Coppell, Texas, image makers initiated a festival to commemorate a historic, food-themed place association for and within the hosting community. Garlic was iconized and festivalized in Gilroy; pigs in Coppell. Pigs certainly are as much fun as, if not more fun than, garlic as an organizing theme, and pigs, notoriously associated with the carnivalesque, seem more readily open to festivalization. Nevertheless, the Gilroy Garlic Festival was an immediate success and Coppell's PigFest disappeared from the community calendar after only a few years. The stories of Gilroy as Garlic Capital of the World and of Coppell's image makers' failed attempt to establish a pig-themed communal identity provide two strikingly different and equally compelling examples of the processes and consequences of branding small cities as festive foodscapes.

Garlic Capital of the World

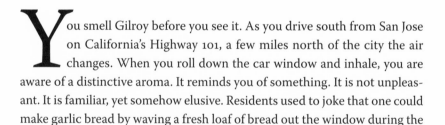

CHAPTER ONE

Making a Foodscape

Gilroy and the Iconization of Garlic

Y ou smell Gilroy before you see it. As you drive south from San Jose
on California's Highway 101, a few miles north of the city the air
changes. When you roll down the car window and inhale, you are
aware of a distinctive aroma. It reminds you of something. It is not unpleasant. It is familiar, yet somehow elusive. Residents used to joke that one could
make garlic bread by waving a fresh loaf of bread out the window during the
garlic processing season.[1] Yes, that is the smell, garlic—not burnt and acrid,
not raw and peppery, but toasted and soft.

Miles of highway bisect the expansive Santa Clara Valley. To the east
and west of the thoroughfare near Gilroy are nurseries, tree farms, orchards,
horse farms, and other visual signs that agriculture is a vital component of
the area's economy. Along one stretch on the west side of the highway north
of Gilroy is a golf course, the manicured fairways of which are in stark juxtaposition to the fields and buildings that comprise the agricultural landscape.
On the east side of the highway, parallel to Gilroy's downtown, are a series of
shopping plazas and outlet malls. In the distance to the west, barely visible
from the highway, are steeply angled roofs of recent housing subdivisions

that suggest the changing character of the area.[2] Although there are few visual cues about the importance of garlic to the city, Gilroy's distinctive seasonal smell is an olfactory reminder that Gilroy bears the title "Garlic Capital of the World."

Every year during the last full weekend in July, traffic along Highway 101 backs up each morning and remains congested throughout the day as thousands of people descend on the otherwise quiet city of Gilroy to eat garlic, braid garlic, observe a garlic cooking contest and cooking demonstrations, watch garlic being topped, and buy garlic-themed ephemera. How did Gilroy image makers settle upon a food item in general, and garlic in particular, as the icon around which to build a communal identity? Why would image makers proclaim a city as Garlic Capital of the World? How has the association of Gilroy with garlic and the yearly Festival celebrating that association transformed Gilroy into a festive foodscape? Why is a festival venerating these small, nonindigenous cloves long eschewed by Anglo-Americans so popular? This work contemplates these questions by exploring the creation and perpetuation of Gilroy's identity as a *foodscape*, a food-themed place.

・ ◆ ・

When the association between a place and a food item is abstracted, highlighted, and promoted, the communal landscape becomes a *foodscape*. Gilroy is a foodscape because its identity as a place is marketed to and often recalled among a diverse public by its association with a particular food item. Civic and local business leaders created a themed identity by promoting an association between garlic, which is grown and processed in Gilroy, and the city of Gilroy. Although Gilroy's economy comprises much more than garlic, it is the garlic association that is marketed in diverse media. Consequently, garlic tends to be what people know about Gilroy, whether or not they have been there. In nearly a decade of researching, writing about, and attending the Gilroy Garlic Festival, I mentioned it to hundreds of people. Most often, my mention of the Festival is met with recognition, and frequently with an enthusiastic recollection of or desire to attend the event; even if the speaker has never been to the Festival, she or he is familiar with the food-place association. This is especially true among former and current Bay area residents and with foodies. The former, no doubt, have seen marketing that targets them as potential Festival goers; the latter tend to know about popular or funky food-themed events because of the exposure such events receive in food-niche media. These two examples of populations knowing about a food-place association even if theirs is not a personal familiarity exemplifies the success of Gilroy image makers' efforts to market the city as a foodscape.

When a locality is known primarily for a festive performance of its food-centered identity, the locality is a *festive foodscape*. Accordingly, not only is Gilroy a foodscape, it is a festive foodscape: through frequent and successful promotion of the Gilroy Garlic Festival by image makers, including city leaders, the Visitors Bureau, and media that feature stories about the Festival, what people "know" about Gilroy is that it hosts the Gilroy Garlic Festival. Garlic and the Festival put Gilroy on the tourism map and into the popular imagination. Gilroy is not a themed city like Las Vegas, but the tenacious association between garlic and Gilroy enables me to assert with confidence that it is a city branded as a festive foodscape.

The term *foodscape* seems a simple combination of the words *landscape* and *food*. Although it is a combination of those two familiar words, *foodscape* is more complex than such reductionism suggests. *Foodscape* represents "a marriage between food and landscape, both the conceptual notion of landscape and actual, physical landscapes" (Adema 2007a); the concept necessarily incorporates each component's complexity, and the components coalesce into a new entity. *Foodscape* implicates the multiple informative historic and contemporary personal, social, political, cultural, and economic forces that inform how people think about and use (or eschew) food in various spaces they inhabit.[3]

Foodscape has no single provenance but evolved from and reflects interest within multiple academic disciplines in ways people ascribe meaning to the physical spaces they inhabit. Foodscapes articulated through place-specific food associations, the subject of this book, are one example of such ascription. *Foodscape* incorporates the geographic notion of landscape as a physical space and the sociocultural forces that inform how people deliberately or unselfconsciously use that space. Affixing the suffix −*scape* to *food* assigns the terms with multidimensional layers, what contemporary social theory recognizes as "perspectival constructs, influenced by the historical, linguistic, and political situatedness of different sorts of actors . . ."

(Appadurai 1990, 296). Accordingly, *foodscape* incorporates the dynamics of global exchange, including the translocal and transnational character of modern food practices. Embracing the term's powerful ambiguity, scholars increasingly use *foodscape* in their discussions of the social and political economies of food (Cummins and Macintyre 2002, Ferrero 2002) and, perhaps less reflectively, the food industry uses the term, for example, for food service software (www.foodscape.com).

Foodscape, like landscape, is much more than just the physical space to which it can refer. Like many ontological concepts, landscape has a tangible manifestation that can be touched, smelled, and heard. *Landscape*, however, may not refer to a specific patch of land, but more generally to an unbounded place like a geographic region, or an imagined place. Significantly, landscape also has an intangible essence that can evoke affective responses, memories, and spark imagination. Many scholars embrace the multiple sensory textures offered by landscapes, expanding beyond visual readings and toward fuller sensory awareness of them.[4] An appreciation of the multisensory "language of landscapes" facilitates an awareness of how landscapes "evoke feelings and instill memory" (Spirn 1998). The affective responses that food evokes are important aspects of individuals' and groups' food-place relationships, and while they can be challenging to access, authors including Rick Dolphijn (2005), C. Nadia Seremetakis (1994), and David Sutton (2001) demonstrate that they are assessable. Whether it is an individual's memoryscape or an association perpetuated through popular culture, the alliance of food and place creates foodscapes.

Foodscape is a useful framework for discourses about food and sites of various sizes and scales, ranging from the personal space of a body, to the social spaces of a kitchen or community, to the public spaces of a city, region, or nation. Corporeal foodscapes can include the small space of the mouth or the expansive space of the body. Similarly, the scale of personal foodscapes can range from one's body to the domestic kitchen to a foreign city where one sampled the food emblematic of that locale. The interpretive framework of foodscape reads physical landscapes, from bodyscapes to nationscapes, that have been transformed ideologically and/or literally into food-centered spaces while necessarily attending to human interaction with the physical spaces that constitute the foodscape. Foodscape refers to the food(s) peculiar to the locality and/or people under consideration, sites as well as activities like methods of procurement and preparation, consumption practices, and modes of display and performance related to those foods or practiced by those people: "Foodscapes are personal, social, cultural, political, economic, or historical landscapes that, in one way or another, are about food. . . . [They] are symbolic of real and desired identities and of power, social, and spatial relations articulated through food" (Adema 2007a).

Taking advantage of the concept's multivalence, I use it to refer to food-themed communal identities as well as to the physical spaces occupied by the cities that promote such identities. Many foodscape localities host food-themed festivals that commemorate the iconized food. The physical sense of landscape is an essential component of such food festivals for fundamental reasons: most food is derived from the earth, and festivals are situated events defined, in part, by their bounded physical site. As this and subsequent chapters illustrate, Gilroy's assertion of garlic capitaldom, based on multiple connections to the city's past and present economic, physical, and social landscapes, creates and affirms the city's status as a foodscape. The Gilroy Garlic Festival further affirms and perpetuates the city's food-themed identity.

Human use of land—as an agricultural area, as residential and commercial spaces, as festival grounds—writes meaning onto the land. Use of a plot of land as festival grounds may be ephemeral, but, with repeated use, the space can become symbolically charged as festival place. A successful food-place association commemorated through a food festival can come to signify a city, town, community, or region. A city or a neighborhood can be a festive foodscape, known among residents and nonresidents for a particular food item and/or the festival commemorating it. Because this book focuses on community foodscapes, or locality-as-foodscape, I attend not to individual actors but a collective image: the created, perceived, and perpetuated food-centered conceptions of place. In this sense, festive foodscapes are "imagined worlds . . . that are constituted by historically situated imaginations of persons and groups" (Appadurai 1996, 33). Denis Cosgrove might consider foodscapes "ideological landscapes" (1984) because foodscapes reflect and reinforce the power relations of the multiple communities coexisting within the host locales. Importantly, foodscapes as imaged places also reference one aspect of organizers' imagined relationship with nature as agricultural space. Both Appadurai and Cosgrove, I suspect, would agree that foodscapes are symbolic of place, real and desired identities, and social/spatial relations articulated through an iconized food.

Creating a foodscape is part of the spectaclization of place: designating a place as special in order to create spectacle where one previously did not exist. Place spectaclization is about differentiation of and among places, and is the foundation of a locality's promotion of a food-centered identity or other themed, mediated identity. The concept *mediated identity* exploits the rhetorical ambiguity of *mediate*. A mediated identity results, literally, from processes of mediation among residents, town leaders, and other image makers, and among those to whom the negotiated identity is marketed. It also recognizes that identity is constructed in the dialogical interaction between the individual or collective Self and Other. *Mediated* also refers to the unavoidable collaboration between the city leaders and image makers seeking to differentiate a place by creating and promoting an identity, and contemporary media that promote the place-identity. Materials that image makers and civic power brokers put forth when presenting a city, like post-cards, fliers, brochures, and television ads, or what John Dorst (1989) calls auto-ethnographies, portray image makers' desired collective identity or communal Self.

Symbolic theming of place, whether it is a Nike store or a city, is a con-stitutive part of contemporary consumer society (Gottdiener 1997). As such, theming "acts *in concert* with other aspects of political economy, especially production, in the ongoing effort of capital to accumulate wealth, on the one hand, and with cognitive and emotional elements, on the other, in a quest for identity and self-expression" (Gottdiener 2000a, 28; emphasis in origi-nal). Deliberate creation and promotion of a place as foodscape is often one strategy of place making employed to generate a collective place-specific identity or a sense of place. By differentiating a city from others, image mak-ers intend not only to boost pride among locals but to attract visitors—i.e., economic capital—to the locale.

Gilroy, California, Past and Present

Gilroy, California, is located in southern Santa Clara County, approximately eighty miles south of San Francisco. Santa Clara County is home to the Silicon

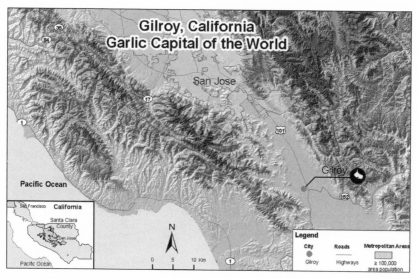

Gilroy, California. (Map by Manuel Peralvo)

Valley and substantial agribusiness.⁵ The Santa Clara Valley around Gilroy is a fertile plain enclosed on the northeast by the Contra Costa Mountain range and on the west by the Coast Range Mountains. The melding of sea breezes from San Francisco Bay and Monterey Bay with the arid heat of the valley provides the valley with a moderate climate.

In the early to mid-nineteenth century, the area around Gilroy was home to thriving ranching, grain farming, and logging and lumber industries.⁶ The California Gold Rush, vast tracts of fertile land kept in tact by a land grant system, and increased demand for grain products for the area's booming population are behind much of Santa Clara Valley and Gilroy's rapid growth as agricultural centers. The town of Gilroy emerged in the 1850s as a stagecoach stop along the San Jose to Monterey Road. Initially known as the township of Pleasant Valley, it was incorporated as the Town of Gilroy in 1868. Two years later it was incorporated as the City of Gilroy by the California State Legislature.⁷ Following the arrival of the railroad in 1869 Gilroy experienced associated commercial growth, as did many small cities throughout the west in this era. During the last third of the nineteenth century, Gilroy began its transition from a rural, farming town to a regional agricultural, commercial, and industrial center.

The railroad depot in Gilroy, circa 1916. The Southern Pacific Depot, built in 1870, was replaced in 1918. Note the hotel and apparently thriving business district. (Photograph courtesy of the Gilroy Museum)

Monterey Street in Gilroy's business district, circa 1927. (Photograph courtesy of the Gilroy Museum)

Among the changes taking place at that time was a diversification of Gilroy's population. Joining the European settlers busily establishing the town as an agricultural and commercial center were Chinese displaced by the completion of the transcontinental railroad. Eager for cheap labor, Gilroy-area farmers and businessmen hired these Chinese workers to work in the grain, tobacco, fruit, and seed industries. Newspaper articles report that James D. Culp's Gilroy-based Consolidated Tobacco Company employed some nine hundred Chinese laborers to pick, cure, and roll tobacco. The firm reported making one million cigars a month in 1873 ("Before Garlic, Cigars Ruled" 1996). Not long after, however, rising anti-Chinese sentiments and legislation forced Culp to downsize and relocate his business. Despite anti-Chinese labor and immigration legislation, by the early 1900s, Gilroy's Chinese population numbered around two thousand. Their presence was significant enough for residents to recognize one area of downtown as Chinatown, with businesses including a Chinese laundry and a Chinese herb and drug store. In addition to merchants, many of Gilroy's Chinese worked as tradesmen, domestic servants, and service personnel in the city's numerous hotels. In the mid-1920s, Gilroy's Chinatown suffered a devastating fire, forcing many residents to Chinese neighborhoods in San Jose or San Francisco. Most never returned and although a few Chinese businesses continued into the mid-twentieth century, Gilroy's Chinatown became a memory, recorded in the Sanborn Fire Insurance Maps and vaguely remembered in local lore.

Arriving in the Santa Clara Valley amid the anti-Chinese movement were Japanese farmers. Eventually the Japanese replaced Chinese as farm workers (Lukes and Okihiro 1985). Like their Chinese counterparts, many of these farmers were migrants searching for work. The first Japanese farmers arrived in the Santa Clara Valley in the mid-1890s, during what Lukes and Okihiro label the Valley's "orchard phase." Legally excluded from owning land, many of the Japanese, unlike the Chinese, became tenant farmers. Their farm clusters constituted the beginnings of more permanent communities. By 1902, Gilroy recorded Japanese residents; more came to the area after losing their homes and businesses in the 1906 San Francisco earthquake. The population gradually increased in number and significance within the area's agriculture industry. In 1919, the young Kiyoshi Hirasaki leased 130 acres of land and began what would become Hirasaki Farms. After a decade of growing seed, he switched to crops including lettuce, celery, and garlic. Buying land in his children's names (since they were born in the United States, they were citizens and therefore eligible to own property), Hirasaki gradually built a farming empire employing hundreds of Japanese workers.

Local recorded history notes that the southern Europeans who arrived in Gilroy in the 1890s planted row crops for their own consumption. Among their homegrown foods were tomatoes, peppers, onions, and garlic. Foreshadowing the city's industrial and identificational future, in 1897 the first commercial dehydrator was built. At that time it was used for transforming Gilroy's bumper crops of plums into prunes, facilitating Gilroy's reputation as the prune capital. That early dehydrating operation grew into what is today Gilroy Foods, a division of ConAgra.

Italian residents of Gilroy who planted garlic for their own use were the main garlic growers in the area until Japanese farmers like Hirasaki began growing it for commercial purposes. Farms raising food crops shared the valley with fields of floral crops being grown for a burgeoning commercial seed industry. Following the early success of the now-defunct Pieters-Wheeler Seed Company, founded in 1911, commercial seed farm operations such as Goldsmith Plants, Inc., became stable fixtures in the Valley around Gilroy. The flowers grown on the seed farms were pretty, but garlic seemed more noteworthy and defining for the city. By 1940 Hirasaki's Gilroy farm was the largest commercial garlic farm in the United States.

Since the late 1940s, Gilroy's population has consistently expanded and its economic base has changed accordingly. All of Gilroy's Japanese residents were either interred or "voluntarily" relocated during World War II. Their absence was temporary, however, as many returned to Gilroy and reestablished themselves in the community. Many of the Portuguese and Italians whose truck farming businesses grew during the war also stayed in Gilroy, further transforming the area's demographics. Gilroy's mid-twentieth-century growth spurt reflects the national post–World War II population trend as families of military men left their bases and settled in nearby towns. Monterey Bay, just forty miles from Gilroy, was home to Fort Ord as well as a U.S. Naval Reservation. Like many other towns in the area, Gilroy experienced a significant postwar flow of military personnel from Monterey Bay (table 1.1, table 1.2). The subsequent baby boom contributed to Gilroy's remarkable population increases through the 1950s. Gilroy's rapid popula-

Table 1.1.

Gilroy Population, 1940–2000

Year	Population	% Change within Gilroy	% Change within Santa Clara County
1940	3,615	+3.2	—
1950	4,951	+37.0	+66.1
1960	7,348	+48.4	+121.0
1970	12,665	+72.4	+65.8
1980	21,641	+70.8	+0.09
1990	31,487	+45.5	+15.6
2000	41,464	+31.7	+12.1

Sources: Doug Kuczynski, California Department of Finance, Demographic Research Unit, December 6, 2005; California State Department of Finance, "California 1990, 2000" U.S. Census Bureau, "Gilroy (city)" U.S. Census Bureau.

Table 1.2.

Racial Composition of Gilroy, 2000[a]

Racial category	Number of respondents	% of local population
White	24,426	58.9
Asian	1,810	4.4
Black or African American	745	1.8
American Indian and Alaska Native	661	1.6
Native Hawaiian and other Pacific Islander	105	0.3
Other races	11,499	27.7
Two or more races	2,218	5.3
Total population	**41,464**	**100**

Sources: ("QT-P3. Race and Hispanic or Latino: 2000, Gilroy city, California," U.S. Census Bureau)

[a]According to self-identification data provided by Census 2000 respondents. Inconsistencies in the number totals are a confusing aspect of census data. Percentage numbers may equal less or more than 100% because individual respondents may report more than one race. Such inconsistencies in numbers are explained as "nonsampling error." These numbers potentially are problematic and inaccurate reflections of Gilroy's real population. For numerous reasons, including in particular fear of legal repercussions in the case of undocumented agricultural laborers, people may not complete census information or may not report accurately. City officials may not challenge inaccuracies because, as Don Mitchell demonstrates, historically, non-white Latino workers have been undercounted and "lumped together" by power brokers in the interest of creating representations of California's beautiful landscape. See Don Mitchell, *The Lie of the Land: Migrant Workers and the California Landscape* (Minneapolis: University of Minnesota Press, 1996).

tion growth through the 1970s and 1980s is attributable to explosive expansion of the high-technology industry in neighboring San Jose. Gilroy's population steadily increased as it evolved into a bedroom community for San
Jose. Throughout the 1980s and 1990s, agricultural ranches increasingly
were converted into single-family home subdivisions, development that
continues apace into the early years of the twenty-first century. Repeated
visits to Gilroy suggest that the land immediately around the swelling
city is more valuable for housing, retail, and industry than it is for farming. Accompanying the upscale housing boom has been the appearance
of upscale specialty markets and national chain retail outlets as previously
open spaces continue to be transformed into spaces of domestic and retail
consumption.[8]

By the mid-1950s, changing land use patterns that reflected Gilroy's
transition from a predominantly agricultural town to a bedroom community
for San Jose were well underway. The transformation of the old Eschenburg
farm prune orchards into the Eschenburg Park subdivision in 1957, for
example, foretold the city's imminent residential boom. The City Council
had the foresight to incorporate growth-controlling limits amid increasing conversion of ranch land into upscale planned residential communities. Beginning in 1979 with Ordinance 79-28, the council adopted its first
Residential Development Ordinance (RDO) intended to control growth and
to balance land use, jobs, and "community," though the document neglects
to define what is meant by the last term. Initially reviewed annually, the
"modern RDO," as it is now called, is incorporated into the City's ten-year
Consolidated Plan. In the RDO the City Council specifies the maximum
number of housing unit building permits to be issued for the coming years.

Consideration of the ongoing need to provide housing for migrant workers who are vital to Gilroy's economy accompanies local planners' concerns
about the environmental and economic impacts that the rapid increase in
the number of large, expensive single-family housing developments are having. A section entitled "Farmworker Housing" in the 2000 *City of Gilroy
Consolidated Plan* indicates awareness by city officials, or at least those who
drafted the plan, that the housing needs of migrant worker families require
special attention. Many of these workers find seasonal and ongoing employment in Gilroy's agriculture and agribusiness-associated industries, the key-

stones of Gilroy's economy. The garlic industry is the city's largest private employer. Christopher Ranch, L.L.C., the country's leader in fresh garlic production, and Gilroy Foods, the world's largest supplier of dehydrated garlic, onion, vegetables, and capsicums, together employ more than eleven hundred people, nearly four hundred more than the next largest nongovernment employer.[9]

Prior to the Gilroy Garlic Festival, Gilroy had more negative than positive associations defining its identity among Bay area residents. Drivers along Highway 101 passed Gilroy on their way to other places. Gilroy was where Highway 101 reduced from a four-lane, divided highway to a two-lane road for southbound drivers. This resulted in frequent traffic jams during peak travel times and speed traps where a speed limit reduction corresponded to the reduced road size. Regional lore recalls Gilroy's reputation in the early 1970s for generously handing out speeding tickets to passersby.[10]

Gilroy was also known for its smell. During harvest season and the months immediately following, scent emanating from tomato canneries and prune and garlic dehydrators filled the air. The industries' olfactory by-products, particularly garlic, drifted up and down the Valley, and beyond. Local author Kathryn McKenzie reports some residents recounted the smell traveling "as far north as Blossom Hill Road in San Jose, and as far south as Salinas—both locations some twenty-five miles away."[11] When a city official in San Jose complained about the odor to Christopher Ranch's Don Christopher, he replied "I can't believe we are not charging you for that!"

While many disliked the lingering aromas from the production plants, some locals are nostalgic about the days when Gilroy still had a tomato cannery, reminiscing that the smells of tomatoes and garlic combined into a smell evocative of a pot of spaghetti sauce, with extra garlic. Among them is Rhonda Pellin, who told me she remembers when the stimulation was so strong that she sometimes went home and cooked spaghetti sauce and garlic bread. The last tomato cannery closed in 1997, leaving garlic as the dominant olfactory aspect of Gilroy from June through October each year.

Despite Gilroy's sensory distinctiveness, San Jose's appropriation of its Silicon Valley identity through the late 1970s and into the 1980s overshadowed other non-technological aspects of Santa Clara Valley's identity. Eventually San Jose became synonymous in the popular imagination with

high-technology industries. Silicon Valley connoted the financially successful urban world of computers and start-up companies. A little to the south,
Gilroy continued through these years as an agricultural center, although
the nature of its agricultural industries shifted as an increasing residential population required supporting retail and services, and agribusiness
expanded.

Gilroy now struggles with seemingly bipolar aspects of its identity:
an agricultural past that has evolved into a commercial food-processing
present, and a growing suburb for an increasingly affluent population of
nonagricultural workers. Contemporary Gilroy is really two distinct Gilroys;
which part of the city you visit informs how you perceive the city's population. To the west are Gilroyans who live in the new homes built in gated
residential developments, shop in the newer strip plazas, and do not venture
beyond the unmarked precincts of these professional, often-commuting,
new residents. The other Gilroyans live closer to the extant downtown, in
the Victorian homes, 1920s bungalows, and 1950s ranch-style houses that fill
heavily treed neighborhoods, not far from the one-story motels and small
businesses along the two-lane Monterey Street, the main street through
downtown. The area close to downtown, like that of many other cities, is
dichotomous: not far from lower-income housing are well maintained prop-
erties on the National Historic Register.

The luxury-home suburbanization has had negligible impact on Gilroy's
downtown. Although residents commuting northward to San Jose and the
Bay area on high-speed trains (running only Monday through Friday) benefit from the modern Caltran train station with ample parking, there is little
other visible evidence that the families of commuters spend time or money
downtown. There are ongoing efforts by the City Council to revitalize the
diminished commercial center, including redesigned sidewalks intended
to invite pedestrian traffic and plans for mixed-use buildings.[12] But these
changes are offset by empty storefronts and a jumbled array of stores: a
vacuum cleaner shop, a bowling alley with a Japanese-owned lunch room, a
low-income medical clinic, antique stores, Garlic City Coffee Shop, and the
Chamber of Commerce and Gilroy Garlic Festival offices. Over the course of
the seven years I visited the city, many storefronts were increasingly weath-
ered and uninviting despite the beautifully redesigned sidewalks.

Aggrandizement and the Commodification of Place

In 1978, Gilroy's image makers put a clever positive spin on their garlicky reputation by declaring Gilroy as the Garlic Capital of the World. To kick off their capital campaign, they organized a garlic-themed festival, re-representing Gilroy and garlic as fun—if a bit offbeat—entertaining diversions. With media assistance, word of Gilroy's food-theme place brand spread to wider and more diverse audiences. Gilroy's identity as *the* garlic capital rapidly entered the popular imagination, especially among foodies, food festival fans, and festival organizers.

Actually, Gilroy is one of several self-proclaimed garlic capitals of the world. Making a similar claim is Stroudsburg, Pennsylvania.[13] Though much smaller and younger than Gilroy's Festival, Stroudsburg's annual garlic festival, the Pocono Garlic Festival, commemorates the town's affinity for the stinking rose, in particular, for garlic grown in the Pocono Mountains. Many other towns and cities pay homage to the bulbous herb with an annual festival. From Tonasket, Washington's Okanogan River Garlic Festival to Saugerties, New York's Hudson Valley Garlic Festival, localities throughout the country organize garlic-centered festivities. From Ontario to British Columbia, Canadians similarly orchestrate garlic-themed festivals. The Isle of Wight, United Kingdom, is also home to a multi-decade tradition of celebrating locally grown garlic with a yearly festival. Arleux, France, perhaps the only town whose claim to garlic capitaldom predates Gilroy's claim, has been celebrating its relationship with garlic through a festival since 1961.

The phenomenon of places—towns, cities, states—claiming to be the capital of a particular food item as a strategy of place differentiation is ubiquitous throughout contemporary America. These attempts to differentiate localities with such titles exemplify what I term *aggrandizement*: rhetorical, symbolic, and physical attempts at place differentiation. More specifically, aggrandizement refers to the way image makers, event organizers, and/or town leaders attempt to distinguish their event or town from others. Communal aggrandizement is expressed through claims like "World Capital," "Biggest," "Best," "Oldest." Such claims are part of festival's "vocabulary of intensification" (Abrahams 1982). Often aggrandizement is, or is intended to be, humorous; other times a claim is taken quite seriously by those who make it. The motivations behind place differentiation most often are economic, directly linked to promotion of place in the interest of local boosterism and increased tourism. Thus, strategic aggrandizement is one component of negotiating identity and a central aspect of place-making. In addition to spectaclizing place for consumption by tourists and potential future residents or businesses, image makers often mediate a locality's identity as part of their effort to create or improve senses of community and place among residents.

Increased attempts among image makers to attain place differentiation by emphasizing a local or regional product, or a segmented local or regional identity illustrate the seductive allure of *neolocalism*. Neolocalism is a response to and a foil for the distancing and depersonalizing effects of globalization: "[Americans] miss having a sense of community and region to provide an anchor of identity. One upshot of this is a renewed commitment to experiencing things close to home" (Shortridge and Shortridge 1998, 7). Accompanying the rapid flow of information and people that constitutes modern globalization is a diminution in the importance of spatial barriers. The absence of spatial limitations has produced an increased interest in celebrating the uniqueness of place, indicating that "the elaboration of place-bound identities has become more rather than less important . . ." (Harvey 1993, 4). As a deliberate effort to create a new identity by celebrating things "close to home," neolocalism is articulated in diverse ways, including renewed interest in local history and politics, historical reenactments, and patronage of local or regional producers and markets such as farmers' markets.

Mediated food-place associations and place-specific food festivals are also manifestations of neolocalism. Both highlight a food with a historic connection to the place, often by recontextualizing the food item. The symbolization of garlic for Gilroy exemplifies this recontextualizing process, as does the 1990s symbolization of chile peppers by image makers in Pueblo, Colorado (Haverluk 2002). In addition to bolstering a collective identity, by translating into a festival the food symbolization, image makers aim to attract visitors lured by the festival frame and food. Through festival events and publicity they commodify an existing relationship between a food item and the locale's geography, history, and residents. The subsequent consumption of the locale's identity by residents and visitors is the image makers' intention. Just as clothing retailers create differentiated spaces of consumption (Crewe and Lowe 1995), image makers seek to create differentiated places for consumption through aggrandizement.

Because food is regarded as a malleable commodity with potential for broad appeal, food is frequently iconized in the processes of place differentiation and commodifying place. Through food-centered place branding and aggrandizement, the food-place association is exoticized. Within the place-food festival frame, the iconized food is further exoticized through events such as cooking contests that feature the iconic food, queen and baby pageants whose winners become food royalty, references to popular culture that already link the food to the world outside, and parade floats that incorporate the food and its popular culture symbols. The production and consumption of communal identities come together in the symbolic consumption of identity and in the literal consumption of iconic foods. Both modes of consumption are promoted by place branding and are articulated through year-round sale of iconic foods at local shops and restaurant, for example, as well as through annual celebrations such as place-based food festivals.

Aggrandizement draws attention to a perceived exoticism, even if what is elevated by iconization to exotic is a quotidian item such as garlic. Food-centered aggrandizement is analogous to the appropriation of exoticism explored by Susan Stewart (1984) in her consideration of the tourist impulse of acquisition. A quest for the exotic serves as a means of distinction for the consumer and a means of distinction for that which is situated as exotic.[14] Differentiation of place works only when social space is compared to other places and offers something different—a food, a landscape, an event—that cannot be experienced elsewhere. Yet, "[o]nce the exotic experience is readily purchasable by a large segment of the tourist population, either increasingly exotic experiences are sought (consider travel posters advertising the last frontier or the last unspoiled island) or, in a type of reverse snobbery, there is a turning toward 'the classic' of the consumer's native culture" (Stewart 1984, 148). As symbolic landscapes that represent a food-place association, foodscapes muddle the exotic/classic binary: iconizing a food item that is or was grown in the locale exoticizes it while at the same time evokes nostalgia for an agrarian, pastoral past. The suggestion of and potential pleasure from literal consumption of food associated with festive foodscapes further complicates the exotic/classic model: festive foods are exotic, because the types and quantities of food offered are extra-normal, and simultaneously classic, because food offers comfort and may carry familiar or familial connotations. I contend that such ambivalence is part of the attraction of place-based food festivals, and food events in general. Although ambivalence often is considered confounding, and therefore negative, its liminal nature is part of its attraction: a place or a situation laden with ambiguity can be variously interpreted, offering multiple levels of experience and meaning within a single experiential frame, thus broadening its appeal.

Like other aspects of the tourist experience, events and places are understood by the juxtaposition of contrasts (MacCannell 1989, Urry 1990). Place-marketing, a component of the tourist experience, is a modern manifestation of differentiation. In the mid-1970s, for example, industrial cities experiencing industrial decline turned to differentiation as a strategy of self-promotion (Holcomb 1993). During that time of economic recession and massive deindustrialization, local authorities in cities such as Cleveland and Pittsburgh turned to marketing the cities as products to be consumed, as commodities for the marketplace. By isolating unique parts of the cities, what became known as "tourist bubbles," and ignoring other less desirable areas and features, image makers sought to differentiate each city, and differentiate within each city, in the tourism and commercial marketplaces. The fiscal crisis of the late 1980s and early 1990s caused by further deindustrialization, falling tax base, and declining public expenditure were driving forces for the emergence of a new style of local economic development that privileged image promotion over other possible tourism foci (Hannigan 2003, see also, Judd and Fainstein 1999). Such image-driven place-marketing emerged as part of concentrated attempts at urban regeneration.

The commodification of place, however, is not limited to urban environments. Rural regions such as Appalachia have been and continue to be commodified (Stephenson 1984). Numerous towns across the United States, faced with a declining rural-based agricultural or light industry economy, turn to tourism as an "alternative economy." Leavenworth, Washington, exemplifies how the rise of heritage tourism, of which food-place themed aggrandizement is part, amid increased competition to secure tourist dollars is linked with the production of cultural or symbolic capital (Frenkel and Walton 2000). The quest for distinction in attempts to lure potential businesses, residents, or visitors is what draws chambers of commerce throughout the United States to assign labels of aggrandizement to their towns. The forces behind, and economic and social consequences resulting from, "selling place" are many.[15] Selling place bundles economic and social opportunity with the commodification of place, commodification that can be literal, as in selling Grand Canyon package tours or ethnic foods in New Glarus, Wisconsin, or ideological, as in selling the ethnic-themed identity of Leavenworth, Washington, or a food-themed identity symbolized in a food festival. As Barbara Shortridge asserts in her study of purposefully reinvented heritage destinations like Lindsborg, Kansas, and New Glarus, Wisconsin, food is "a major participatory component of [visitors'] ethnic exploration" (2004, 268).

The theming of a town—whether it is a complete restructuring as in Leavenworth, Washington, or promotion of a food-themed symbolic identity—endows the town with identity capital. That is, what is highlighted as part of the strategy of place branding becomes a symbolic and potentially tangible resource for differentiating the locality. In contrast to what tourism scholars term "theme towns," Gilroy has not undergone much, if any, physical restructuring as a result of its theming as a foodscape, yet it is ascribed identity based on the iconization of a particular food. Promoting place as a foodscape is one strategy of place aggrandizement. Inherent in place aggrandizement is competition: competition among the place(s) asserting uniqueness and all other places.[16]

The commodification of place and aggrandizement achieved through place branding articulates a competition paradigm. Yet, there is something more. What inspires image makers not only to differentiate a social space but to do so by asserting that it is the "biggest" or "weirdest" or "capital" of something? Karal Ann Marling suggests that an American infatuation with colossus is attributable to an "aesthetics of awe" and anxiety about the vastness of the American frontier. Although her focus was on Minnesota roadside statuary, her discussion of how these larger-than-life objects "convey a sense of a town's unique claims to recognition" is applicable to this discussion of place branding through assertions of capitaldom. A place-differentiating claim of capitaldom, like a roadside colossus, becomes "a resonant mark of local presence, a magnet drawing travelers off the westward course of history and highway, into the mythical realm of the American Midwest"

(1984, 4). Remove the regional specificity, and the analysis can apply to other attempts at place differentiation that present anomalies.

Claims of uniqueness such as "Garlic Capital of the World" vaunt superiority, just as, as David Lowenthal (1994) and Barbara Kirshenblatt-Gimblett (1998) remind us, claims of cultural heritage imply superiority. As a mode of cultural production, heritage "distills the past into icons of identity" (Lowenthal 1994, 41), but it is always a selective past. Displays of a select past, whether in a museum or as a themed tourism destination, endow that past with value and shape public memory.[17] Commemorating an agricultural heritage through a festive foodscape is another example of exploiting a real, fabricated, or idealized cultural past. This is not to suggest that the binary of real/ideal is the only conception of the past from which image makers draw. There are any number of possibilities along what might be considered a continuum of pasts from real to fictionalized, including the melding of elements from each (real and fabricated) that would result in a new representative reality.

Barbara Kirshenblatt-Gimblett acknowledges that "[t]o compete with each other, destinations must be distinguishable, which is why the tourism industry requires the production of difference" (1998, 152). Highlighting heritage is a way of producing what she calls a "hereness." Marking heritage establishes a place as a destination; it converts a place from somewhere tourists pass through on their way to elsewhere to a place they head toward. Asserting that Gilroy, California, for example, is the Garlic Capital of the World assigns a "hereness" to the city; it marks it as an anomalous place, different from other towns along the highway.

Inherent in titular celebrations of place is the contradiction that the same rhetoric that extols the uniqueness or virtues of one place is used to differentiate other places. This is the paradox of aggrandizement: in an attempt to mark distinction and differentiate a place, image makers cannot help but employ the same language of differentiation used by other image makers, thereby generating a degree of similitude. In fact, "the practice of selling places may even generate sameness and blandness despite its appearance of bringing geographical differences into the fold of contemporary economic and political discourse" (Kearns and Philo 1993a, 21). With so many self-proclaimed Capitals of the World—Castroville, California, and artichokes; Ketchikan, Alaska, and king salmon; North Loup, Nebraska, and popcorn;

Wenatchee, Washington, and apples—there is a limit to how unique or original such claims can be. It seems that the individuality of a place matters less than cultivating an image of a place with what are perceived as unique or exotic attributes.

Indicative of how popular the strategy of aggrandizement is among image makers seeking to differentiate locales is the presence of multiple web-based resources listing places' "claims to fame."[18] The ubiquity of the practice indicates how strongly image makers are drawn to aggrandizement as a strategy for local differentiation.

While Gilroy asserts its claim of capitaldom, across the country, image makers in Stroudsburg, Pennsylvania, make the same assertion. Luckily for Gilroy, the Gilroy Garlic Capital of the World place-branding campaign was relatively early in the trend of food-themed place promotion, giving it the attraction of novelty and exoticism. And, not only did the image makers claim capitaldom, they orchestrated a festive celebration of what had been a marginal food. How could the media and public help but be curious about the festivalization of garlic?

CHAPTER TWO

The Festivalization of Garlic

Creating and Celebrating Community in Gilroy

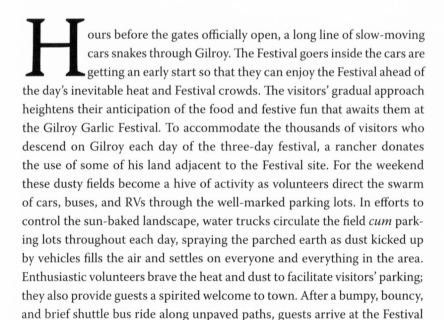

Hours before the gates officially open, a long line of slow-moving cars snakes through Gilroy. The Festival goers inside the cars are getting an early start so that they can enjoy the Festival ahead of the day's inevitable heat and Festival crowds. The visitors' gradual approach heightens their anticipation of the food and festive fun that awaits them at the Gilroy Garlic Festival. To accommodate the thousands of visitors who descend on Gilroy each day of the three-day festival, a rancher donates the use of some of his land adjacent to the Festival site. For the weekend these dusty fields become a hive of activity as volunteers direct the swarm of cars, buses, and RVs through the well-marked parking lots. In efforts to control the sun-baked landscape, water trucks circulate the field *cum* parking lots throughout each day, spraying the parched earth as dust kicked up by vehicles fills the air and settles on everyone and everything in the area. Enthusiastic volunteers brave the heat and dust to facilitate visitors' parking; they also provide guests a spirited welcome to town. After a bumpy, bouncy, and brief shuttle bus ride along unpaved paths, guests arrive at the Festival gates, where another team of vivacious volunteers sells entry tickets and Festival program books.

The positive energy is palpable as people queue to enter the Festival grounds. Smells of garlicky foods season the rapidly warming air and enhance everyone's mounting anticipation. The physical transition from non-festival space through the dusty car park to the actual Festival site combined with intangible details like the ambient festive spirit and the garlicky air creates the "sensory gates" that signify entry into distinctly separate time and space (Seremetakis 1994, 29). Welcome to the Gilroy Garlic Festival.

. ♦ .

It took a visionary outsider to appreciate the novelty and marketability of what was perceived by many as a communal liability. In 1978, Dr. Rudy Melone was a relative newcomer to Gilroy. As fund-raising chairman of the local Rotary Club, he was charged with devising new ways for the civic-minded group to support community organizations. According to the Festival's official history (Midtgaard), Melone saw economic and social potential in promoting Gilroy as a center—if not *the* center—for garlic pro- duction. He learned that Arleux, in northern France, proclaimed itself to be the Garlic Capital of the World and attracted eighty thousand people to its annual garlic festival.[1] Suspecting that Gilroy produced and processed more garlic than Arleux, Melone set out to convince the local power brokers that Gilroy would do well to celebrate rather than try to ignore this vital and often maligned economic resource. He saw promise in commemorating the city's main agricultural product and anticipated fund-raising potential in the festival format.

Dr. Melone and Don Christopher, owner of Christopher Ranch, asked Val Filice, an established local cook, farmer, and garlic lover, to prepare a special garlic-laden lunch for an upcoming Rotary meeting at which they would promote the idea of organizing a garlic festival. Attending this lunch would be local leaders and invited media guests, including food editors and writers. Betsy Balsley, then food editor for the *Los Angeles Times*, was one of the guests who enthusiastically supported the idea of a festival. Initially the idea met with hesitation from the mayor, who admitted to not liking garlic, and from Christopher himself who wondered if there was enough interest in garlic to support a festival. There was skepticism about the Festival's success outside Gilroy as well: Don Christopher recalls that a county official thought it would attract such a small number of attendees that he did not bother to enforce sanitation standards. Despite reservations and with encouragement from Balsley and others, Melone and Christopher proceeded with organizational planning. They put Filice in charge of what would become the culinary backbone of the Festival, the area called Gourmet Alley, where garlic-laden foods are prepared by local volunteers and sold to hungry attendees.

The inaugural Festival took place August 4–5, 1979. Those dates were selected so that the Garlic Festival would not conflict with previously scheduled Bonanza Days events and because the garlic harvest is complete by August, allowing organizers to conceive of the Festival as a harvest festival. The Festival would be a full sensory experience: because Gilroy Foods' dehydrators would be processing the season's crop in August, they would be generating the distinctive aroma for which Gilroy was already famous. The first Festival was held on farmland donated by a local resident. Visitors walked over broken and dried garlic stalks as they visited booths sponsored by local civic organizations and businesses that offered "everything imaginable related to garlic: fresh garlic (pee-wees to colossal), garlic braids, all forms of dehydrated and processed garlic, books and information on garlic uses and its health aspects, folklore, garlic hats, tee shirts, belt buckles, garlic roses, garlic jewelry, paperweights, plaques, pet garlic and more" (Melone 1979a). The garlic-Gilroy association being promoted through the Festival was reinforced by olfactory as well as visual, physical, and gustatory stimulation.

In addition to informational and retail booths, there was entertainment including country-western and rock musicians and minstrel singers, belly dancers and gymnasts, a magician, and roving mimes. Activities that are no longer part of the Festival calendar were tours of local garlic fields, packing plants, and processing plants, all discontinued because of liability concerns. Among the activities that continue to be incorporated into each year's Festival are the recipe contest and the garlic topping contest, considered in a subsequent chapter. But, as Melone noted, "the real drawing card—the unique quality of the Festival—is the GARLICKY FOOD" (Melone

1979a). Most of the garlicky foods made in the open air kitchen of Gourmet Alley then and now are Americanized versions of Italian dishes: *calamari*, *scampi*, pasta with pesto sauce, garlic bread, Italian sausages, and garlic seasoned beef, reflecting the influence of Val Filice's Italian heritage on the Festival menu.

Organizers expected between five thousand and ten thousand people to attend the inaugural Festival: they were nearly overwhelmed by fifteen thousand attendees. Val Filice humorously recalls having to send runners out to buy more food because there were so many more people than anticipated. He ordered men to drive to nearby Monterey for more prawns and squid. The beer chairman found himself in a similar bind. According to Festival history, partway through the first day the beer chairman called the distributor and said, "Heck, forget the kegs. Start sending us the trucks" (Midtgaard, Tognetti 2003).

Mr. Filice attributes the Festival's success to timing, to people's willingness to learn about a then-underappreciated food. He explains that in the late 1970s, "[p]eople were ready to learn about new foods, to learn about garlic. People didn't know how to use garlic." Among those who did use garlic, he suggests, many were ashamed to admit it. Because of the Festival, Mr. Filice laughingly says, the public "finally let [their enjoyment of] garlic out of the closet."

Since 1979 Gilroyans of all ages have participated with ebullience in the Gilroy Garlic Festival. Each July, Christmas Hill Park, an expansive public park southwest of town where the Festival has been held since 1980, is transformed into multipurpose outdoor performance venues, kitchen amphitheater, working kitchens, concessions venues, children's theme park, art fair, and general gathering place where people eat, drink, listen to music, and shop under the glaring watch of the inland California sun. The first Festival site was about one acre; since its move to Christmas Hill Park, the Festival site has expanded to seventeen acres, with an additional approximately ninety acres dedicated to parking.

Over the years the focus of the Festival has changed. By organizers' own admission, Festival activities in its early years leaned toward hosting a rowdy party, including serving copious quantities of alcohol, in the interest of generating positive perceptions of garlic and Gilroy. The party atmosphere led to safety concerns, especially after a 1993 knife fight resulted in thirteen arrests.

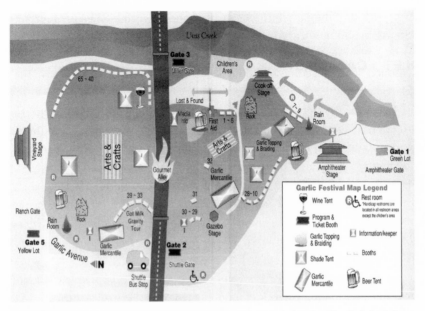

Garlic Festival map, from 2003 program booklet. (Image used with permission from the Gilroy Garlic Festival Association, Inc.)

Since then, food, merchandizing, and entertainment have been emphasized more than drinking and partying. To create and sustain a family atmosphere, organizers expanded the children's area, selected entertainment suitable for a family venue, and reduced the centrality of the beer tents in promotional materials and by their physical placement on the Festival site.

As attendance increased, so have the number and diversity of the Festival's consumer offerings. In 1998, organizers formalized merchandizing of Gilroy Garlic Festival ephemera by opening the "Garlic Merchantile," controlled-access tented areas functioning as the on-site stores for official Festival merchandise. The number of independent vendors increased from 141 at the 1981 Festival to 181 at the 2004 Festival; in 1981 there were sixteen bands and entertainment acts booked for the Festival as compared to the more than forty bands, strolling musicians, and entertainers scheduled for 2004. Cook-off contest emcee Narsai David commented during the 2003 Cook-off that the Gilroy Garlic Festival is "more and more like a state fair . . . [with] different stages, different venues or areas" for food sales, music, children, and shopping.

Banner for Gourmet Alley. Visible just below and behind the banner are the booths from which garlic-hungry diners order and receive their food, 2005. (Photograph by author)

A flare-up at Gourmet Alley, 2000. (Photograph by author)

One of the main attractions of the Festival is Gourmet Alley, a covered area that literally bisects the Festival grounds. In the Alley, "pyro chefs" work over huge propane burners and grills cooking garlic-infused foods for guests and workers. The volunteer cooks are noted for producing dramatic "flame-ups" or "flare-ups," tall pillars of flames emanating from large sauté pans, dramatic visual displays loved by visitors and media.

The foremost enticement of Gourmet Alley is gustatory. Massive quantities of garlic-laden food are prepared and consumed each year using literally tons of garlic. In 2002, for example, Festival visitors consumed 32,186 servings of garlic bread, 15,589 pepper steak sandwiches, and 10,079 orders of garlicky mushrooms. In 2003, some 132,000 visitors consumed ten tons of garlicky beef in the form of steak sandwiches, seven tons of the pasta that served as the vehicle for garlicky pesto sauce, four tons of garlic-rich shrimp scampi, and four tons of garlic-laced crisp calamari; the cooks in Gourmet Alley used over two tons of garlic in three days. (For better or worse, such numbers are not available for garlic ice cream, a highly sought-after taste treat at each year's event.) Each year's press release boasts food sales numbers from the previous year's Festival, further reinforcing the importance of food as the event's focus. In addition to highlighting the centrality of the garlic-laden foods prepared at Gourmet Alley by local pyro-chefs, such media attention glorifies the Festival's carnivalesque excess. Such braggadocio exemplifies *aggrandizement*, the strategy employed to create distinction. For Gilroy, the Festival is an enactment of their Garlic Capital of the World assertion; it is the celebration of a garlic-centric aggrandizement campaign.

Festivals, Time, and the Enactment of Identity

Communities throughout the country host food festivals, many focusing on a single food item. Examples abound from all corners of the nation: from Gilroy, California, where visitors to the Gilroy Garlic Festival celebrate the most odorous member of the lily family, to Rockland, Maine, where people gather at the Maine Lobster Festival to commemorate and consume the beloved crustacean.

Why are food festivals so popular among community leaders seeking to distinguish their towns? Perhaps it is the absence of a historical event to commemorate, or not wanting to highlight a single ethnic group to the exclusion of others. Maybe it is recognizing the economic or nostalgic value of agricultural heritage, or knowing that visitors are drawn to food-themed events. Most likely, it is a combination of these considerations that accounts for the persistent popularity of food festivals among event planners. Somehow, community leaders determine that a food item will stimulate enough interest to make such a festival worthwhile. The sheer ubiquity of festivals that iconize food on community calendars across America warrants critical attention.

Place-specific food festivals, like contemporary community festivals in general, are descended from traditional agricultural fairs. The American agricultural fair is a composite social institution, "part Roman carnival, part medieval market fair, and part English cattle show" (Marling 1990, 77). American agricultural associations, which emerged in great numbers after the 1840s, and the agricultural fairs they spawned, are regarded as "the paramount forms of collective activity among the rural population and the fair the dominant institutionalized expression of that activity" (Neely 1935, 89). The evolution of the agricultural fair over the course of the nineteenth century from a "practical farming community event into a more complex leisure and profit-oriented event" (Borish 1997, 155) reflects the century's general societal, economic, and population shifts. Even as populations relocated increasingly to cities during the late nineteenth century and into the twentieth century, agricultural fairs retained their appeal: in 1935, Wayne Caldwell Neely observed that fairs had become "an intimate part of the immediate social scheme," so much so that " '[g]oing to the fair' ha[d] become a significant recreational event in the social life of many generations of the human family" (1935, 184–185). Contemporary community festivals persist in being significant recreational events for many families, and their ubiquity on community calendars across the country suggests that civic leaders recognize their appeal.

If the nineteenth-century American agricultural fair was a metaphor for rural society, as Linda Borish (1997) asserts, the modern community festival is a metaphor for contemporary society. At community festivals, as in urban and suburban America, agricultural elements are enclosed, contained, and spectaclized (e.g., petting zoo), consumption of food and entertainment are highlighted, and competition is privileged in carnival amusements and themed contests. Community festivals continue to be a metaphor for and an articulation of the host-locale's collective identity, or, rather, the identity that image makers and festival organizers hope to affirm among residents and have associated with the locale for visitors. Food festivals share these defining characteristics, but with heightened symbolic and programmatic attention to food.

Food and festivals embody both traditional and contemporary cultures; they are simultaneously personal and communal, global and local, dynamic and stable. Food and festivals are ephemeral cultural expressions, but, like tangible cultural products, the effects of food festivals extend beyond their physical presence. However temporary a place-based food festival may be, the effects of a deliberately created communal identity promoted through a festival potentially are enduring. The food-land-place association established through a place-specific food festival may linger in the imaginations of local residents and visitors long after the festival, suggesting the tenacity of food as an identificational symbol.

The processes of promoting and celebrating collective and place identities both inform and are informed by the identities. That is, identities are never static; they are always being shaped and modified, and shaping and modifying. Displays of these dynamic processes constitute enactments of identity.[2] Community festivals as a category rightly are considered performances of collective identities. More specifically, they are enactments of multidimensional, desired collective identities determined by image makers.

Festivals are a "'time out of time,' a special temporal dimension devoted to special activities" (Falassi 1987). That festivals are a time out of time does not diminish their importance as part of everyday life of the host community. On the contrary; they often embody a hyper-awareness of communal life or of an idealized cohesion as residents and visitors come together in the spirit of play, suspend the rigors and conflicts of daily life and, for a short time, participate as a collective of individuals in an experience that reinforces a sense of a shared past and present. Festivals "provide *the* occasion whereby a community may call attention to itself and, perhaps more important in our time, its willingness to display itself openly" (Abrahams 1987, 181; emphasis in original).

Festival denotes a particular framed experience as well as an interpretive framework through which this articulation of expressive culture can be studied.[3] Just as a picture frame delimits background and directs the viewer's focus and perception, the festival frame informs the way attendees experience the festival. The festival frame keys participants' and observers' expectations, making the medium part of the message. A structured expressive form, whether it is framed as ritual, play, or a hybrid genre, is "a deliberate and artificial demarcation" that brackets behavior and informs meaning, thus making the medium part of the message.[4] To participants and observers, *festival* implies that predictable, though variable, activities will take place during a distinct time period, in a demarcated space.

Another constitutive element of the festival frame is that festival events are most often affectively charged with positive energy. The festival frame predicts playful and positive moods, and connotes rules for behavior different from daily non-festival life. Within the festival frame—that is, during the bracketed festival time—there is the potential for affirmation of, challenges to, and inversions of social norms. Until social inversion happens, and often even when it does, the positive affective mood of the festival frame dominates participants' and visitors' expectations, expectations that are informed by prior lived and learned experiences. Lived festival experiences perpetuate expectations that community festivals are appealing, fun, and affirmative events. And these experiences affirm the mediated identity being commemorated through the festivities. Visitors to the Gilroy Garlic Festival not only partake in the festive fun, they literally and ideologically consume the Gilroy-garlic association.

Festival also implies social interaction, social license, and foods different from those that comprise most daily diets. As with other performative genres, festivals "provide an intricate counterpoint to the unconscious practices of everyday life insofar as they are stylistically marked expressions of otherness" that situate habitual activities in an alternate frame; as such they "are characterized by a higher than usual degree of reflexivity" (Kapchan 1995). This sort of reflexivity is inherent in county fair domestic arts competitions: "By locating in a time and space dedicated to a special purpose related to but removed from everyday life and by adopting stylized procedures, judging and exhibition reorder, highlight and comment on the everyday occupational and domestic experiences of fairgoers' lives" (Prosterman 1995, 16). In addition, within the festival frame, undertaking quotidian activities like eating and cooking is temporarily reframed: there is license to abandon normative food-related behavior, thus allowing for enjoyment of exotic or unhealthy foods like garlic ice cream or funnel cakes, excessive consumption, and spectaclized eating and cooking through contests.

While annual festivals are "a time out of time," as recurring events they also are part of the host locale's community calendar, and thus are part of its routine life. That festivals function in part to affirm communal identities makes festival time part of everyday life. Although it may initially seem contradictory, festivals are both within the realm of the everyday and special, differentiated experiences outside the realm of the everyday. Annual community festivals like Gilroy's exemplify that the constructs *everyday life* and *special events* are not mutually exclusive but are relational, existing only as complements to and in contrast to each other.[5] In fact, one factor that contributes to the success of the festival genre as a strategy for identity affirmation is the juxtaposition of everyday/special that coalesces in this traditional form. Roger Abrahams articulates a similar view when he notes that "there is a continuity and a dialectic between everyday activities and these [enactments or marked behavior such as festival and rituals] heightened events" (1977, 100). Part of what makes the Gilroy Garlic Festival such a strong affirmation of the city's mediated food-themed identity is its time out of time-ness: the once-a-year Festival affirms the city's everyday (self-proclaimed) status as Garlic Capital of the World. As long as a community festival remains vital to its host community, the affirming dialectic and continuity continues.

An unsuccessful "annual" event—one that is so poorly attended or not well received within the host community that it is not repeated—interrupts continuity of identity formation not only by disrupting the community's calendar but by derailing the organizers' attempt, through the festival, to create historical continuity for the community and to affirm a promoted identity. Even if a festival does not evoke a specific moment in the locality's past, its promotion as an "annual" event implies a connection to the past and to the future. The higher the number of years an annual festival can claim, the greater its implicit and explicit links to the past. Contributors to Eric Hobsbawn and Terrence Ranger's celebrated anthology (1983) ably demonstrate that although historic continuity might be largely fictitious, that may be of little concern to organizers or attendees. Linnekin and Handler (1984) alternatively suggest that traditions, whether regarded as genuine or spurious, are social and cultural constructs reflecting discourses of power, representation, and interpretation. Indeed, whether or not an event is interpreted as an authentic tradition depends in part on how it is variously presented and interpreted by organizers, participants, and observers.

Each of these approaches to interpreting tradition is useful when studying how people engage traditional forms of creative expression, including the community festival, to facilitate senses of place and senses of community. Most important is recognition that all traditions are social or cultural constructs that reflect relationships of power (individual and/or group relations; hegemonic, subversive, or a changeable combination of both) and that the traditions' meanings will change over time, just as social and power relations change over time.

A useful way to embrace the dynamism inherent in discussions of tradition without getting bogged down in the rhetorical danger of "authentic" so often associated with "tradition" (Bendix 1997) is to embrace the complementary notion of a "useable past": the application of creative imaging to the interpretation of a group's heritage and collective memory that results in re-presentations of a potentially artificially constructed past in the service of community building. The evocation of a usable past to invent, justify, or explain communal traditions as an element of identity negotiation and affirmation is one possible strategy utilized by community leaders and sometimes embraced by individuals to ascribe meaning and establish a sense of communal identity and place. Again, the Gilroy Garlic Festival presents a salient example. Image makers organized the inaugural Festival in an attempt to put a positive spin on their city's malodorous reputation. Because it was successful, image makers established the Festival as a city tradition, thus affirming and promoting a positive association between Gilroy and garlic. Celebrating useable pasts through inventing traditions can also provide sociocultural refuge amid rapid social change, affirming local identity when external forces seem to threaten it (e.g., Bendix 1989, Conzen 1989, Hobsbawn 1983, Hoelscher 1998, Teluja 1997).

Whether they are invented or rooted traditions, community festivals are part of the process of individual and collective self-authentification. They can be a means of integrating individuals into the spirit of a collective identity and celebrate as well as enhance individual, group, and place identities (de Bres and Davis 2001, Schultz 1994). A festival is one way a locale calls attention to itself. Part of the appeal of the community festival is that it serves multiple functions in the economic and symbolic lives of individuals and locales: when successful like the Gilroy Garlic Festival, a recurring event brings people together in the spirit of celebration at a definite time and in a situated place, generates financial gain, and, similarly, generates a sense of community.

Place-specific, food-themed festivals, like the Gilroy Garlic Festival, orchestrated to promote a locale's foodscape identity are cultural performances. As such they are enactments that display culture in action. As framed, symbolically charged intensifications of experience, they become venues where people enact individual and collective identities and expectations (Singer 1959, Turner and McArthur 1990). Cultural performances are constructed from the same complex historical, political, and social processes that inform daily life, aesthetically reconfiguring the worlds of those who produce them; they are collective representations of social desires, sacred longings, and personal motivations of their performance communities (e.g., Flores 1995). Whether local festivals or grand spectacles like the Olympics, such displays are "occasions in which as a culture or society we reflect upon and define ourselves, dramatize our collective myths and history, present ourselves with alternatives, and eventually change in some ways while remaining the same in others" (MacAloon 1984a, 1).

The cultural performance model recognizes dramatic displays as reflecting, interpreting, and influencing the society matrix within which they are enacted.[6] This approach facilitates interpretations of social dramas, spectacles, rites, festivals, and other performative events as part of the ongoing processes of identity formation and negotiation. Performance theorists "read" these events as semiotic texts variously employing the familiar tropes of metaphor and, drawing on Mikhail M. Bakhtin, the carnivalesque, correctly recognizing that these two processes, as well as others, can occur within the same event (Brown 1997, Geertz 1973, Lavenda 1997, Noyes 2003). Cultural performances are part of a dialectic between structure and agency, may exhibit symbolic reversal of hegemonic social and power relations, express identity, are liminal so potentially transformational, are potentially counter-hegemonic, and may affirm the existing social order (e.g., Brandes 1988, Erlman 1996, Fernandez 1986, Limón 1989, Turner 1982). The Gilroy Garlic Festival illustrates that these processes are not necessarily mutually exclusive: several of these processes are at work at any given time within most cultural displays. Multidimensional events warrant multilayered readings. MacAloon's (1984b) analysis of the Olympic Games exemplifies this approach: in developing a theoretical paradigm for complex performative events, he outlines the synchronism of the four central performative genres (spectacle, festival, ritual, game) that coexist within the metagenre of the Games.

Creating and Sustaining Community

The Festival brings together Gilroy residents from all sectors of the community who volunteer their time for Festival planning and events. Their efforts raise funds for local nonprofit organizations, charities, and school groups. Their repeated volunteer participation instills and reinforces a sense of communal spirit year after year. As 2002 Gilroy Garlic Festival President Kurt Chacon reminded visitors in the Festival program book: "As you enjoy your day here, please keep in mind that this wonderful event is put on by over 4,000 volunteers who donate their time (42,000+ volunteer hours) to more than 150 non-profit groups. Over the last 23 years, the Festival has awarded almost $6 million to these groups. In addition to the economic benefits derived from this event, the Garlic Festival has taught us that giving of ourselves to the community has made our Community one that we are all extremely proud of" (Chacon 2002). Mention of the 4,000+ volunteers "clocking" from 38,000 to more than 42,000 volunteer hours, as well as a general reference to the more than 150 charities who benefit from funds raised at the Festival, consistently appears in the President's Message in each year's program.

The Gilroy Garlic Festival, like most community festivals, is not held solely for the entertainment of and economic gain from outsiders. In addition to tangible financial gains are intangible benefits felt especially among the locals whose volunteer efforts make the event successful. These benefits come in the forms of friendship among volunteers and individuals' sense of contributing to the betterment of the city, both of which engender communal spirit. Gilroyans' voluntary participation is a form of civic engagement that Robert Putnam (2000) argues has been in decline in America, especially since the 1970s. Yet community festivals throughout the country are staffed by local volunteers whose efforts exemplify Putnam's contention that individual civic participation leads to the betterment of the collective. The repeated volunteerism of Gilroyans challenges Putnam's argument about the decline of civic engagement: the 4,000-plus volunteers—nearly 10 percent of the city's population—who staff the Festival each year demonstrate that civic engagement is alive and well, at least in Gilroy, at least for this town's annual identificational event.

Many people return year after year as volunteers, often working in the same area each year. Young Gilroyans whose parents volunteer often end up assisting with Festival tasks themselves at a young age and develop zealous aspirations to work their way up the volunteer chain of command. Among the young volunteers with whom I spoke is Lauren Bevilacqua who, for example, began volunteering at the Festival when she was seven years old, working alongside her father as he helped set up and man the massive parking lots. When she was fifteen years old, Lauren aspired to be the first female chair of the parking committee by the time she was twenty-two. Each year Lauren took on additional responsibilities within parking lot operations, working the week before the Festival as well as all three days of the Festival. At eighteen years of age she was no longer determined to be the Parking Lot Committee Chair, although she did admit that it was "still kind of a goal . . . it would still be pretty cool to be the diamond in the rough so to speak." In addition to raising money for local nonprofit groups and learning leadership and management skills, Lauren commented that it is the camaraderie shared among fellow volunteers that keeps people returning year after year: "you go to the same place because you know and are practically family with the people out there." She says that she and a few other parking lot volunteers get together at least once during the year to recall anecdotes and memories they've collected working together over the years. Many other Festival volunteers see each other only once a year, at the Festival, thus endowing those intensive days together with a spirit of reunion and stressing the Festival's time out of time-ness.

The contagious energy of volunteering is what brings people back every year to stand in the dusty parking lot or work over hot flames for hours and hours. Longtime resident, former Festival Board of Directors member, and continuing volunteer Jodi Heinzen commented to me that many of her friends volunteer at the Festival, where "strong bonds are made when people work together for a similar goal." Besides, she continued, "it's a fun place to be. Everyone there is happy and having a good time. It feels good to make other people happy."

Amid all the hard work and fun, the volunteers' interactions produce a sense of community, the fuzzy yet desirable sense of belonging in a physical place as well as belonging to a group. The more than four thousand volunteers can be understood as a temporary, imagined community, one that contains multiple imagined subcommunities. A sense of community emerges that sustains volunteer workers through the intensive days before and during the Festival. This temporary and intensive sense of community is similar to *communitas* explored by Victor Turner (1979 [1969]). Initially conceived as emerging during the liminal phase of rites of passage, Turner's notion of communitas is applicable more broadly: it can refer to groups of individuals that come together for a defined period of time during which intensive, focused, and heightened positive or negative emotional energy and activities facilitate a spirit of oneness. Going through such an intensive, mutual experience produces a sense of community, one that is potentially transitory or periodically revived. The sense of camaraderie Festival volunteers articulate exemplifies how shared participation in an intensive experience can generate a sense of community. Some volunteers, like Jodi Heinzen and Lauren Bevilacqua, sustain the fellowship throughout the year; others partake only in the temporary community generated during the Festival.

Visitors similarly create a temporary community, albeit one even more short-lived and amorphous than that of the volunteers. They also participate in the temporary community created by the volunteers. An important element of the visitor-volunteer Festival relationship is their reciprocal exchange that is an essential thread connecting people in a community. At the Gilroy Garlic Festival, volunteers and attendees engage in important material and ideological reciprocal exchanges. At the most basic level, in exchange for the ten-dollar entry fee, Gilroyans reciprocate by providing opportunities to consume Gilroy's imaged identity. The hosts provide their guests with food (garlic-laden foods iconic of Gilroy, for an additional fee), entertainment (live music, the opportunity to dance, cooking demonstrations, children's games), mementoes of the visit (a plethora of garlicabilia, for an additional fee), and the experiential pleasure of being at the Festival.

Each of these exchanges involves interaction between the Festival participants and visitors. Through these exchanges, locals and guests strengthen
the significance of the temporary communities defined by the festival frame.
The consumption of garlic-laden foods and participation in or observation
of the garlic-themed events, as well as consumer transactions in the Garlic
Mercantile where garlicabilia are sold, affirm Gilroy's identity as a foodscape
and contribute to the perpetuation of Gilroy as a festive foodscape.

The volunteers are hosting a party to which thousands of people come
and, as Lauren Bevilacqua so astutely said, "the community feels the need to
come through for all the people who enjoy it. There is something exhilarating about knowing that you are needed to pull together a huge event. . . ." In
addition to being hosts, the volunteers are affirming the value of their city as
a branded place and of the people who inhabit it: "there are the true devotees who love to do it [volunteer] because they simply love Gilroy and love
Garlic and love what Gilroy stands [for] and how it looks compared to the
rest of the country," Bevilacqua continued. That the volunteer efforts raise
money to assist community groups adds another positive dimension to the
volunteers' sense of contributing to and being part of a community. And it
adds another layer of reciprocity: volunteers give of themselves for the betterment of the local organizations, which in turn contribute to the quality of
life for residents of Gilroy.

Not everyone catches the contagious positive communal spirit of the
Festival. Since its inception, some city officials and residents have been
ambivalent about, inconvenienced by, or disenfranchised from the Festival.
One community leader, speaking strictly "off the record," critiqued the
importance granted to garlic and the Festival by those with "tunnel vision."
This person wondered what the life of a garlic festival could be. Charged with
some aspects of long-term planning for the city, this business person opined
that city leaders should be considering the changing economies of Gilroy
and of the region, and that they should be looking beyond garlic rather than
focusing on it to the seeming exclusion of other profitable local industries
and businesses.

Longtime resident George White's family began raising garlic in Gilroy
early in the twentieth century. Even though he thinks the Festival makes a
"big deal of nothing," he conceded the he "likes anything that brings people to Gilroy" (Vashel and Eggers 1986, 11). Even ardent supporters of the

Festival like Heinzen do acknowledge that although "the attitude of most Gilroyans is positive . . . there are always some grumblers." It is especially the residents of Eagle Pass, one of the newer residential developments west of town, who don't like the Festival because modified traffic patterns and traffic jams during the Festival congest the roads leading to and from their upscale development.

Although the voices of dissenting residents are few, they are part of the local discourse. Absent from conversations and from most of the festivities are the workers who labor long hours harvesting and processing the garlic. Late summer is the busiest time of the year for Christopher Ranch and Gilroy Foods, as it is for most agricultural enterprises. The workers who produce the iconic food that defines Gilroy as a festive foodscape exist in the background. Like the "army upon army of migrant workers" in California that have been part of "the material production of landscape and the production of landscape representations" (Mitchell 1996, 1), these workers contribute to but are not a significant presence in the celebration of garlic.

The organizers, volunteers, and paying attendees are, for the most part, several steps removed from the processes of garlic agriculture. There are important exceptions including, notably, Bill Christopher from Christopher Ranch, who has been and continues to be involved with multiple aspects of Festival planning and presentation. Dissenting voices are few and faint. Organizers, city leaders, and residents affirm that the Festival's economic and intangible benefits far outweigh the power of those whom it inconveniences or disenfranchises.

Since its inception the Gilroy Garlic Festival has been a celebration of the locality and the intangible yet palpable sense of small-town spirit that exists in this city. As one observer commented, Gilroy has "the town spirit of boosterism that makes its glory in such agrarian championships [as claiming to be the Garlic Capital of the World], a kind of naïve civic optimism that stretches back to its roots" (Steinhardt 1979).

If Imitation Is Flattery . . .

It is not just the Festival's rapid and tenacious success or Gilroyans' demonstration of civic pride that makes Gilroy's status as a festive foodscape noteworthy. The Gilroy Garlic Festival is particularly appropriate to study because other festival organizers look to the Gilroy Garlic Festival as a highly successful model. Gilroy and its Festival were included in a U.S. Department of Housing and Urban Development publication "The Urban Fair: How Cities Celebrate Themselves" (Office of Public Affairs 1981). As the title suggests, fairs and festivals are regarded as vehicles for communal self-affirmation through celebration of community identity. The publication is designed to facilitate self-evaluation of existing urban festivals, and aid city leaders who want to organize new ones, for "the betterment of the community." Inclusion of Gilroy in this publication provided official, external validation of and for the festival as well-run, and as a model of successful city-boosterism.

If imitation is the most sincere form of flattery, organizers of Gilroy's Festival indeed should be flattered. Further validating Gilroy Garlic Festival's success is its acceptance among festival planners from other cities as a model to emulate. Visitors from across the country and throughout the world study Gilroy's Festival. For example, in 2002, representatives from the Philippines Province of Llocos, including officials from the Philippine Department of Tourism, visited the Festival. Other years, members of CalFest, the Californian and Nevada Festival and Events Association, have come to study the intricacies of producing this Festival. In anticipation of interpreting or mimicking the Gilroy model for the betterment of their hometowns' celebrations, visiting festival organizers meet with Festival administration, talk with volunteers, and take behind-the-scenes tours. At the 2005 Festival, I joined a representative from the Delray Beach, Florida, Chamber of Commerce on a VIP tour, led by Gilroy volunteer Jodi Heinzen. During the tour we had access to areas off-limits to regular Festival attendees and were encouraged to ask questions about all aspects of Festival production. Providing an example of imitation bordering on repetition, consider nearby Stockton's Asparagus Festival which is modeled after the Gilroy Garlic Festival and is complete with their vegetable-themed version of Gilroy's famed Gourmet Alley, "Asparagus Alley" (Lewis 1997).

Gilroy's image makers worked without the assistance of professional festival organizers, yet their event became the envy of image makers determined to produce community festivals throughout the world. That they could create a festive foodscape based on an ingredient on the fringe of mainstream American foodways attests to their creativity and commitment, and people's curiosity. Residents' repeated participation in all stages of the Festival facilitated and continues to reinforce their sense of Gilroy as home and as a valued public space.[7] Once established, personal and communal connections to place seem natural, even innate. If well marketed, presented, and received, a food-place association can seem organic as well. Such is the case with Gilroy and garlic. The Festival's ongoing popularity substantiates Festival organizers' anticipatory assertion that Gilroy is the Garlic Capital of the World.

CHAPTER THREE

From Foreign to Fad

Garlic's Twentieth-Century Transition

Gilroyans who are sentimental about the days when Gilroy's air reminded them of spaghetti sauce are also realistic. They know that not everyone appreciates the ever-present olfactory stimulation that blankets southern Santa Clara Valley during processing season, and that a negative reputation can spread further and linger longer than Gilroy's distinctive smell. Food columnist Elizabeth Mehren incorporated comments of derision about Gilroy's "pungent presence" into newspaper articles published in Los Angeles, Washington, D.C., and Chicago, emphasizing the city's odoriferous reputation (Mehren 1979a, 1979b, 1979c). Former garlic farmer, local chef, and Festival cofounder Val Filice reminisced that years ago, as he stood watching water run through his farm's irrigation system, tourists driving along Route 152 would stop to inquire about the "terrible smell"—the smell of "Gilroy's gold," garlic, being dehydrated. It wasn't just the smell of garlic processing that caused many people to wrinkle their noses and reinforced Gilroy's negative reputation. Mr. Filice recalls that outside the Italian community, "people were embarrassed to use garlic . . . because [it caused] bad breath and [because of] its odor." Prejudice against garlic as an ingredient and widespread mockeries of Gilroy's smell left Gilroyans with low communal self-esteem. Festival cofounder Rudy Melone noted that upon his arrival in Gilroy in the late 1970s, "[t]here was a general air of embarrassment about garlic—an absence of pride" (Midtgaard).

The inaugural Festival facilitated the transformation of Gilroy's association with garlic from negative to positive. Not only did Gilroy's place image change, so too did garlic's. The quirky Garlic Festival accelerated garlic's transition from a food on the dietary and social margins into mainstream American foodways.

· ◆ ·

That food is a metaphor for identity is readily accepted when related to regional and ethnic identity. Foodways are acknowledged "as a ticket to understand the power sustaining the continuity of ethnicity and region as matrices for the membership of individuals in groups" (Brown and Mussell 1984, 3). Many contemporary scholars correctly recognize ethnicity as a social process rather than a fixed category, and situate foodways within the performative process of identity (e.g., Kalčik 1984). Associations of ethnic groups with particular foods, perpetuated through "ethnic" restaurants and at ethnic food festivals, reinforce a general perception among members of the group as well as among outsiders or tourists that food is emblematic of ethnic identity (Heldke 2003, Magliocco 1998). Whether consumed at an ethnic eatery or an ethnic food festival, food is perceived a "safe" way to experience the exotic Other (Kugelmass 1990, Van Esterik 1982).

It is not just tantalizing flavors that attract image makers to food as an organizational theme: the simultaneous intrigue and seeming symbolic neutrality of many food items are among its attractions. Because food is regarded as a safe medium for experiencing the Other, be it a people or a place, organizers can avoid potentially divisive issues such as ethnic identity or contested history. Group or community identity can be unintentionally or deliberately consolidated into a food item and, through that item, outsiders and insiders figuratively consume the identity while literally consuming the iconized food. Food festivals and the food served at them are food-culture consolidation in a festival frame. As Sally Moore and Barbara Myerhoff note, "[c]eremonies that make visible a collective connection with some common symbol or activity can minimize for a ceremonial moment their disconnections and conflicts . . . even while depicting them" (1977, 6). Festival organizers create ceremonial food events in hopes of drawing people together, even temporarily, to generate a sense of communal spirit and identity based on the perceived accessibility of food. Food is encoded with multilayered systems of meaning and symbolism, however, making it "different from run-of-the-mill commodities, both in the depth of meaning ascribed to it and in the complexity of the system that produces it" (Charles 2002). But, like that of most commodities, food's symbolization is dynamic and subject to change.

Concisely stating a truism, Howard Marshall comments that "like dialect and architecture, food traditions are a main component in the intricate and impulsive system that joins culture and geography into regional character" (1979, 400). Over time and through intergroup interactions, traditional foods of one group, be it a cultural or a geographic group, may take on varied or new meanings: encoded meanings can change, reinforcing the dynamic character of symbolic signification. The post–Civil War transition of Maine lobster from a low- to high-status food (Lewis 1998) and the evolution and mainstreaming of a Southwestern cuisine (Bentley 2004) exemplify the changeability of food's emblematic significance. Place-food associations, such as Maine and lobsters or Michigan and cherries, like many ethnic-food associations, are often unquestioningly accepted. As natural as they may appear, however, place-food associations become familiar through deliberate manipulation and promotion. A casual tour through any grocery store reveals labels promoting a relationship between place and food product. Even the produce section, mostly devoid of labels, bears witness to the custom of associating certain products with specific places. For example, the consumer might find Idaho baking potatoes, California berries, New York and Washington state apples. Regional specialties increasingly find homes in mainstream markets, but in general the markets continue to stock items popularly associated with specific places. Place-food associations are imaged and reinforced through commodification, from food labels (de Wit 1998) to festive foodscapes.

Immigrant Foodways, Nativism, and Dietary Reform

The embarrassment about which Melone spoke and that people felt toward garlic predates Gilroy's negative press and odoriferous agribusiness. It was rooted in culinary egocentrism lingering from the colonial era and reinforced during the period of massive southern European migration to the United States in the decades around the turn of the twentieth century.

Italians have been coming to the American continent since one of their countrymen was instrumental in documenting previously uncharted lands in the Western Hemisphere. The greatest number of Italian immigrants came to the United States between 1896 and 1910, with some three hundred thousand recorded as arriving in 1907 alone (Federal Writers' Project 1938). While most stayed in northern and eastern cities to live and work, some were taken or went by choice inland to work the land or help develop the unsettled spaces of the American West. Substantial Italian immigration to California began around the time of that state's gold rush, facilitated by passenger ship service between Italy and San Francisco that began mid-century (Gumina 1978). As California's economy shifted from mining toward agriculture and industry, Italian settlement patterns shifted as well. Drawn by the gentle climate and availability of rich farmland, many Italians from San Francisco moved toward the agricultural counties of San Joaquin, Santa Clara, and Sonoma, contributing knowledge and labor to these counties' nascent agricultural industries.

Despite the cultural diversity of California's population, prejudices against certain immigrant groups informed the social landscape, as they did throughout the country. One manifestation of cultural bigotry came in the form of culinary egocentrism. Such "deviations from the logic of the table," notes Reay Tannahill, historically "had very little to do with food. They were political or social gestures" (Tannahill 1988, 347). She observes that those in "the Western world who canalized their ordinary human need to feel superior" did so through intolerance of "homosexuals, Jews, people who ate garlic or colored their hair, Catholics, blacks . . ." (ibid., 348). The presence of garlic eaters among her list of people discriminated against indicates how widespread the distaste was for both the food and the people who ate it.

Since people articulate individual and collective identities through incorporation of or aversion to particular consumables, it follows that rejection of specific foods can be really a prejudicial dismissal of the people associated with that food. Hence, the early aversion to garlic among Anglo-Americans, particularly those of northern European descent, was an expression of their prejudice against garlic-eating immigrant populations. The historical anti-garlic sentiment can be understood as a minor articulation of nativist ideology, what John Higham (1955) described as nationalism guided by an antiforeign spirit and related fear of internal threats to the nation (see also Anbinder 1992, Billington 1974, Jacobson 1998, Knobel 1995).

This antiforeign spirit has its roots in America's colonial heritage, specifically pre–Civil War anti-Catholic sentiments expressed by Protestants, a prejudice carried with the colonists from England (Higham 1955, Tannahill 1988). The antiforeign spirit among the people who were themselves recently transplanted foreigners evolved into a sense of American exceptionalism. Early feelings of American exceptionalism were a natural outcome of the Puritan conception that their "city on the hill" was a fulfillment of scriptural prophecy.[1] The ideological seeds of American exceptionalism slowly germinated and manifested in the nativist movement. Throughout American history, the targets and expressions of nativist prejudices, though not always called that, have varied. In the mid-nineteenth century, an antiforeign spirit was articulated in political and social ways, including the short-lived Know-Nothing Party and longer-lasting reform efforts intended to expedite the Americanization of immigrant populations. At the turn of the twentieth century through the First World War, the population that commanded much of nativists' attention was the Southern European immigrants, including especially Italians. Reflecting the opinion of the time, Jacob A. Riis wrote in his muckraking exposé that the "swarthy Italian immigrant," who is also "honest" and "lighthearted," "claims a large share of public attention, partly because he keeps coming at such a tremendous rate" (1971 [1890], 47, 45). So widely known and shared among Riis's readership were the Italian's "conspicuous faults" that Riis was not inclined to enumerate them.

The concern felt by nativists over controlling the flow of immigration, and their anxiety about exerting control over those immigrants already living in America, informed official and unofficial activities in the interest of Americanization. A multitude of reform efforts attempted to expedite

Americanization of the immigrant masses. This is not to suggest that all reform efforts were articulations of nativist ideology; they were not. Yet many reformers linked foodways with one's fitness to be an American citizen. These reformers interpreted the continuing practice of immigrant populations' native foodways as un-American.

Several historical contingencies informed nativists' inclination to reform immigrants. A sense of cultural and ethnic superiority among some Anglo-Americans of northern European descent, bolstered by a festering fear of losing political power as the population was diluted by these immigrant populations, fed the flames of the rekindled nativist movement. The flood of Catholic immigrants, specifically immigrants from southern European Catholic countries such as Italy, was perceived as a threat to the American political system and national identity. Labor clashes, right-to-vote issues, and muckraking that revealed the squalor in which many urban immigrants lived brought concerns about assimilation or lack thereof to the fore, resulting in what was perceived as an immigration problem. The turn of the twentieth century witnessed increased distrust of immigrant populations. The steadily increasing distribution and readership of newspapers and magazines perpetuated and spread the negativity. The prejudicial title and content of a 1901 article in *American Kitchen Magazine* exemplify the era's prejudice against immigrant foods. In the article "Queer Foreign Foods in America," the author called immigrant foods "coarse and unsavory compared with the food of his [the immigrant's] adopted land" (Shapiro 1986). Dr. Allan McLaughlin of the U.S. Public Health and Marine Hospital Service was a frequent commentator on immigrants and "the immigrant problem" in the early years of the twentieth century. In his authoritative magazine articles he perpetuated detrimental stereotypes of several immigrant "races," including the Italians (e.g., McLaughlin 1904, 1903).

Food reform was one of several avenues pursued by Progressive Era (~1890–1920) reformers seeking to improve the lives of urban immigrants. That era's attitudes toward food reform were a continuation of earlier health-diet reform efforts. Sylvester Graham (1794–1851) was one of many early nineteenth-century health reformers whose teachings emphasized vegetarianism, temperance, and sexual abstinence. Like many other dietary reformers of that period, he advocated a diet devoid of all condiments and spices because they overstimulated the body (Haber 2002, Nissenbaum 1980).

Following in Graham's footsteps were many whose health-motivated, dietary reform teachings had long-lasting influences on the American diet. Other nineteenth- and early twentieth-century reformers, including especially Wilbur Olin Atwater (1844-1907, who introduced the calorie to Americans) and John Harvey Kellogg (1852–1943, creator of Kellogg's cereal), talked about food and morality without reference to taste, tradition, or context; for them food was regarded solely as fuel for the body (Carson 1976 [1957], Coveney 2000, Whorton 1982). The teachings of these early dietary reformers forever changed the ways Americans think about and consume food (Schwartz 1986, Stacey 1994). As the health-dietary reform movement secured a foothold among nineteenth-century Anglo-Americans, they began to turn their reform-mindedness toward others. Believing their foodways and lifestyles to be superior to those of the increasing numbers of immigrants from southern and eastern Europe, reformers sought to Americanize immigrants' diets.

Reformers involved in settlement houses and the home economics movement regarded foodways as an appropriate medium through which to instill American values among immigrant populations (Jass 2004). Reformers targeted food because they equated healthy eating with the health of the nation. Robert Woods, who ran one of Boston's settlement houses, expressed the reformist ideology that foreign foodways were ill-suited to the American way of life; in a 1904 charity organization publication he wrote that the Italian's "over-stimulating and innutritious diet is precisely the opposite sort of feeding from that demanded by our exhilarating and taxing atmosperic conditions. This fact suggests [that dietary reform is] the first and perhaps the chief step in bringing about the adaptation of the Italian type of life to America" (1904, 81). Visually and odoriferously distinctive, Italian immigrants' foodways were particularly conspicuous to those concerned with assimilation. Continued use of exotic flavors was interpreted as resistance to Americanization and, therefore among radical nativists, a threat to national security. As Harvey Levenstein noted, "[t]he acrid smells of garlic and onions wafting through the immigrant quarters seemed to provide unpleasant evidence that their inhabitants found American ways unappealing; that they continued to find foreign (and dangerous) ideas as palatable as their foreign food" (2003, 104).

Several other undercurrents were swirling about during the Progressive Era that informed dietary reform efforts. One of the social forces directing reformers' attention to foodways was the "cult of domesticity" that fortified early nineteenth-century domestic life (Cott 1997 [1977], Sklar 1973). The cult of domesticity empowered women with superior moral sensibility and positioned their domain, the domestic sphere, as critical to the development of strong individual and therefore national character. This ideology fostered belief in the civilizing capacity of women among many of the era's elite and the emerging middle class; and it was women in these strata of society who had both the time and the inclination to participate in reform movements. As the century matured, the belief in women as keepers of morality was absorbed into American ideology. The idea that women and women's work, such as domestic food preparation, can shape and control the morality of society is at the foundation of much of the late nineteenth-century social reform ideology. Settlement houses and classes taught there, including cooking classes, were perceived to be for the good of the immigrants and of the nation; resistance in the form of failure to assimilate was interpreted as disloyalty to the immigrants' adopted home and a threat to the strength of the nation.

Reform efforts in the decades around the turn of the twentieth century were inspired also by tremendous changes taking place in nearly all aspects of food science and technology. Among the many influences shaping Americans' perceptions about food and consumption at that time were the discovery of vitamins, the nascent field of nutritional science, the advent of scientific cookery, the emergence of home economics as a respectable source for domestic management advice, the growth of corporate food purveyors, and the increasing importance of food advertising.[2] Scientific discourse within the domestic science movement about food and the body resembled those of previous dietary reformers: food was sustenance and fuel, pleasure and taste simply were not part of the rhetoric.

Additional undercurrents informing the evolution of American attitudes toward food and dietary reform included a tenacious vestige of Puritan ideology and lingering influences of British culinary tradition. Waverly Root describes "a Puritanical disapproval of self-indulgence and a feeling that there was something sinful about enjoying one's food" (1995 [1976], 162). This Puritan spirit may be so firmly planted in Americans' psyche that, as he suggests, it nourished the nineteenth-century moralistic dietary reform movement, and continues in the contemporary apprehension toward foods that are offered and consumed more for pleasures of the palate than for nutritional sustenance.

In his exploration of American culinary heritage, Harvey Levenstein (2003) notes that, despite the presence of non-British immigrants, American foodways during the colonial era through the nineteenth century were most significantly influenced by British foodways (see also Harris 1979 [1974]). Consistent with the restraint displayed toward the use of spices among the British middle and upper classes during the eighteenth century, the new Americans eschewed heavily seasoned foods. Garlic and other strong flavors were regarded as dangerous to the moral fiber of society because spicy foods were thought to stimulate the body, which in turn led to sinful sexual thoughts and excessive consumption of alcohol. The association between Italians and garlic was so firmly implanted in the popular imagination that an aversion to garlic expanded into a negative attitude toward Italian immigrant foodways (Levenstein 1985). The Italians were certainly not the only immigrant population whose traditional foodways embraced garlic, nor the only ones subject to culinary ethnocentrism. In his study of changing foodways among Greek immigrants to America, Robert Theodorataus (1981, 1983) stresses the potent negativity among Anglo-Americans toward garlic and its eaters in general, and toward Greeks in particular: "No food has raised more ire among anglicized Americans than has garlic. Both garlic and those who ate it were viewed as offenders against public decency and morals." His research concludes that after 1960, however, as other ethnic foods (notably Italian and some Spanish) became more popular, Euro-Anglo American acceptance of garlic became more "liberal." By the 1970s, he continues, garlic was used in Greek recipes in larger amounts and with increased frequency. Since there were so many more Italian than Greek immigrants settling in the United States around the turn of the twentieth century, it is no wonder that the association between garlic and Italians was more firmly established in the popular imagination than an association between garlic and other immigrant communities.

The well-intentioned reformers did not anticipate that their efforts would meet resistance. Despite reformist pressures and the challenges of procuring familiar ingredients, Italian immigrants generally clung to their foodways. Food is, after all, a sensual link to one's homeland, and familiar foods are all the more comforting for those living in a new or foreign country.

Italians immigrants used food—traditional Italian foods, or American foods prepared in traditional Italian ways—as what Tracy Poe (2001) calls "portable systems of ethnic unity," and tangible symbols of their mother country. In cities like New York, and in small towns like Roseto, Pennsylvania, Italian immigrants tended to live in close-knit communities with other Italians. In San Francisco, for example, there existed a "small colony with a physiognomy all its own . . . [that] was essentially self-sufficient, in small part, of its own volition, in much larger part, because it was socially and economically constrained to be so. The presence of this homogeneous core of Italians naturally re-enforced habits, customs and modes of thought . . ." (Radin 1935). Adding to the fact that food played "particularly important roles in Italian family life[,] . . . it was extremely difficult to gain entry into Italian family home and kitchens or to coax the women out of them" (Levenstein 1985).

Dietary reform efforts had little impact on changing Italian foodways also because reformist ideology and practices, taught primarily through cooking and nutrition classes, undermined the role and significance of Italian women as domestic authorities and knowledgeable cooks. As Hasia Diner summarizes in her study of immigrant foodways, "Discussions of Italian women as cooks, and good ones at that, and as the ones who stood by their food as the symbol of their indispensability, ran through the remembered details of immigrant and first-generation life" (2001, 77). The fact that these women had to learn to use new ingredients and new appliances made them likely candidates for the cooking classes offered by reformers at settlement houses and by home economists at public schools. But such classes were viewed with disdain. Although they attended other classes such as sewing with enthusiasm, few participated in classes on nutrition, cooking, and food budgeting.

> This general pattern predominated in most settlement houses and other sites for immigrant adult education. American ameliorative organizations tried hard to appeal to Italian women to modify their cooking habits. But Italian women mostly ignored them . . . [because] attending a class on a particular subject amounted to an admission of ignorance, incompetence, a need to improve. Since Italian women in America defined much of their personal worth in terms of cooking, cooking classes were cultural land mines. . . . For a woman to sign up for a class would be tantamount to a public declaration that her family somehow found her cooking skills wanting.[3]

From Culinary Periphery to Food Fad

The lingering suspicion toward particular spices and seasonings, and reform-ist prejudice against foreign diets continued well into the twentieth cen-tury. Yet despite the best efforts of social reformers and lingering foodways prejudice, garlic slowly infiltrated mainstream American cookery. Garlic's gradual incorporation into revised editions of Fannie Farmer's *The Boston Cooking-School Cook Book*, the cornerstone of classic American cookery instructional books, reflects incremental assimilation and acceptance of the pungent bulb. The book's first edition in 1896 neither included garlic among the list of condiments "used to stimulate the appetite by adding flavor to food," nor was garlic an ingredient in any of the five tomato sauce recipes, including "Sauce à l'Italienne" (Farmer 1896, 241). The only recipe in the 1896 cookbook that called for garlic was "A Chapon," a piece of bread rubbed with raw garlic and incorporated into a tossed salad to season salad. Garlic was not included in the "Seasoning" section of the 1912 edition (Farmer 1912 [1906]). Yet by 1933 garlic was listed as an ingredient in a few dishes includ-ing a recipe for "Mexican" tomato sauce, which called for one clove of garlic; surprisingly no garlic was among the ingredients for that edition's "Italian" tomato sauce (Farmer 1933). The 1951 revised edition finally included garlic in its "Spices and Seeds" section, noting that "Garlic adds particularly appe-tizing seasoning to many dishes" (Farmer 1951, 36). Garlic is also present as a key ingredient in several dishes, among them "Garlic Olives," "Garlic Bread," and "Sauce for Spaghetti."

Despite a gradual incorporation of more recipes with garlic in the 1959 tenth revised edition, editor Wilma Lord Perkins advised caution, noting that "Many foreign recipes owe much of their special quality to unusual sea-sonings. Use unfamiliar seasonings with discretion" (Farmer 1959, 15). Other cookbooks printed in America included recipes with garlic, indicating that it was not a completely unfamiliar or wholly eschewed ingredient. For exam-ple, *Miss Corson's Practical American Cookery and Household Management* (1886), penned by New York Cooking School founder Juliet Corson, included a recipe for "mock-caviare" made by pounding boned anchovies with a clove of garlic.

Amid dramatic changes in American foodways during the first half of the twentieth century, ambivalence toward some foreign foods, including garlic, remained. In his social history of eating in America, Levenstein claims that American culture's phobia about garlic made it "a particular embarrassment" (2003 [1993], 29). The author of a 1939 article about the charismatic and hugely popular New York Yankee Joe DiMaggio affirms that he is "well adapted to most U.S. mores," specifically mentioning that he used water instead of olive oil to slick his hair and that he "never reeks of garlic" (Bunch 1939, 69). Even though garlic retained its negative aura among non-Italians, Levenstein (1985, 2003 [1993]) also notes that some "Italo-American" dishes were so resistant to reformist Americanization that they were adapted and incorporated into the mainstream foodways. Rather than being Americanized out of existence, dishes like spaghetti transgressed cultural boundaries, were adapted (thus Americanized by modification), and were incorporated into mainstream foodways. The incorporation of spaghetti and meatballs into restaurants frequented by non-Italians and onto domestic and commercial menus of non-Italians exemplifies how Italian foodways contributed to an evolving twentieth-century American cuisine.[4] In 1946, Hector Boiardi sold his Chef Boyardee canned spaghetti business to an American conglomerate, a move that exemplifies the "uncoupling of enclave foods from enclave businessmen": going corporate marked the transition of "ethnic foods into the national marketplace and the cultural mainstream of American life" (Gabaccia 1998, 150–151).

In the mid-twentieth century garlic was continuing its gradual transition from a food on the margin of mainstream American foodways to a familiar ingredient. A recipe for garlic bread was not included in *The Boston Cooking School Cook Book* until the 1951 edition. By 1956, the author of an article in *Collier's* magazine seemed to be complaining that garlic bread had become so ubiquitous in restaurants and on domestic dining tables throughout the country that it "borders on the commonplace" (MacDougald Jr. 1956). Consumption of fresh garlic rose from about 4.5 million pounds in 1945 to over 36 million pounds by 1956 (ibid.). Even allowing for population growth, those numbers indicate an impressive rise in use, and suggest that Americans were acquiring a taste for the pungent product. A few years later, the American Dehydrated Onion and Garlic Association sponsored a consumer survey, the results of which were noteworthy because they "disprove[d] some widely held theories about the use of garlic in the home" (Gentry Foods 1961). From the survey Gentry Foods, a producer of dehydrated garlic, concluded that "Garlic, in all its forms, is a growing market, with greatest use among younger families . . . . Garlic is a sophisticated product, appealing more strongly to persons of above average economic status and education . . . . And garlic is now socially acceptable, being used almost as often for 'company' meals as for family meals, and is being used by over 90 percent of all families." That a garlic-processing company published such optimistic statements about one of its products is self-serving, but, even if their optimism was hyperbolic, they were commenting on an existing food trend: the increased use of previously eschewed ingredient.

Historians position the late 1950s and early 1960s as pivotal years for American food culture (e.g., Belasco and Scranton 2002, Shapiro 2004).[5] Ongoing developments at all levels of farm and food industrialization since the last decades of the nineteenth century facilitated the industrialization of cooking and consumption practices from the 1950s onward (Symons 2000). Two disparate events took place within days of each other in 1963 that bolstered an ongoing transformation of American foodways and domestic cooking landscapes: the airing of Julia Child's television show *The French Kitchen*, and the publication of Betty Friedan's *The Feminine Mystique*. Jessamyn Neuhaus summarizes that "the 1960s saw the rapid 'gourmetization' of United States food culture" (2003, 323).

Early popular American celebrity chefs such as James Beard and Julia Child did much to promote the use of garlic among American home cooks. Included in James Beard's 1965 cookbook, *Menus for Entertaining*, were numerous recipes incorporating garlic as a primary seasoning agent, among them several breakfast dishes. His encouragement of home cooks to incorporate garlic into the first meal of the day, especially dishes prepared for company, indicated his willingness to set aside previously popular notions of restraint in favor of flavor.[6] Julia Child's 1968 *The French Chef Cookbook*, based on her wildly popular PBS television program, included a recipe for *Aïgo Bouido*, Provençale garlic soup. Although there is only one garlic-centric recipe in the book, its inclusion indicated her interest in getting American domestic cooks to be less inhibited about using garlic. Beard's and Child's enthusiastic incorporation of ingredients previously regarded with suspicion served to expand domestic cooks' and diners' willingness to work with and eat such ingredients.

Before becoming widely accepted by the American public, garlic developed a cult-like following. Among its leading proponents was Lloyd J. Harris who, in 1974, founded the organization Lovers of the Stinking Rose to spread the gospel of garlic. In addition to an annual newsletter called "Garlic Times," Harris authored two books about garlic that became classics among devotees: *The Book of Garlic* (1979 [1974]) and *The Official Garlic Lover's Handbook* (1986). In 1976, at the suggestion of Harris, Berkeley restaurateur and chef Alice Waters organized a garlic-themed Bastille Day dinner at her Chez Panisse restaurant. Already known in culinary circles for her commitment to using only seasonal, organic foods long before it was trendy, Waters's theme meal elevated garlic to an ingredient worthy of critical acclaim among other chefs and foodies.

By the mid-1970s, the number of garlic fans was increasing and cooking with garlic became a fad. The emergence of a genre of garlic-themed cookbooks around this time reflects garlic's status as a food fad ingredient. Early in the publishing trend were *The Great Garlic Cookbook* (Meyer and Cato 1975) and *Garlic Cookery* (Shulman 1984). The Gilroy Garlic Festival Committee contributed to a growing garlic-centric literature, self-publishing *The Garlic Lover's Cookbook* (1980) followed by several others, including *Garlic Lover's Greatest Hits: 20 Years of Prize-Winning Recipes from the Gilroy Garlic Festival* (1998). There is no shortage of garlic cookbooks in the contemporary marketplace, indicating garlic's popularity among American eaters, or at least among cookbook authors and publishers.[7] Documentary filmmaker Les Blank commemorated garlic's apparent Bay area cult-type following in his 1980 film *Garlic Is as Good as Ten Mothers*. Included in the fifty-one-minute film is footage from the first Gilroy Garlic Festival as well as from the Chez Panisse garlic dinner. Garlic is the main ingredient not only of books, videos, and theme dinners, but also of some restaurants, most notably San Francisco's famed garlic restaurant, The Stinking Rose: A Garlic Restaurant. The restaurant's owner Jerry Dal Bozzo published his homage to the bulb, *The Stinking Cookbook: The Layman's Guide to Garlic Eating, Drinking, and Stinking* (1994), which is sold, along with other garlicabelia, through the restaurant's web site (www.thestinkingrose.com) and in a San Francisco retail store.

The measurable change in garlic's acceptance is partly the result of changing attitudes toward the populations who used garlic. The steady flood of immigrants from Southern Europe that contributed to what had been conceived as "the immigrant problem" slowed during World War I. Immigration restrictions in the 1920s further curtailed the influx of immigrants from southern Europe. With the passage of stricter immigration laws, interest in Americanization reform waned.[8] A postwar desire among Anglo-Americans for national unity likely contributed to increased tolerance of southern Europeans already living in the United States, although ongoing prejudice against Asians belied the presumed wish for national unity. Social, political, and economic crises, including the Great Depression, World War II, and Cold War ideology diverted attention away from Americanization to matters of survival and national unity, especially between Anglo-Americans and the European immigrant communities they previously considered outsiders. Changes in immigration law and immigration patterns continued to inform American foodways. As the population changed, so too did what constituted mainstream foodways. For example, increased immigration of Mexicans and Latin Americans in the late 1960s and 1970s facilitated exposure to and availability of new foods and flavor combinations, some of which gradually entered the mainstream.

Renewed health concerns in the 1960s had middle-class Americans thinking about food differently and initiated a quest for ways to cook and eat with less fat and less salt.[9] Using spices, including garlic, to season food was presented as a healthier way to cook and eat for health-conscious Americans. The ethnic revival of the 1970s elevated ethnic clothing, dialect, and foodways. It also stimulated Americans to think about ethnicity in new ways, as negotiable, voluntary and, therefore, not quite so foreign.[10]

Gradually garlic entered the world of gourmet foods and from there it rapidly transitioned, as do many foods that mark distinction, to the mainstream. Genovese pesto, a sauce made from garlic, fresh basil, pine nuts, and parmesan or pecorino cheese blended with olive oil, for example, now is readily available in jars at grocery stores throughout the country.[11] Increased international travel also roused an interest in what previously had been foreign flavors. All of these factors exposed an increasing number of people to different foods and foodways, including garlic, which less than a century ago was the subject of condemnation.

By 1979, garlic was still on the fringe of American foodways, but it was less negatively charged as an identificational icon than it had been. The immediate success of the first Gilroy Garlic Festival indicates that at least fifteen thousand people were curious about garlic and to see what Gilroyans would do with garlic. The Festival owes its success, according to Mr. Filice, to people's willingness to try what he called an underappreciated food. That culinary curiosity is attributable to garlic's gradual incorporation into American foodways and the willingness of Bay area residents to attend a quirky food festival. Many forces coalesce to inform the constantly evolving American culinary landscape; likewise, many forces contributed to Gilroy image makers' successful branding of the city as a festive foodscape.

CHAPTER FOUR

Garlic Galore

*Festival Inversion, Subversion, and the
Enactment of Labor Relations*

Twice each day during the Festival, a crowd gathers around a hay bale–defined circular demonstration area centrally located on the Festival site. Fully exposed to the sun's glaring rays, Festival goers sit on the hay or stand in uneven rows behind it, anticipating a show. At noon and again at three in the afternoon, Bill Christopher, one of the owners of Christopher Ranch and son of Festival cofounder Don Christopher, enters the circle and begins introducing the contestants, all of whom are already kneeling on the ground preparing their work space. "Let's give a big round of applause for Marie!" shouts Christopher enthusiastically. "And this is Juanita, let's hear it for Juanita!" he continues, as more of the crowd claps and cheers. After introducing each contestant, the contest begins. For the next five minutes, the audience applauds and whistles and calls out to the contestants, cheering them along as they work furiously fast to top garlic. Whoever finishes with the heaviest bushel baskets wins cash and the glory of victory.

This is the Garlic Topping contest, the most unique event on the Festival program. Actually, the topping contest has a second component, one just as popular as the competitive display of garlic workers. Even though it is not advertised in the program book, most of the audience, many of whom are repeat visitors to the Festival, know about it and come prepared. Each facet of the topping contest is a fascinating cultural enactment of how social order and power relationships are framed, affirmed, and challenged within the festival frame.

· ◆ ·

Community festivals embody the processes that inform daily life. The community festival as a whole and each of its constitutive elements are cultural enactments because they are intensifications of daily life through which participants affirm, challenge, or subvert normative behavior and expectations. At agricultural fairs and food-themed community festivals, some events also express participants' and observers' relationships with each other and their relationships with food production.

Among a festival's constitutive elements are drama and contest (Stoeltje 1989), events through which societal norms are challenged and affirmed, and through which known and latent conflicts might be expressed. A familiar feature of the dramatic display of festival contests is the inversion of normative roles and behaviors. In such venues, however, tension—expressed through inversion—can be expressed safely because festival time is not "real" time, but a playful, liminal time out of time. Within cultural enactments like festivals, "Play is both unreal and yet productive of a greater sense of reality" (Abrahams 1977, 88): cultural enactments simultaneously call attention to the seriousness of that which is being enacted, and are an intensification of the playful not-realness of the display. Although what occurs within dramatic displays doesn't "count" as real life, it is very much part of real life and such displays are important venues through which relations are acted out, challenged, and affirmed.

Among the crowd-pleasing, garlic events at the Gilroy Garlic Festival are the garlic braiding interactive demonstrations and the garlic topping contests. These two events, unique to the Gilroy Garlic Festival, warrant critical attention because of their uniqueness and, more importantly, because they present a microcosm of labor and consumer relations, and participants in them witness and partake in Festival inversion. Through these two events, participants enact their relationship as consumers with an agricultural product and the workers who labor to produce it. Although there is a near-complete erasure of labor at the Festival, these two events remind visitors that garlic is an agricultural product.

The garlic braiding contest and the garlic topping contest each involves garlic in its natural state—"fresh from the field" dried bulbs. One is an informal, hands-on class during which Festival goers manipulate dried garlic; the other is a competitive event during which Festival goers watch others manipulate the dried bulbs. Before attending to garlic braiding and topping, however, the Garlic Queen and her Court warrant attention, because no discussion of a community festival would be complete without consideration of festival royalty. Like festival queens in general, the Garlic Queen and her Court symbolize the enduring social and moral standards of the host community.

It's Not a Beauty Pageant

As with any living tradition, the Festival retains its vitality by changing over time. In the Festival's early years an extensive menu of preliminary satellite events, such as the Tour de Garlic bike tour and the Reek Run foot race, were used to generate additional interest and participation in the Festival. As participant involvement waned, satellite events were dropped from the calendar. The calendar of prelude events associated with the Festival has dwindled; in fact, the Festival Association does not organize any pre-festival public events. They do, however, participate in other community events: the Festival Association sponsors an entertainment stage and has a food booth at an annual classic car show called the Garlic City Fun Run that is organized by a local car club, held two weeks before the Festival. According to Chris Filice of the Festival Association, the association's participation at the automobile Fun Run does not provide much publicity for the Festival but it is a "good will gesture." The association's participation in community events is part of the cycle of civic engagement that seems to thrive in Gilroy.

Among the events that remain vital to the Festival is the Gilroy Garlic Queen Pageant. The drama of selecting Miss Gilroy Garlic and her Court takes place in early May, well ahead of the midsummer Festival. The selection of Gilroy's Festival royalty is similar to contests in other rural towns in that it is a display produced by locals and, importantly, for local consumption rather than for visitors or tourists.[1]

The young women who vie for the honor of being the "Belle of the Bulb" are judged on personal interviews (40 percent), talent (20 percent), evening gown poise (20 percent), and garlic-themed speeches or skits (20 percent). The personal interviews are conducted privately and individually, in front of just the five judges, each of whom is a Gilroy resident with some experience in the fashion industry or with many years of Festival participation. The remaining components are performed in front of an audience of local family and friends at the culminating pageant, held in an auditorium at the local community college. Audience members do not hesitate to express their enthusiasm by clapping, yelling out, and cheering for individual contestants as they display themselves on stage. To one side of the auditorium is a television camera: community members who are not able to get tickets to the pageant or want to relive the excitement of the evening can watch it on community access television throughout the coming year. Upon completion of the competition the judges, who are seated at a long, rectangular table between the stage and the audience, select the winner and runners-up.

The Garlic Queen and her Court embody communal and societal ideals— stable yet dynamic, implicitly accepted yet ambiguous standards. Through the pageant, collective expectations about traits upstanding young women should exhibit are articulated. Inherent in the pageant genre, for example, is the expectation that the contestants will be physically attractive. Gilroyans, however, are quick to state that "it is not a beauty pageant."[2] The lack of emphasis on physical appearance among audience members and in the evaluative scoring at the Garlic Queen Pageant is offset by the inclusion of additional, seemingly less superficial standards important to the well-being of the community: that she is or will be attending college, will do community service, and will represent the town in a positive way.

As place-based food festival royalty, the queen personifies the locality's food-place association. She and her court come to symbolize Gilroy and its garlic, further strengthening garlic's role as the vehicle by which citizens of Gilroy affirm community values. The Garlic Queen and her Court are obligated to represent the community in the weeks leading up to the Festival and, most importantly, for various activities throughout the Festival days.

Among the Garlic Royalty's responsibilities are entertaining the audience at the Cook-off while the judges' scores are tallied, and congratulating contest winners as they are announced. Here, 2000 Gilroy Garlic Queen Leila Alicia Wright hands the second-place plaque to Susan Runkle, of Walton, Kentucky, for her entry, Crispy Garlic Salmon Cakes with Roasted Corn Salsa. (Photograph by author)

Through their royal activities, these young women display to a wider public the moral and societal standards most valued by Gilroyans.

Ongoing incorporation of king and queen pageants into community festival programs indicates the contest genre's ongoing relevance to the host communities. While they do affirm social values, they also contain elements of festival play and Bakhtinian carnival license. In contrast to normative behavioral paradigms, the participating young women are allowed, and in fact encouraged, to parade themselves as spectacles, to flaunt their talents, and to articulate reasons each is "better" than her competitors. The potential danger of undermining established authority by crowning a new leader (albeit food royalty) is mitigated because the coronation and the enactment of the royal duties take place within festival's liminal time out of time. The ongoing inclusion of queen pageants in the American festival repertoire is mimetic recognition that judgment and competition are central aspects of

American ideology, and more specifically, that American society judges her youth, rewarding those who embody societal ideals. The temporary nature of the Gilroy Garlic Queen's appointment—each Garlic Queen and Court reign for one year before being replaced—mimics the reality of recurring judgment and frequent replacement of media stars within American popular culture. Despite the brevity of community festival royalty's reign, the continued presence of festival queens affirms the importance of female authority in American culture in general, and even in the absence of a ruling monarchy, of royalty in particular.

The young women who become garlic royalty and their subsequent performances in that role affirm the collective expectation of young women among Gilroyans while also affirming the significance of garlic as iconic of positive elements of Gilroy as a community.[3] They and their activities also affirm Gilroy's brand identity as a garlic-themed festive foodscape.

Garlic Galore I: Braiding

At Garlic Grove, a centrally located garlic information booth, interested visitors can obtain free garlic growing kits: canvas bags bearing the name ConAgra, the parent company of Gilroy Foods, containing two bulbs or heads of garlic. Volunteers manning the booth offer spoken and printed instructions on how, where, and when to plant the garlic, how to care for it, and when to harvest it. On display at Garlic Grove are photographs showing commercially raised garlic at various stages of its growth, harvest, and production. The visual displays, garlic growing kits, and the topping contest are the only conspicuous indications that garlic is an agricultural product that requires human involvement to get from the field to the table.

Also at Garlic Grove, a limited number of Festival guests can obtain tickets to one of the coveted garlic braiding classes. On the Festival schedule since 1982, the interactive braiding demonstrations have proven a very popular attraction: every year the free tickets are gone by mid-morning. Repeat visitors to the Festival know to get to Garlic Grove early if they want to participate in a braiding class. Only fifty Festival attendees at a time can be in the noncompetitive demonstrations, held twice each day, during which they learn to braid garlic.[4] Those with tickets meet at their appointed time at the

Gilroyan Elaine Bonino instructs Beth and Tom Johnston of Delray Beach, Florida, how to braid garlic, 2005. Looking on is Festival volunteer Jodi Heinzen. The garlic used for the demonstrations, some 2,100 bulbs, is grown and donated by Ms. Bonino's nephews. (Photography by author)

hay bale–defined circle. There, enthusiastic Gilroyan Elaine Bonino greets them with bushel baskets brimming with untrimmed dried garlic. After the guests hand in their tickets and collect a handful of garlic stalks, Bonino proceeds to demonstrate the simple braiding technique, one involving three strands or three stalks of garlic. This is not a difficult task, but it does require some coordination, especially for those who have never braided before. She walks among the students, most of whom are sitting on the hay bales, offering assistance and encouragement. Within thirty minutes, most participants have some semblance of a garlic braid, or at least a cluster of loosely woven garlic stalks.

Part of the attraction of this event is that it is one of the few interactive Festival activities and it is the only "free" (i.e., included in the cost of Festival admission) one. Of course, visitors can admire arts and crafts, listen to music, and watch the cooking contest and demonstrations, but these activities are relatively passive. Shopping and eating are interactive, but they require spending additional money. At Garlic Grove and during a braiding class are the only chances visitors have to touch actual garlic bulbs. Another attraction of the braiding demonstrations may be that participants get to take home their braids, or their attempted braids.

The braiding class is described in program books as "a crash course" to learn "the time honored tradition of Garlic braiding."[5] Over the years the amount of text in the Festival programs dedicated to describing this event has decreased, with the space given instead to photographs from previous years' demonstrations. The increased space for photographs of smiling garlic braiding students, most often Caucasian, suggests Festival organizers' commitment to highlighting visitors' interaction with the icon of Gilroy's branded identity. The pictures in each year's Festival program of amateur attempts at garlic braiding also serve as visual reminders that it takes skilled manual labor to produce the garlic braids for sale at the Festival and in local shops. Unlike the workers who make the retail braids, the people pictured in the programs are sitting at a festival, voluntarily engaging in the chore for only a few minutes. The demonstration classes temporarily situate Festival goers/consumers as manual laborers, performing the repetitive task of commodity production. The garlic braiding classes are an enactment of classic festival inversion (Abrahams and Bauman 1978, Babcock 1978, Bakhtin 1984 [1969]): what is in reality work is situated as play, and those who normally enjoy the fruits of others' labors do the labor themselves. Like festival inversion in general, the braiding class inversion is not a threat to established norms or labor-consumer roles. The engagement of the Festival goers as braiders is defined and limited by the Festival's temporal structure and the spatial boundary of the hay bale–defined circle.

Garlic Galore II: The Garlic Topping Contest

When garlic is pulled from the ground, long stalks and short roots are attached to each bulb. If the garlic is to be sold or processed dry, it is left to "cure" or dry in the fields, lying atop the dirt in rows adjacent to the row from which it was pulled. When the bulbs are dry, they are topped. "Topping" is the process of trimming the roots and stalks from the dried bulbs and is normally done in the field where the garlic has been drying. Working up and down the rows, men and women top the garlic before tossing it into

Dried garlic with roots and stalks. (Photography by author)

bushel baskets. The baskets are weighed before being taken to the plant for additional sorting and processing.

The topping contest is an articulation of a familiar festival theme: the competitive display of occupational skills, occupational skills reframed as spectacle and entertainment. It is a diversion from everyday life for observers but is condensed intensification of everyday life for contestants. The topping contest transforms a mundane task—topping garlic—into what Beverly Stoeltje (1987, 1993) calls a ritualized drama.

The garlic topping contest has been on the schedule since the inaugural Festival. In the early years of the Festival, the topping contest was a two-person competition, with each person representing a different local garlic-growing company. In those years it was a genial display of corporate rivalry.[6] For several years into the 1980s, text in the Festival program invited visitors to "enter this friendly competition." The invitation came with a caveat, however: "This is grueling work, and certainly a test of your skill" (Gilroy Garlic Festival Association 1986, 13). Although it is unclear how many years the visiting public was invited to try their hand at this difficult and dangerous task, text in the program booklets suggest that this format was in place well into the 1990s.[7] By the late 1990s, injuries from the special topping shears amplified participant safety concerns, and the contest returned to being a demonstration by skilled laborers rather than a participatory event.

Since the late 1990s, participants in the topping contest are preselected men and women employed by Christopher Ranch, the Gilroy-based company that is the country's largest producer of fresh garlic products. Bill Christopher, who organizes the contest each year, explained that some of his workers volunteer to be in the contest, and when more are needed, he asks others to participate. In the years that I watched the contest, several of the same men and women participated year after year. In exchange for their participation in the contest once a day for three days, he continued, the contestants are provided with food and refreshments in the Hospitality Area, have access to the Festival site, and sometimes are given Festival tickets for their families.

The topping contest takes place twice a day, daily at noon for female contestants and again at two p.m. for male contestants.[8] Festival goers sit on hay bales that define the perimeter of the competition area, a circle approximately forty feet in diameter. The contest draws such a large crowd that observers also stand several people deep behind the ring of hay bales. Some years a large, freestanding umbrella offers a few people shade; but most spectators and all the contestants are fully exposed to the scorching heat of the midday sun. At the scheduled times, Christopher, who serves as emcee, introduces the contestants by their first names to attentive audiences.[9] After a brief review of the rules, which do not change year to year, the contest begins.

With encouragement from Christopher, the crowd cheers as the contestants skillfully "top" hundreds of bulbs of garlic that have been strewn on the ground, as it is in the garlic fields. The contestants, all of whom are of Mexican or Hispanic descent, work at an alarmingly rapid pace, clearly adept at using the very sharp hand shears they brought with them for the contest. As a bulb is topped, the contestant tosses it into a nearby bushel basket. With efficient, repetitive movements most contestants quickly fill at least one and are well into a second bushel basket of trimmed bulbs before

Spectators cheer on (from nearest to farthest) Lucilla Diaz, Rosa Vasquez, Margarita Diaz, and Maria Flores Diaz at Friday's women's topping contest, 2005. (Photograph by author)

Alfredo Vasquez (center), Gustavo Flores (left), and Manuel Caneles (right) compete during the men's topping contest at the 2005 Festival. (Photograph by Beth Johnston)

During the judging of the competition, male contestants wait while their topped garlic is weighed, 2000. (Photograph by author)

Christopher calls "Time's up!" At the end of five minutes, baskets are collected and weighed; the man and the woman with the heaviest baskets wins—fifty dollars for first place, twenty-five for second, and fifteen for third.

The laborer-contestants are doing difficult and potentially dangerous work, just as they do in the fields during one phase of the garlic production cycle. And, like their work in the garlic fields, the contest winners' financial compensation is determined by the measured weight of the garlic they top. The reality of their work in the fields—the faster they work and the more garlic they top, the greater their take-home pay—is condensed within the festival frame, and presented as entertainment for visual consumption.

• ◆ •

The landscape of the topping contest is a microcosm of the labor, power, and race relations of garlic production in Santa Clara County, and of worker-consumer relations in general. At the Festival, as in their daily work environment, non-Anglo laborers are being judged by nonlaboring observers. The contest takes place in a defined space within which subordinate workers are overseen by an Anglo managerial superior. During the contest the workers are also being observed by an audience comprised of people who normally purchase the products of their labors. The diverse audience is representative of the general consuming public who, through their acquisition of garlic from grocery stores and other retail outlets, judges the work of the laborers. Unlike other secular rituals that represent challenges to the status quo (e.g., Turner 1977), the organization and realization of the topping contest affirms existing power relationships.

These observations, particularly with respect to the topping contest as a condensed version of labor relations, parallel those of Robert Lavenda (1992), who notes that although small-town festivals in theory are conducted to promote a unified community identity, in practice they often reinforce social divisions. While the contest is a playful presentation of topping for the audience, it also affirms the hegemonic relationships between laborer and producer/manager and between laborer and consumer. In the hay bale–defined circle, workers are marginalized, objectified, and made into spectacles. Gilroy's topping contest exemplifies the politics of cultural performance: from a singular cultural display, one can extract principles of race, occupational specialization, and social attitudes. The topping contest is a microcosm of California's historic and contemporary agribusiness labor relations (cf. Mitchell 1996).

These relations are represented in the Festival writ large. Mostly absent from the Festival audience are people involved with the manual labor of garlic processing. In late summer they are busy in the fields and plants processing the harvest. In comparison, some local employers of nonagricultural workers give employees Friday off so that they can attend the Festival. The local historical museum is closed, for example, and staffing is lower at some local offices because so many Gilroyans are involved as volunteers in Festival production—that, and they want to beat the larger crowds that descend on the Festival on Saturday and Sunday.

In addition to symbolizing power relationships, the topping contest demonstrates one of the processes required to transition garlic from a field crop to a consumable ingredient. Through this demonstration, the topping contest reconnects Gilroy's iconic garlic with the natural environment from which it comes. In the process, it reminds the thoughtful observer of the reality that manual labor is required to get the food item from field to market.

Through their introduction to the contestants, audience members might get to "know" agricultural workers. Yet their familiarity with the worker-contestants is necessarily superficial: the worker-contestants are present in the enclosed competition circle once each day for little more than five minutes, the duration of the competition. Although they are not prohibited from interacting with the audience before or after the contest, I have never seen them do so. Rosa Vasquez, a stay-at-home mother who works as a part-time seasonal garlic braider, has participated in the topping contest for ten years and is a frequent winner. She says she is aware of the audience during the contest, and it makes her nervous, but she likes it when the crowd is involved. Yet there is no real interaction between contestants like Vasquez and the audience. My attempt to speak with the male contestants on Friday one year was brief and rushed because, I was told, they were hurrying to get their meals so Alfredo Franco, who assists Mr. Christopher and provides their transportation, could get them back to work. Since they are paid piece-meal, any time away from work is time they are not earning money—except for the contest winners.

Audience members are further detached from the workers by the social and symbolic gesture that the latter are introduced only by their first names. The physical structure of the hay bales and the linguistic practice of introducing contestants only with their first names serve to keep distance between the audience and the participants, emphasizing the physical and social distances between laborers and consumers in daily life. As Beverley Stoeltje and Richard Bauman note, "Display heightens the process of objec-tification by setting things off in special contexts, marking them with special intensity by being on view, available for examination, contemplation, reflec-tion, whether the object is woman, flag, agricultural product, or association" (1989, 170).

The hegemonic affirmation apparent in the contest does not mean that there are not subtexts eroding the suggested symbolic order. The topping context is a discursive space that allows for multiple layers of expression and meaning. Presenting manual labor as entertainment problematizes the denatured presentation of garlic that dominates the Festival. More specifi-cally, the presence of the workers demonstrating their occupational skill highlights the reality of the labor required in the field-to-table process, and this problematizes the un-peopled garlic-themed identity put forth by Gilroy's image makers. If, as Bakhtin asserts, what is officially excluded becomes symbolically charged, then the near complete erasure of garlic as an agricultural product and of the labor required to keep this inexpensive product in the markets becomes extra-significant.

. ♦ .

What follows the topping contest is just as important as the display of power that the contest symbolizes. Once the weighing is complete and the contestants have received their prize envelopes, the freshly topped garlic is tossed back into the ring and spread around the ground. Knowing audience members are on the edge of their hay bale seats, ready for what comes next; first-timers are captivated by the excitement even though they cannot anticipate what is about to happen.

On command from Christopher, audience members lunge forward to grab the garlic bulbs scattered on the ground. Many return Festival visitors come prepared with empty plastic bags; others scoop garlic bulbs into their arms or make reservoirs in the fabric of their oversized shirts. Clambering around on the ground are people who paid the ten dollars per person Festival entry fee. They scurry to retrieve bulbs sold in nearby markets for around one dollar a pound.

The significance of the garlic retrieval lies not in economics but in what it symbolizes. This post-contest competition is structured and unstructured mayhem. Structure is provided, literally, by the hay bales that define the space in which the disorder occurs. The presence of an officiating and authoritative supervisor (Christopher) also lends structure and the suggestion of order. Although the post-contest free-for-all is not listed in the Festival program, it is an established event and is therefore part of the Festival's schedule. As with other instances of festival inversion, this nonofficial event allows participants to temporarily suspend social norms and etiquette. In this case, those who had been consumer/observers become spectacle/participants. The contestants are part of the inversion as well. Looking mildly amused, they stand just outside the circle and watch for a moment as the audience members-turned-foragers throw themselves into the mayhem. When I asked some of the toppers, who had just completed the contest, about the spectators' mad dash for garlic, several of them concurred that watching

Post-topping contest mayhem. The initial crush of people are eager to pick up freshly topped garlic, 2000. (Photograph by author)

A happy garlic grabber, 2000. (Photograph by author)

this spectacle is funny; with mild bemusement, one competitor expressed surprise that people got so emotional over the free garlic.

That the worker-contestants get to chuckle at the audience-scavengers is significant because "festive folk laughter presents an element of victory not only over supernatural awe, over the sacred, over death; it also means the defeat of power, of earthly kings, of the earthly upper classes, of all that oppresses and restricts" (Bakhtin 1984 [1969], 92). Their laughter, seen through a Bakhtinian lens, reveals not merely amusement; it is an expression of their authority and temporary superiority over the consumer-audience-scramblers.

Each year I engaged fellow audience members in casual conversation about the topping contest and the subsequent scavenge.[10] Most of the people with whom I spoke expressed some discomfort with the spectaclization of the laborers. One woman said that she felt bad for the contestants, whom she referred to as "migrant workers." She tempered her initial remark by suggesting that if the workers were having fun, then she thought it was okay for us, the audience, to cheer them on. Even if the contestants were comfortable being on display, she continued, she thought the prize money should be more, since they worked so hard. With another particularly contemplative observer, I discussed the possibility that the discomfort we were expressing might be "white man's guilt," an inversion of "white man's burden": rather than feeling obliged to improve the lives of others, we felt guilt for making spectacles of them. In a subsequent conversation, this Festival visitor reflected that watching the topping contest with spectators cheering as others toiled made her feel like she was in ancient Rome cheering on the gladiators.

When I asked locals about the contest, I got a very different sort of response. In general, they did not seem to think negatively about the contest but enjoyed it as an entertaining spectacle. Melissa Noto's comments typify those of other locals: rather than finding it "derogatory," she considered the contest as "giving them [the worker-contestants] respect for what they do." She also opined that because she grew up around garlic workers in general, and the topping contest in particular, she "doesn't think anything about it [the contest]." A first-time visitor to the Festival was taken aback as the audience transformed from spectator to spectacle; while she did find it humorous, she also found it mildly embarrassing for people to scavenge. Another person remarked that the behavior affirmed her belief that people will do anything to get something for "free."

Why would watching this contest be unsettling to some audience members? No doubt it is in part some discomfort with the spectaclization of what is perceived to be a marginalized population. Additionally, the topping contest presents an aspect of the food chain that consumers are not used to seeing or thinking about: the reality that people toil in fields and factories. Garlic topping is what Erving Goffman (1974) would call a backstage activity, in this case an activity done out of view of the consuming public. Within the circle of hay, however, it is front and center, putting on display that which is normally kept out of sight. But in just a few minutes, the contest is over and the audience, many of whom are clutching garlic stalks, disperses around the Festival to continue their merrymaking.

Various components of the Gilroy Garlic Festival exhibit the central paradox of festivity: a form that seems to provide a break from ordinary routine, one that at times may even seem chaotic and formless, may actually promote order and social control by reinforcing power relationships and moral guidelines (Brandes 1988). The festival paradox certainly is present in the performative frame of the topping contest and post-contest garlic free-for-all.

· ◆ ·

The power relationships articulated in the topping contest are not without contestation, although opposition is rarely public and has not been recorded in the Gilroy Garlic Festival's official history, the history to which the public has access. One year, though, there was a very public display of disquiet among the farm workers that made visible to Festival visitors some normally behind-the-scenes labor politics. The brief episode was an important reminder that no landscape or foodscape produces itself.

In 1980, Val Filice still was farming garlic. That summer, he recalls, during harvest time, leaders from the United Farm Workers of America (UFWA) came to Gilroy and tried to unionize the laborers. A wage dispute, the focus of their incitement, led many workers to go on strike, shutting down some of the harvest and production work ("Gilroy, Calif." 1980). Members of the UFWA no doubt recognized that picketing at the then two-year-old Festival, taking place on August 2 and 3 that year, would be a tremendous opportunity to publicize their cause.

On July 24, Rudy Melone got word that the UFWA planned to picket the Festival.[11] Within days he was meeting with Marshal Ganz, a leader in the California branch of UFWA. Mr. Melone made it clear to Mr. Ganz that the Festival, administered by the Gilroy Garlic Festival Association, was not an activity of the garlic growers, the employers with whom the UFWA was having the labor dispute. Despite Mr. Melone's request that the UFWA recognize the distinction between the Festival, which had no agricultural employees and therefore should not be a target of the UFWA's attention, and the garlic growers, Mr. Ganz persisted in asserting that the UFWA would picket the Festival.

In anticipation of possible violence that might ensue during the picketing, and bad publicity that picketing would generate, the Festival Association sought legal counsel. They prepared several legal documents, including a restraining order and a complaint for injunction and damages.[12] Discussions of security measures and law enforcement procedures dominated association and Board of Directors meetings in the days before the Festival.[13]

Festival goers' access to the Festival that year was slightly obstructed by the crowd of picketers gathered just outside the entry gate and the law enforcement officers standing by in case the situation warranted their services. The story of the UFWA incitement made national news: a *New York Times* article reported that "several hundred striking members of the United Farm Workers of America, many of them children, stood a vigil outside [the Festival], holding the red and black flag of the union" ("Gilroy, Calif." 1980). It is noteworthy that on the same date this short article appeared about the labor dispute's impact on the Festival, just five pages before in the same section, there was an article nearly ten times as long praising the second annual Festival (Lindsey 1980). The latter article made no mention of the labor dispute, strike, or picketers. Three days later a very short article noted that an interim agreement ending the nineteen-day strike had been reached "in the garlic-growing capital of the nation" ("Settlement in Garlic Strike" 1980).

In addition to holding flags, picketers were handing out a flier with the header "WHY WE PICKET THE GILROY GARLIC FESTIVAL." On the one-page, typed flier was a line drawing of a dark-haired young boy and a dark-haired young girl hand-picking garlic in a field. The single-spaced text informed readers that

> The Garlic Festival means different things to different people.
>
> For the growers it means profits and prestige. For those of us who harvest the garlic it means our children must work in the fields so families can eat. . . .
>
> Since July 21, 2,000 farm workers around Gilroy and Hollister [a neighboring town]—including 1,200 garlic workers—have been on strike for a better life and for representation by Cesar Chavez's United Farm Workers. . . .
>
> We called on the companies where workers have voted for the union to meet immediately and discuss ways we can end the strike. The growers refused!
>
> That is why we are striking. And that is why we are picketing the Garlic Festival.
>
> We feel the time to have a garlic festival is when all people in our community can share in the bounty and celebration, not just the growers and their friends. . . .
>
> Contribute the money you were going to give to the growers to attend the garlic festival to the garlic workers' strike.

One visitor who witnessed the strike was disturbed enough to write to the Festival Association upon his return home. In a handwritten letter, composed on the back of one of the AFWU fliers, this Festival guest had several complaints. Not only were there higher prices and more traffic than he had experienced when he attended the first year's Festival, he disliked being "greeted by all those strikers, 'Farm Workers' passing the bucket to get some money and trying to boycott the festival etc."[14]

Apparently not all visitors understood the strikers' message. Don Christopher remembers that some non-Hispanic guests thought the people greeting them at the entry gates were calling out "Welcome!" and that the display was part of the Festival. In fact, what the picketers were yelling was "¡Huelga!", the Spanish word for strike.

The 1980 picketing was a vivid reminder of the often behind-the-scenes human work involved in getting an agricultural product from field to factory to table. The 1980 picketers, and the ongoing interactive braiding demonstration and topping contest are the only times during the Festival when visitors are faced with the reality that they, like the garlic they eat, are part of an agricultural process. Garlic's iconization and festivalization removes garlic from its agricultural context. By making it a plaything, the Festival reinforces a general lack of awareness among American consumers about the processes by which their food gets from farm to table.

The foundation of a festival that commemorates a food-place association is agricultural. Just as eating is an agricultural act (Berry 1992), attending the Garlic Festival also is an agricultural act. Through their participation, as with deliberate and unconsidered choices at the grocery store, Festival goers sanction the status quo of agricultural production. Unlike county fairs that directly connect food to its source, the Gilroy Garlic Festival and other similar place-based food festivals are not overt celebrations of the connection between landscape and the product of the land. The connection is implied—displays at Garlic Grove, bushel baskets filled with strands of field-fresh garlic lining the Cook-off stage—but it is not a focal point of the Festival, marketing materials, or media coverage of the event. In most instances, festival frivolity overshadows the agricultural connection, often to the point of erasure. Who wants to think about the details of agribusiness when walking around a food festival? The topping contest, however, makes evident the agricultural reality of garlic by workers demonstrating garlic-specific occupational skills.

Foodscapes as Landscapes of Consumption

In her analysis of rodeos, Beverly Stoeltje (1987) explains how the livestock that is usually part of the work and business worlds of the host community become instruments of play in the rodeo. Through their play at the rodeo, members of a ranching community display their social organization. At the Gilroy Garlic Festival, garlic, an integral part of Gilroy's agribusiness economy, becomes a literal and symbolic instrument for play. It is played with by cooks on the Cook-off stage, played with by jewelers making earrings that resemble little bulbs, played with by the cooks doing Flare-ups at Gourmet Alley, played with by visitors attempting to braid dried stalks at the braiding class. Garlic is "played with" during the topping contest in a ritualized way

A booth selling garlic ice cream, one of the many garlic-flavored novelty foods at the Gilroy Garlic Festival, 2000. (Photograph by author)

that is mimetic of how garlic is worked in a non-play setting, with workers being watched and judged, and being paid according to the weight of what they top.

For most people the festival frame connotes leisure, a time out of time. As time free from the obligations of labor and production, modern leisure such as a festival "is seen as quintessentially the time of consumption" (Appadurai 1996, 79). The consumption can be literal, consuming sustenance, or ideological, consuming ideas. At the Gilroy Garlic Festival, participants and attendees literally consume the iconic food in various forms, from garlic pickles to garlicky pesto to garlic ice cream. They also consume ideologies about place, power, and agricultural production embedded within and performed through Festival events. Foodscapes represent and offer for consumption, in abbreviated and symbolic form, landscapes of production: production of consumer goods, of ideologies, and of identities. Participation in the Festival affirms the various community identities articulated through and performed in the festival frame. As such, the Gilroy Garlic Festival is a temporary but recurring site for creating and reinforcing multiple senses of community and identities, including that of Gilroy as a festive foodscape.

CHAPTER FIVE

Place Branding and Selling Place

Creating and Marketing Identity Capital

W hen Rudy Melone proposed the Gilroy Garlic Festival, he had two agendas. He asserted that "the garlic festival will proudly celebrate the worth of garlic and help create a positive and favorable image of Gilroy" (1979b). The secondary purpose was to generate revenue to help the Gilroy Chamber of Commerce become independent of City support. As it turns out, the latter did not happen but the former did. During my interviews with Gilroyans, I heard time and again versions of this narrative: "I was on vacation and someone asked where I was from. Before the Festival no one knew where Gilroy was. But now, everyone knows where Gilroy is and they know about the Garlic Festival, even if they have never been to Gilroy." Not only did the Festival propel garlic and Gilroy into the headlines, it also generated among residents a sense of communal pride in the city and in garlic.

It was not just the Festival that catapulted Gilroy into public awareness; it was media coverage before, during, and after it. In the weeks following the first two Festivals, articles appeared in newspapers throughout the country. Much of this post-Festival press had a tone of amused jocularity. Recalling garlic's odorous reputation, newspaper stories incorporated catchy phrases such as "Fame's nothing to sniff at in Gilroy" and "Garlic Town Savors the Smell of Success."[1] Gilroy's civic and city leaders, now among the city's image makers, did not seem to mind the tongue-in-cheek publicity; rather, they were delighted that the press embraced their quirky Festival. *Gilroy Dispatch* editor Pat Anderson was ebullient over the national and international attention bestowed on Gilroy:

> It seems that just about all the California metro papers, including both the Los Angeles Times and [San Francisco] Herald-Examiner, treated our local extravaganza as a major happening (that is to say, they did it justice). Then came those big spread[s] in the Chicago Tribune and Washington Post, and someone even said he saw a piece in the New [Y]ork Times. Even Time magazine mentioned it. Topping everything so far, however, was the report from Mayor Norman Goodrich at the Gilroy City Council meeting Monday that he had received a letter from a man living in Coventry, England. . . . (1979b)

While the small group of Gilroy business leaders had sought primarily to reverse Gilroy's negative image, what they initiated was on ongoing campaign of selling place. Their efforts commodified Gilroy's imaged garlic-centric identity, an identity signified in the Garlic Festival. After image makers created and promoted the food-themed brand identity, ongoing media campaigns enhanced their place marketing efforts. Gilroy's story illustrates one example of selling place as festive foodscape.

• • •

The praxis of selling place is not unique to the United States, nor is it a modern phenomenon. Some trace its historical roots to Viking Leif Ericsson's quest for settlers (Ashworth and Voogd 1990), and the Hanseatic League and the Italian city-states in medieval Europe (Harvey 1989b). The legacy of American boosterism stems from Americans' conception of land as a purchasable commodity and the growth imperative to settle the American West (Boorstin 1965). In fact, it was the marketing of frontier towns in the United States that marked "the beginnings of place selling in the modern sense, where places were marketed via the printed word and the new mass media—the handbill, the pamphlet, the poster and the newspaper" (Ward 2003, 9). As land speculators and newly formed government bodies competed to attract settlers, they, often in collusion with railroad companies, engaged in aggressive campaigns of selling place.

Gilroy in its early years was typical of many western nascent cities. Citizens heralded the March 1869 completion of the railroad line from San Jose as a harbinger of the city's growth and prosperity. A number of civic improvements followed after the railroad's completion, including establishing a volunteer firefighting unit (July 1869), and franchise or contractual agreements for gas and water service (1870). In an 1873 promotional pamphlet, *Gilroy as a Home*, Gilroy image makers described the city's commercial and industrial assets as well as her star tourist attraction, L. H. Dyer's Hot Sulphur Springs, in hopes of attracting additional investors, tourists, and residents (Hogan 1980). In 1888, the Gilroy Board of Trade published another promotional pamphlet, *Gilroy, the Most Favored Section of Santa Clara*, extolling Gilroy's growing population and rising property values. The cover page of a subsequent boosterism publication glorifying the city's charms boasted Gilroy as "an ideal land for tourists, homemakers and the healthseeker" (*Souvenir Magazine* 1905).

The tradition of boosterism continues in Gilroy. The late twentieth-century image makers commodified the city and her identity by assigning her a food-theme brand. Marketing transforms ideas and goods into commodity forms, Robert Goldman and John Wilson explain: advertising "both enhances the exchange value of existing goods and transforms into commodities those goods and services we might not have considered commodities before" (Goldman and Wilson 1983, 120). The transformative capacity of marketing applies to commodities as diverse as perfume (the subject of their interrogation), sense of community, food, place, and identity. The creation or magnification of ethnic identity is a familiar choice in some communities seeking to fortify tourism (e.g., Frenkel and Walton 2000, Hoelscher 1998). In Taos, New Mexico, a contemporary reinvigoration of an ethnic identity became social and economic capital as part of the city's tourism economy (Rodriguez 1990). Whether it is by magnification of ethnic identity or promotion of a food-place association, local identity can be commodified and consumed. As a commodity form, the foodscape Gilroy can be consumed literally, through eating garlicky foods sold throughout the city and at the

Festival, and ideologically, through perpetuating the Gilroy-garlic association by visiting the Festival or absorbing themed marketing and media.

Through self-inscription and promotional materials, the commodified identity, multitasking as social, symbolic, economic, and cultural capital becomes identity capital.[2] Identity capital is what image makers for a locale choose to draw upon or highlight in their ongoing presentation, representation, and promotion of a locality. There are abundant examples of a communal resource promoted as identity capital to mark place distinction in the service of securing economic capital: consider natural resources (the Grand Canyon, which serves as an attraction to surrounding towns); human-made resources such as amusement parks, shopping centers, or other cultural divertissements that become the focal point of a locality's identity (Orlando, Florida, as the gateway to Disney; Las Vegas, Nevada; Bloomington, Minnesota, as home of the Mall of America); or imagined or real histories upon which image makers choose to capitalize and promote place identity (Leavenworth, Washington, and its manufactured Bavarian-ness). In the case of Gilroy, business leaders cultivated the natural resource of the valley to draw economic capital in the form of jobs related to the garlic industry. City leaders then drew upon that capital, transforming it into an icon of collective and place identities. By assigning symbolic or sign value to garlic, Gilroy image makers transformed the locality's agricultural and industrial resource into an amalgamation of symbolic, social, and identity capital.

To enhance their claim of distinction, Gilroy image makers drew upon the identity-affirming and traditionalizing form of festivals. Since the mid-nineteenth century, town leaders throughout America have recognized the capacity of festivals to evoke civic pride, affirm community solidarity, and differentiate one locality from another. Festivals were organized throughout the American West, for example, to differentiate among emerging young cities with the goal of attracting new residents (Banner 1983). Festivals and other festive special events continue to be regarded as integral to tourism development and marketing plans because of each event's innate temporal differentiation from everyday life (Getz 1989), and because through the festival form, a collective identity is commodified and presented for consumption.

In becoming identity capital, garlic is abstracted from its growth and production, as well as from the context of its long-standing association with particular ethnic foodways. Through recontextualization that changed people's perceptions, garlic became a denatured and symbolically neutral fun food to be cooked, eaten, worn, painted, sung about, and made into jewelry and assorted ephemera. As a commodity form, garlic transitioned from an ingredient to an object suitable for fetishization and festivalization.[3]

Records indicate the breadth of media coverage for the first two Garlic Festivals included Public Service Announcements on seventy-two radio stations in California, articles in magazines such as *Food and Wine* and *Sunset*, and television coverage on multiple local and regional stations. To promote the second Festival, Val Filice, Mayor Norman Goodrich (who had decided that he liked garlic after all), and the first Miss Garlic, K. T. Bendel, appeared on Dinah Shore's nationally syndicated show, *Dinah!*. Through extensive media exposure, the city's identity rapidly evolved from a place drivers bypass to a place of intriguing distinction.

Within a year, Gilroy acquired its new identity as Garlic Capital of the World; the media blitz leading up to and after the second Festival cemented the new identity. Image makers deliberately created a place-specific, food-centered communal identity perpetuated by aggressive promotion of the Festival. Diverse media and audiences ate up the novelty of fetishizing garlic, the spirited Festival, and garlic puns. Gilroy had become a festive foodscape. The obvious success of the inaugural Festival convinced city leaders that promoting the town's crop would secure a positive identity for Gilroy. And of course the Festival, and the lingering positive association it generated, would reap financial benefits for Gilroy. Gilroy city officials and the media positioned the city as a place to be consumed through its garlic-centered identity.

Festival attendance swelled from 15,000 in 1979 to 90,000 in 1981 to 132,000 in 2003. The Festival's ongoing success and media coverage of it confirm the tenacious association both have created and continue to generate between the city of Gilroy and garlic. Ongoing recognition in local, national, and international media publicizes the city and the food-place association celebrated through the Festival. In 1998 QVC, the twenty-four-hour television shopping network, broadcast live from the Festival for two hours midday on Saturday. The program was part of the network's "Local Flavors Tour." The Festival, and through it Gilroy as a festive foodscape, were promoted while garlic and garlic-related products were sold. Telecast to more than

Julia Adema displays a garlic clove hat, one of many nonedible garlic-themed items for sale at the Gilroy Garlic Festival, 2000. (Photograph by author)

"Mr. Gilroy" Gerry Foisy talks with 2003 Garlic Queen Melissa Noto before the 2005 Festival. (Photograph by author)

fifty-eight million homes in the United States, Europe, and Japan, this short feature provided tremendous exposure for the Festival and for Gilroy. Food Network's *All American Festivals* program features the Festival, providing national exposure to a food-niche audience.[4] The Director of the Visitors Bureau knows when Food Network airs the program featuring the Gilroy Garlic Festival because the bureau receives dramatically more phone queries than usual about the city and the Festival. Similarly, in 2005 the Festival Association office received some four hundred e-mail queries after the Food Network program aired. According to its 2003 Official Sponsor Package, the Festival "has been awarded more than 36 industry awards for excellence" including multiple Pinnacle Awards from the International Festival and Events Association. Magazines and web sites commend the Festival for its family atmosphere. For example, in 2004 it received the "Best Family Fairs and Festivals" award from *Bay Area Parent* Magazine.

The Festival, which consistently draws more than 120,000 people to town one weekend a year, and the associated marketing of it, cement and perpetuate the city's identity as a festive foodscape. Several local businesses capitalize on the association, incorporating garlic into their business names. From Garlic City Billiards to Garlic Farm Travel Park, "garlic" is scattered throughout the yellow pages and streets of Gilroy. It is no wonder that businesses capitalize on such a palatable association; such names are humorous and catchy, especially to outsiders. South Valley Internet, an area Internet connectivity provider, secured garlic.com as its domain address and provides e-mail service that incorporates garlic.com as the e-mail address suffix, spreading Gilroy's food-place brand via e-mails throughout the World Wide Web.

Gilroy's branding as the Garlic Capital of the World not only provides clever names for local businesses; it also has significant economic and infrastructure consequences. Community organizations and nonprofit groups benefit from the ongoing success of the Festival. Festival proceeds, approximately $250,000 in 2002, are used to fund community projects, charitable groups, and service organizations. Five years after the first Festival, the Gilroy Visitors Bureau was created and, twelve years later, the Gilroy Economic Development Corporation formed. In the column "The Gilroy Advantage, Lifestyle for the 21st Century" published in their 2000 and 2004 newsletters and on the "Community Profile" section of their web site, the

Low-tech media like roadside billboards contribute to perpetuating Gilroy's branded identity. This sign stands along Highway 101 just south of Gilroy, visible to northbound traffic. This sign informs people about the city's claim of capitaldom, 2005. (Photograph by author)

Economic Development Corporation positioned the formation of these two entities as part of Gilroy's steady movement toward becoming a tourist destination with the following: "The City has kept pace with the awakening of the tourism industry in California. Since 1979, when the first Gilroy Garlic Festival was held, Gilroy has steadily moved in the direction of becoming a tourist destination. The Gilroy Visitors Bureau, created in 1984, and the Gilroy Economic Development Corporation formed in 1996, are ongoing funded commitments made by the city as they orchestrate the long-range goals that guarantee the community's future economic vitality."

This text suggests that the Economic Development Corporation regarded increased tourism as a guarantee of Gilroy's future economic vitality, and recognized the food-centric Festival as a significant component in advancing Gilroy as a tourism destination. The Economic Development Corporation recognizes the importance of place differentiation to attract tourism and development dollars. The aggrandizement achieved through the Festival and the claim of capitaldom is part of the strategy of place differentiation and marketing distinction.

Place Marketing, Marketing Place

Place marketing takes a selective representation that "distills the essence of a place, and 'imagines' an identity that is attractive to tourists and residents alike" (Chang 2004). Marketing place is about product packaging where the product is an appealing, imagined geography. In the case of Gilroy, the product is Gilroy's identity, represented by the moniker Garlic Capital of the World and the Festival; the packaging is auto-ethnographies and media coverage that tout the city's claim of capitaldom and the Festival; and the consumers are current and potential local residents and businesses, potential future employers, visitors to the town and, more specifically, local and tourist Festival attendees.

Like food packaging designers (Heller 1999), whose success is measurable by consumer activity, place marketers hope to affect place-specific spending activity among consumers. The impact of their campaigns is measured in visitorship and dollars spent. Area hotels are filled months in advance every year for the duration of the Festival. In addition to contributing to hotel and tax revenue, Festival attendees and vendors spend money at area restaurants, markets, gas stations, and other retail outlets. These measurements are relevant for another group of potential consumers of the branded identity: prospective Festival sponsors. The Festival's success and media exposure are significant not only to affirm Gilroy's collective identity as a foodscape and attract visitors to the city, but also to secure sponsorship for the continued success of the Festival. Sponsors ranging from local retailers to Pepsi® help make the event financially viable just as individual commitments in the form of volunteerism make the Festival civically viable. Like the media, some corporate sponsors incorporate levity into their marketing by playing off garlic's age-old and rightfully earned odor-inducing reputation: in 1998 Sweet Breath Ice Chips, a candy-like breath freshener, was "The Official Breath Freshener of the Gilroy Garlic Festival." Product representatives handed out free samples to all interested Festival attendees and that year's official Festival press kits included a package of Sweet Breath Ice Chips. The Jelly Belly Candy Company, another sponsor, took advantage of garlic's capacity for manipulation by creating roasted garlic Jelly Belly® jelly beans. They distributed samples of the distinctive garlic jelly beans at

the 2004 Festival. In trash cans and on the ground just past the Jelly Belly®
booth, readily apparent to the nose and eye, were slightly chewed remains
of the sampled roasted garlic jelly beans. Apparently visitors underappreciated this garlic delicacy. Despite the apparent lack of appeal to Festival
guests, roasted garlic Jelly Belly® jelly beans continue to be sold at the Jelly
Belly® store in Gilroy's Premier Outlet Mall. They are one of many edible
souvenirs of Gilroy available throughout the year that affirms the garlic-
Gilroy brand.

The impact of a festive foodscape's identity-affirming festival is not limited to the duration of the festival. In fact, successful place branding and its
associated marketing will have tangible and intangible consequences year-
round. Intrigued by good marketing, people will be drawn to the place and,
while there, will spend money. This assumes, of course, that the food-place
association is a positive one. Gilroy's garlic campaign could have been unsuccessful: people might not have been intrigued by the initial garlic festival, or
they may have attended and left with a negative impression of the food and
the place. But neither of these things happened. The ongoing success of the
Festival is evidence that the product is well packaged and marketed, and has
secured customer brand loyalty.

A growing body of literature among scholars of urban and tourism studies attests to the rapid expansion of place branding as an identity-marketing
phenomenon and as a nascent field for professional consultants.[5] Place
branding is a local strategy working amid global forces to reimagine a city so
that it secures a competitive edge against other cities vying for tourist and
investment dollars. It is a marketing tool that is usually discussed as it relates
to themed environments, regions and larger cities such as Disney World,
Las Vegas, or New Orleans (e.g., Gotham 2002). The branding of Gilroy as
the Garlic Capital of the World is an example of successful place branding
on a smaller scale.

Place branding "implies a new way of representing reality, a new practice of Lefebvre's *l'espace conçu*," literally "conceived space" (Pedersen 2004,
79) or how space is imaged and imagined. This means that place branding
is a dynamic amalgamation of real, physical space; conceptual, imagined,
symbolic space and iconography; and experiences and perceptions of space.
Place branding is based on the premise that place identities can be socially
constructed, or as I call it, mediated.

The success of place branding rests on consumer (e.g., festival attendees, tourists, locals, investors) perceptions and experiences of the place. If consumers accept the association between the place and the icon—if they buy into the brand—then the branding is successful. A successful place-branding campaign cannot be done solely from the outside in or from the top down; it necessitates inclusion of locals. Such inclusion is most likely to involve the people who comprise the "inner circle of cultural or political life" and endogenic as well as exogenic image makers' efforts to "influence the influencers" (Pedersen 2004). Usually unheard are the less powerful but legitimate voices, though their participation or quiet nonparticipation in the brand identity is encouraged. In Gilroy, "the influencers" have changed over the years. At first they were the men who conceived of and brought to fruition the first Festival. Recall that initially the mayor, while he did not discourage the Festival, did not have confidence in its ability to draw people to Gilroy. After the first year's unforeseen success, however, he transitioned from being an "influencee" to being one of the "influencers," encouraging others to support the Festival and its associated Garlic Capital of the World branding.

John Hannigan (2003) outlines three "related dimensions" of place branding: instant recognition, playing on a desire for comfort and certainty, and providing a point of identification for consumers. The first and last of these coalesce into what I've called differentiation; that is, differentiation of one place or locality from another. Creating distinction is at the core of successful place branding, and being able to protect a claim of being a world capital of something enhances distinction. Only by differentiating one locale from other locales is a place able to stand out in the competitive quest to secure lucrative manufacturing and commercial industries as well as tourists. David Harvey (1993) explains that interplace competition is about attracting production by preserving a good business environment or realizing profits from speculative development, for example, and drawing consumers by creating a cultural center or attractive landscapes. To that I would clarify that "attractive landscapes" can be enhancements of existing geographic or cultural features, or mediation of a select historical moment or other feature to create a modern imaged–scape for consumption. "Investment in consumption spectacles, the selling of images of places, competition over the definition of cultural or symbolic capital, the revival of vernacular traditions associated with places, all become conflated" as place image makers engage in interplace competition for highly mobile capital (ibid., 8).

Gilroy's brand moniker "Garlic Capital of the World" and the promotion of garlic as iconic of the city can be understood as a consumption spectacle represented in and enacted through the Festival. By attending the Festival, participating in garlic-themed events, and ingesting garlic foods visitors, locals, and guests are part of the performance of Gilroy's branded identity. Media continue to consume and reiterate Gilroy's garlic association and the Festival. Despite the Festival's longevity, media present Gilroy's festivaliza-tion and fetishization of garlic as novel.

In Festival promotional texts there is no mention of the fact that more garlic is grown in neighboring counties than is grown in Gilroy. Although there are only five hundred to seven hundred acres dedicated to growing garlic in Gilroy, most of the eight hundred million pounds of garlic grown in Monterey, San Benito, Santa Clara, Fresno, and Kern counties is shipped to Gilroy for processing. According to a brochure published by Christopher Ranch, California produces approximately 90 percent of all U.S. garlic, much of which comes to Gilroy for processing or dehydration. Additionally, Festival organizers reasoned they could assert the claim of capitaldom because Gilroy is home to two of the world's largest dehydrators.

The Festival takes place only three days of the year, however, leaving Gilroy another 362 days each year to live its brand identity of Garlic Capital of the World. During non-Festival times, visitors are encouraged to consume the identity through acquisition of garlicabelia and ingestion of garlic foods, thus consuming the foodscape identity. To facilitate that, the Gilroy Visitors Bureau created the "Guide to Garlic in Gilroy," a bright orange flier that lists restaurants featuring garlic-laden dishes as well as shops specializing in gar-lic merchandise. The menu at Mama Mia's Ristorante Italiano in Gilroy has a special "Gilroy Garlic Menu" from which diners can choose Garlic Scampi or Garlic Festival penne con pesto, among other garlicky entrees. Tangible reminders of Gilroy's branded identity abound. Retails stores in Gilroy (and their web sites) sell garlicabelia like T-shirts, foodstuffs, aprons, hats, magnets, and many more items that visually reinforce the Gilroy-garlic association. Grocery stores and garlic specialty shops sell dried garlic year-round by the pound, and in decorative wreaths and braids.

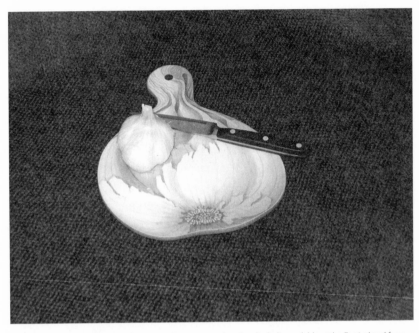

Garlic clove-shaped cutting boards are one of many examples of garlicabelia available at the Festival and from local retailers. (Photograph by author)

Vintage local garlic for sale at Gilroy's Garlic Shoppe, Highway 101, Gilroy, 2005. (Photograph by author)

In a glossy promotional brochure the Gilroy Visitors Bureau capitalizes on Gilroy's fame as the Garlic Capital of the World while reminding visitors and potential investors that Gilroy is about "Garlic! . . . and so much more!" Kristin Carr of the Gilroy Visitors Bureau commented that, despite the "Garlic! . . . and so much more!" slogan, however, the Visitors Bureau refers to Gilroy's "fame" as Garlic Capital of the World "in almost every marketing piece," and not the other features that constitute Gilroy's "so much more." Noticeable by its absence is any mention in the Gilroy Visitors Bureau publications of garlic agricultural or industrial production sites, none of which are open to the public, though fields of garlic and the processing plants are readily visible and smellable from Highway 101.

Automobile travelers approaching the city from the south see two garlic-themed billboards: one is the Garlic Capital of the World sign, the other advertises the web site for the Garlic Shoppe, one of the Gilroy-based garlic-themed retailers. Gilroy auto-ethnographies could—and sometimes do—boast of several other commercial attractions. The city is home to Bonfante Gardens, a family theme amusement park, and the 145-store Gilroy Premium Outlets shopping center. The Economic Development Corporation positions Gilroy as "the regional shopping center destination for South Santa Clara County and beyond" (Gilroy Economic Development Corporation 2004a), thanks to continued building of retail centers that include a warehouse grocery chain, national chain bookstores, two home decoration stores, and other "box" stores, all conveniently situated in expansive plazas immediately east of Highway 101. Such retail outlets lure visitors year-round. Like much of the Bay area, Santa Clara County also boasts several wineries as well as parks, golf courses, hiking trails, and other venues for outdoor activities.

Yet, what differentiates Gilroy from other towns with golf courses, wineries, and retail outlets is its self-proclaimed status as the Garlic Capital of the World. It is not surprising, then, that Gilroy's identity as a foodscape includes little mention of other possible identity-defining industries and few references to the inhabitants who people the city. Such selective inclusion and exclusion is comparable to selective memory strategically evoked by those who create memorials and other commemorative expressions (Bodnar 1991, Kammen 1991, Lipsitz 1990). In the case of Gilroy, the fetishization of garlic is done to the exclusion of recognizing the labor,

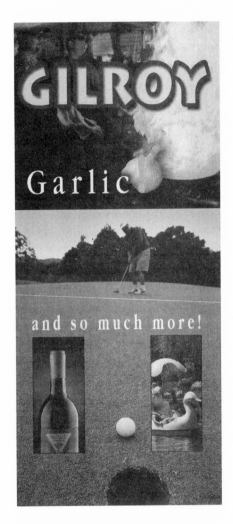

"Garlic! . . . and so much more!" brochure.
(GVB Brochure, author's collection)

agribusiness, and associated industries involved in its production. There is no mention in Festival promotional materials of the predominantly Mexican American laborers who work in the industry, many as seasonal field hands. As with commemorative expressions, cultural forms of self-inscription like community festivals and promotional pamphlets incorporate representations and interpretations of social relations. Through their

Billboard promoting the web site of a Gilroy-based, garlic-themed retailer, 2005. One of the Garlic Shoppe's two stores in Gilroy is located just beyond this sign on Highways 101, south of Gilroy. (Photograph by author)

inclusion and exclusion, these cultural representations legitimize, challenge, silence, and/or celebrate social identities. The noticeable absence of workers from Gilroy texts reinforces extant hegemonic labor relations and the general anonymity of the contemporary food chain. Image makers have successfully established what, for the most part, is an un-peopled food-place association for Gilroy.

Other than the Festival and garlicabelia, there is little more than the distinctive smelling air to connect Gilroy to garlic for visitors. Unlike other themed and branded cities, such as Las Vegas, New Orleans, or Leavenworth, Gilroy is able to retain its branded identity without having undergone much physical transformation. In fact, there has been very little significant physical change resulting from the self-proclaimed capitaldom. Among the tangible changes are road signs, garlic-themed retail outlets, enhancements to the city park where the Festival is held, and the temporary conversion of expansive fields into parking lots during the Festival days. The food-place association is tenacious enough, and entertaining enough, to sustain itself without urban renovation.

Gourmet Garlic? Strategic Ambiguity

Place branding is a powerful marketing tool. Consider place monikers such as "Honeymoon Capital of the World" (Niagara Falls) and "City of Lights" (Paris). Successful brand slogans, whether referring to a geographic or aesthetic feature, popular use, or a desired image of a place, prompt place association. The association made by branding does not need to be contemporaneous. In fact, as the moniker for Niagara Falls illustrates, a place's associational moniker can outlive the reality of the source of the branding. Similarly, the basis or specification of a claim of differentiation can change over time. Around the middle of the nineteenth century, Gilroy was known as the Hay and Grain Capital of California. In the decades around the turn of the twentieth century, Gilroy was known as the Dairy and Cheese Capital of California because four-fifths of the state's cheese production was in the Gilroy area. By the 1920s, Gilroy's extensive plum orchards and extensive dehydration industry prompted its reputation as the Prune Capital. Agriculture and agribusiness continue to be vital to the city's economy, but the principal food is now garlic. Earlier in the century Gilroy town leaders could have promoted the city as the Prune Capital and organized a Prune Festival, complete with a Miss Prune Pageant and prune-centric foods. Imagine the whimsical prune-abelia tourists could have purchased had that food-place branding been successful. Alternatively, Melone and Christopher could have commemorated the prune-centered episode of Gilroy's past when they initiated their campaign in the 1970s. Instead they chose garlic. Garlic was already associated among area residents with Gilroy by smell, it was transitioning from a food on the fringe to a food with a following, and garlic was a key ingredient in the city's physical and economic landscapes. They situated garlic in a festive context, one emphasizing its role as an ingredient by featuring garlic-laden foods and a garlic-themed cooking contest, and promoted the Festival as a premier event.

Since the Festival's inception, Festival organizers have promoted it both as a quirky event and as a gourmet food festival. To be clear, Gilroy is not promoted as a gourmet destination, but the Festival is positioned as one featuring gourmet foods (both those from Gourmet Alley and from vendors) and gourmet food events, most notably the cooking contest and chefs' cooking demonstrations. The term *gourmet* connotes ambiguous but particular associations of food and lifestyle.[6] Gilroy's image makers capitalize on the ambiguity of *gourmet* and the concept's capacity as a marker of cultural capital while also exploiting garlic's capacity for festivalization and fetishization. This juxtaposition of gourmet and frivolity broadens the appeal of Gilroy's garlic identity.

Historically, middle-class Anglo-Americans regarded garlic as malodorous and, "though used by the French, better adapted to medicine than cookery," as Lucy Emerson summarized in her 1801 book *The New-England Cookery* (Root and de Rochemont 1995 [1976], 107). Over the course of the twentieth century, garlic transitioned from an ingredient associated with a marginalized immigrant population and foreigners to an ingredient of mainstream American cooking. As part of its transition, garlic developed a cult-like following exemplified by the Berkeley-based fan club, Lovers of the Stinking Rose. Some garlic devotees express their love of the pungent lily through consumer participation in anything garlic-related, including frequenting the Gilroy Garlic Festival. Despite having a devoted following and being accepted as a principal ingredient by many American consumers, garlic's acceptance is tempered by a subtle ambivalence toward garlic informed by lingering culinary egocentrism, physiological palate preferences, and selective participation in food trends.

In addition to the ambivalence that tempers its popularity as a trendy food, there are several reasons why garlic has proven an unsuitable ingredient among those who pursue food trends as a strategy for marking social distinction. Unlike most other foods that suggest elevated socioeconomic status or culinary distinction, garlic is inexpensive and readily available. That some garlic-laden foods are heartily embraced by the corporate food industry increases their availability to a broad spectrum of the consuming public. For example, the increased availability of commercially packaged Genovese pesto at grocery stores and its frequent appearance on restaurant menus indicate that this garlicky Italian sauce is firmly integrated into American food culture.

When the Gilroy Garlic Festival began, pesto was not widely available outside Italian markets and selected restaurants. Pesto's limited availability and association with northern Italian cuisine, a culinary tradition familiar primarily among foodies and northern Italians, marked it as gourmet.

Among the food offerings at the inaugural Festival was pasta with pesto, a labor-intensive and an unusual food to serve at a festival celebrating an agricultural product. As pesto became a more common food, Festival organizers recognized that they needed to update their pesto offering in order to keep it a gourmet item. Appreciating "the fine line of seeking improvement without altering a highly successful event," 2004 Gourmet Alley cochairman Greg Bozzo came up with a new version, *"Penne pasta con pesto,"* for that year's Festival. "First, and foremost, it's a pesto dish," Bozzo is quoted as saying in an official Festival press release; "But it's more of a gourmet item than our previous entr[é]e. Basil and pesto are primary ingredients, but this will be served in a white cream sauce with the pesto introduced at the very end. And we're adding garden-fresh chopped tomatoes" (Gilroy Garlic Festival Association Press Release 2004). Professional and some home cooks will wonder why this dish qualifies as gourmet, but for the purposes of the Festival, the new dish was presented as such.

The culinary center of the Festival is Gourmet Alley, an outdoor working kitchen where volunteer cooks prepare massive quantities of garlicky foods. Even its name, a clever coupling, juxtaposes the ambiguity and potentially elevating capacity of the term gourmet with the liminal space of an alley. The iconic foods prepared in Gourmet Alley are served in paper or cardboard containers. The absence of picnic tables or benches near Gourmet Alley leaves consumers no choice but to stand or sit on the ground while they eat the iconic foods. It is the foods that are being promoted as gourmet, not the dining experience.

What the rhetoric about the new pesto dish and the titular symbolism of the arterial kitchen suggest are the organizers' dedication to framing the foods served as gourmet. By extension, if gourmet foods are served at the Festival, consuming the Festival's garlic-laden foods could be cultural capital for Festival volunteers, attendees, and garlic devotees. The fact that garlic itself is not regarded as a marker of elevated status and that garlic is not thought of as gourmet within the popular imagination problematizes the ideological equation of the Gilroy Garlic Festival with gourmet. Despite this problematic, having firsthand familiarity with the Festival can and does serve as a marker of distinction among garlic and festival devotees, not a marker of elevated social status so much as a marker of membership in the cultural category of garlic or festival enthusiast.

Most who consider the nuances of the term gourmet would agree that it encompasses ambience as well as actual foodstuffs. While one can partake of a gourmet food experience out of doors, it is debatable whether or not eating garlic bread or garlicky pasta with pesto sauce on a sun-parched patch of worn grass constitutes a gourmet experience. It is the ambiguity of the concept and the individual nature of defining what does and does not constitute a gourmet experience that enables Gilroy Garlic Festival organizers to persist in framing their Festival as a gourmet food festival.

Just as selecting the icon around which to build a place brand can seem somewhat arbitrary or spurious, so too can other claims associated with the branded identity. The fact that Gilroy Garlic Festival organizers continue to conceive of and promote their Festival as gourmet seems specious. Since the last quarter of the twentieth century in particular, food has been a central theme within popular culture, elevating general public awareness of food and altering perceptions of what gourmet signifies. The multitude of ambiguous messages delivered through cable television channel Food Network programs epitomizes the complicated place of food as symbol in contemporary American popular culture (Adema 2000). For Doug Brown (2004), the fact that food journalism is winning industry awards indicates more interest in and embracing attitudes among Americans toward food as more than just sustenance. Along with changing awareness and attitudes come shifts in what might stand as cultural capital. As more people learn about and cook what are considered gourmet foods, the concept *gourmet* must be applied to different or novel foods in order for *gourmet* to retain its status as a marker of distinction. Despite the dynamism of the world of food, and in spite of garlic's incorporation into mainstream American foodways, Gilroy Garlic Festival organizers and community leaders continue to conceive of and market their Festival as a quirky and gourmet food event.

Generating Identities through a Festive Foodscape

Gilroy's branded identity is sustained by the successful food-centered event and place marketing in the forms of auto-ethnographic texts and media coverage. It is important to realize that there actually are multiple identities generated by the Festival and the foodscape place brand. One identity is that of the city as Festival founders intended: "To boost Gilroy's image by claiming the Garlic Capital of the World title." Bill Ayer, president of the 1981 Festival, repeated an often-heard refrain, that the Festival "turned Gilroy around—gave it identification. Once the Garlic Festival happened, the town's people started to gain some pride in themselves and pride in the city" (Ayer 2003, see also, Sutherland 2003). A second collective and multidimensional identity generated by the Garlic Festival is the community of Festival volunteers. A communal spirit is operating and being reinforced on multiple levels as volunteers simultaneously play numerous roles: individual residents, fund-raisers, party hosts, coworkers, neighbors, and most importantly, friends. Just as national contemporaneous communities are expressed through performance of national anthems, the singing of which suggests unisonance (Anderson 1983), members of a locale can express a collective identity through the community festival during which their participation as volunteers suggests the fraternal unisonance that constitutes sense of community.

The Festival is also a participatory institution around which other Gilroyans affirm their identities as members of the collective community, build traditions, and consequently, strengthen attachments to each other and to place. The 2003 Gilroy Garlic Festival Queen Melissa Noto described how she and her friends, many of whom attend college out of town, meet at the Festival each year. Even if they do not determine a time and place to meet, she commented, "it goes without saying, everyone is going to be at the Festival." For many Gilroyans who grew up attending or participating in the Festival, Festival time is an integral part of their conception of home. As a site for midsummer reconnection the Festival becomes a landscape of homecoming for young Gilroyans during their college years. Through their continuity, ritualized display, and inherently collective nature, annual festivals are traditionalizing instruments (Moore and Myerhoff 1977). College-age Gilroyans develop their own traditions of reunion, traditions very similar to those of other former residents for whom the Festival days define a period of homecoming. That the Festival continues to be a site for reunion is readily apparent to anyone walking around the site, where squeals of glee from reuniting friends are followed by excited chatter as they share details of their lives apart. Festival time and space, then, facilitates validation of individual identity and attachment to place just as it validates collective place identity.

The fortuitous combination of good marketing and a receptive public enabled business and town leaders to transform what was a communal embarrassment into positive identity capital. To protect their identity as *the* garlic foodscape, city officials tried to trademark the slogan Garlic Capital of the World as part of the city logo. After a two-year, expensive legal struggle, they conceded defeat. But the association between the city and the moniker, which is used liberally in city, commercial, and tourism materials, is firmly entrenched in the popular imagination. Despite the fact that Stroudsburg, Pennsylvania, declared itself Garlic Capital of the World, Gilroy image makers remain confident that their status as *the* capital is secure because the food-place association between garlic and Gilroy is well-established and repeatedly promoted in multiple media. There is no indication of any contestation between Gilroy and Stroudsburg. In fact, people in Gilroy do not mention Stroudsburg or other garlic festivals, other than the festival in Arleux that was Melone's inspiration. Such is a feature of successful food-themed place branding and foodscapes: once an association becomes firmly entrenched within the public imagination, it is tenacious.

Thanks to successful branding of a food-place association, the city of Gilroy secured name recognition as a foodscape. Image makers bundled the city's identity into their annual Festival, and it is primarily there and through media about it that people consume the commodified place.

The selection of a food item with historic links to the landscape does not guarantee successful place branding. As he faced the task of fund-raising, Rudy Melone was looking for a catch. What he sought was differentiation and aggrandizement—a way to distinguish Gilroy from other towns that would not only elevate Gilroy in the public imagination but would also entice visitorship and investment. An agricultural product seemed logical in part because, to a relative newcomer such as Melone, its presence was so obvious: Gilroy's seasonal scent reminded him that garlic was important to the local economy. Like other localities that evoke a useable past, Gilroy as festive foodscape implies continuity with the past while simultaneously evoking connections to the future: Gilroy—the brand—successfully links Gilroy's agricultural past and present with its industrial and commercial present in hopes of continued recognition of both into the future.

Highlighting an agricultural product draws on the agrarian heritage of the valley, implicitly evoking nostalgia for the illusory simplicity of a farming past while catering to Americans' appetite for a festive and food-themed present. Gilroy's success as a foodscape is attributable to good marketing, people's curiosity about garlic and their willingness to suspend culinary egocentrism, people's seemingly infinite love of food and food festivals, and perhaps most importantly, as Mr. Filice so smartly noted, timing: all these variables came together at the right time, with skillful planning by the right people, in the right place. Americans were ready for another food festival and they were ready for garlic.

In 1979, a successful garlic campaign was far from certain. Twenty-five years later, Gilroy's food-place association has become so embedded in the popular imagination that it seems organic. Gilroy exemplifies successful place branding; hindsight makes it look as though success was inevitable.

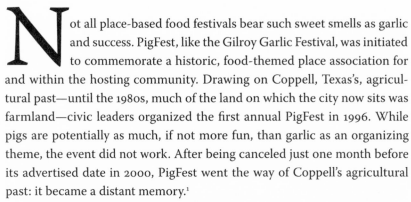

CHAPTER SIX

"This little piggy went to PigFest . . ."

The Paradox of PigFest

Nᴏᴛ all place-based food festivals bear such sweet smells as garlic and success. PigFest, like the Gilroy Garlic Festival, was initiated to commemorate a historic, food-themed place association for and within the hosting community. Drawing on Coppell, Texas's, agricultural past—until the 1980s, much of the land on which the city now sits was farmland—civic leaders organized the first annual PigFest in 1996. While pigs are potentially as much, if not more fun, than garlic as an organizing theme, the event did not work. After being canceled just one month before its advertised date in 2000, PigFest went the way of Coppell's agricultural past: it became a distant memory.[1]

In contrast to the story of Gilroy's branded identity, Coppell's story is of an unsuccessful attempt to create a sense of community and place identity through a place-specific food festival. As an unsuccessful attempt to mediate communal identity, PigFest provides an important comparison to the Gilroy Garlic Festival. The longevity of several widely known place-based food festivals makes their success seem inevitable: the Gilroy Garlic

Festival, which marked its twenty-ninth year in 2007, is a toddler compared to the Maine Lobster Festival, which commenced in 1947, and the Florida Strawberry Festival®, which began in 1930. Consideration of an unsuccessful event evinces that, although many food items are ripe for fetishization and festivalization in the service of place differentiation and community building, place-based food festivals are not guaranteed to succeed. As this ethnographic case study of Coppell's PigFest illustrates, the most significant factors informing a place-based food festival's success or failure are the displayed and implied semiotics of food symbolization and the degree to which organizers allow for communal participation.

"The little piggy went to market": The Making of Coppell

Contemporary Coppell is a suburb of Dallas–Fort Worth, Texas, the ninth largest metropolitan area in the United States.[2] Most of Coppell is situated in northwestern Dallas County, five miles north of Dallas–Fort Worth International Airport. In 1832, early settlers were attracted to the area by a natural spring. They established a small farming community, calling it Grapevine Springs. More than a decade later it became part of the state of Texas. The area was renamed Gibbs in 1873, recognizing prominent Dallas attorney Barnett Gibbs, who had major landholdings in the vicinity. The settlement was renamed once again in 1890 in honor of George Coppell, an engineer whom local lore credits with bringing the Cotton Belt Railroad, part of the St. Louis and Southwestern Texas Railroads, to the area a few years earlier. From the depot in Coppell, the railroad transported local agricultural products, including cotton and food crops such as oats, sweet potatoes, peanuts, and melons to regional markets.

By 1893, Coppell was a bustling railroad town surrounded by active family farms. In addition to the train depot, the town boasted a grocery store, a lumberyard, a blacksmith shop, and a cotton gin.[3] Increased use of automotive transport in the 1920s led to the railroad's decline as the primary mode of commercial shipping and, consequently, initiated a decline in the town's population. As the town of Coppell lost its vitality through the late 1920s and 1930s, farmers still active in the area had to venture to Carrollton, Lewisville,

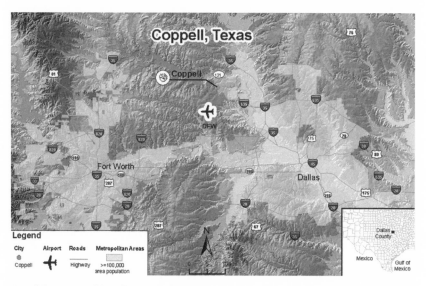

Coppell, Texas, is part of the Dallas–Fort Worth Metroplex. (Map by Manuel Peralvo)

Coppell Depot, built in 1890. (Photograph courtesy of the Coppell Historical Society)

or other nearby towns for supplies. In 1937 a Works Projects Administration work relief effort created a park along the historically significant Grapevine Creek, near Coppell's old town center.[4] Gradually, a small town reemerged near the park and residents again called it Coppell.

Nineteen forties Coppell did not attain the vitality of its late nineteenth-century predecessor. World War II called many area men into service, leaving family farms struggling to survive. Coppell's population declined in the postwar years and the park went unused; the land on which it was built was returned to private ownership and was leased for agricultural use.

By the early 1950s, Coppell's population was again on the rise. It was during this decade that Coppell began a rapid transition from a rural, agricultural community to a bedroom community for the rapidly growing city of Dallas. Concerned about Dallas's interest in land annexation, Coppell residents began the process of securing official recognition as a distinct city. In 1955, by a forty-one to one vote, voting residents elected to incorporate Coppell. By the end of the decade, the city had a mayor and a volunteer fire department, a dial telephone system replaced the central switchboard and operator, Dallas Power and Light built a plant that supplied residents with a steady stream of electric power, and the two main roads through town, Denton Tap Road and Sandy Lake Road, were paved.

Initially only two square miles, contemporary Coppell comprises barely fifteen square miles. For decades Coppell's population steadily and dramatically increased (table 6.1.). Coppell's population growth paralleled that of Dallas County, growth attributable to Dallas's rapid transition from an agricultural center to a manufacturing and financial center for the southwest. The county experienced continued population increase throughout the second half of the twentieth century with Coppell, and many other emerging cities in the area, accommodating new residents.

There were several other features in addition to its proximity to downtown Dallas that made Coppell an attractive destination for new residents. Completion of the North Texas sections of the Dwight D. Eisenhower National System of Interstate and Defense Highways in the 1960s, and the opening of Dallas–Fort Worth International Airport in 1974 stimulated Coppell's population growth. In fact, Coppell's proximity to the airport and major highways is largely responsible for the city's emergence as a thriving bedroom community.

Table 6.1.

Coppell, Texas, Population Data

Year	Population
1960[a]	666
1970	1,728
1980	3,826
1990	16,881
2000	35,958

Source: U.S. Census Bureau, State and County QuickFacts, "Coppell (city), Texas," http://quickfacts.census.gov/qfd/states/48/4816612.html. See also the sources cited in note 2.

[a]Because the city was incorporated in 1955, 1960 is the first year that the U.S. Census Bureau recorded population numbers for Coppell.

In the decade between 1990 and 2000, Coppell experienced an astounding population boom (109.8 percent), far greater than other areas in North Texas. Nearby Carrollton and Grapevine respectively had population increases of 32.7 and 42.4 percent, and neighboring Lewisville blossomed with 67.8 percent population growth. While the city of Dallas experienced a noteworthy 18.1 percent population increase, the populations of suburbs north of Dallas near Coppell grew at a much more rapid pace. Real estate developers knew that Coppell was geographically well-situated to thrive; developers and locals promoted, and continue to promote, Coppell's location as one of its assets. The same highways that made it conveniently close to Dallas and Dallas–Fort Worth International Airport also made Coppell far enough away from the stresses of modern urban living that affluent families could have the American bucolic ideal of a home, a yard, and swaying trees. With carefully worded text, developers suggested that Coppell's "luxury homes" were for an upper socioeconomic segment of the area's population; the people who moved there were predominantly white, with earned income well above those of residents in neighboring suburban cities (appendix A, tables A.2 and A.3). In the 2002 edition of *Destination DFW*, a Dallas–Fort Worth informational-promotional publication, the description of Coppell reads

> Just a few years ago most folks had never heard of Coppell, and those who had didn't think much about it. In 1980 it was just a quiet little town of 3,826; then the fickle finger of development trends began to point Coppell's

way. It's still quiet but no longer little. Not that it looks like a city—it's actually more a dusting of North Texas woods with luxury homes, manicured yards, and rows of shade trees in sway. In short, it's a good place to raise a family. If anything, it's becoming more exclusive with the passage of time. . . . Coppell can generally be described by its enviable bordering freeways: I-635, I-35, and Highway 121. To the south-east is Las Colinas and one of the fastest suburban commuter routes to downtown Dallas. . . . (HPC Publications, 69)

In addition to its location and upscale residential subdivisions, developers promoted Coppell's commitment to incorporating green spaces into its design, specifically "parks, jogging trails, playgrounds and the Riverchase golf course" (Samuel L. Wyse Associates 1973, 69). Included among the preserved open spaces is the Works Projects Administration park, Grapevine Spring Park, which, after being donated by private owners for city use, was restored and rededicated as a historic open space park—complete with a historical marker erected by the Coppell Historical Society—in 1993. Aggrandizement texts like the *Destination DFW* magazine also mention the quality of the city's school district, praising expanding enrollment, a new high school complex, and campuses rated "exemplary" by the Texas Education Association. Inclusion of the school district in Coppell's autoethnographies affirms developers' intention of attracting young families.

Coppell's Community Information Officer Sharon Logan speculated that people are drawn to the city by its carefully planned aesthetic design, including dark brick facades on most homes and government structures and landscaped medians along public thoroughfares. No doubt all these features are some of the "amenities of community life [intended] to attract new residents" alluded to in the 1972–1992 Comprehensive Plan.

Coppell is accessed easily via one of the multilane highways that define its boundaries. The city's proximity to Dallas–Fort Worth International Airport facilitated building of "industrial parks" comprised of warehouses, merchandise transfer centers, and corporate headquarters along the city's southern edges. These oxymoronically named "parks" abut the few extant fields, reminders of the not-so-distant past when much of the land was dedicated to family farms. The area's continued population growth and the ease of access afforded by the extensive network of highways encircling the city have led to the construction of sizable apartment complexes and expansive shopping centers along Coppell's northern edges.

Once off Highway I-35, I-635, or Texas State Highway 121, drivers find themselves on smoothly paved roads divided by the aforementioned, well-maintained landscaped medians, amid shopping plazas and subdivisions with names that allude to a pastoral ideal or one of the area's displaced natural features. Most of the commercial and residential buildings visible from the main roads are large, dark brick structures. Although there is architectural variety among the homes in residential subdivisions bearing names like "Magnolia Park" and "Stonemeade Estate," there is remarkable visual homogeneity among the various subdivisions and in the retail plazas along the main thoroughfares.

Readily apparent while driving around Coppell is the commercialism that accompanies suburban growth in America: strip plazas with grocery stores, cafes, dry cleaners, and national chain drug stores. Like many suburbs, the city and its businesses are designed to accommodate modern American car culture. Social relations are atomized by Coppell's car-dependent town plan and homes with alley-access garages, neither of which facilitates daily spontaneous interaction among residents.

Coppell's wide roads are easily negotiated, but they do not lead to a geographic town center. The absence of a town common means that there is no central social and commercial gathering space, what often becomes the heart and soul of a small city. There is an area called Town Center, but it is neither a geographic center nor a social gathering place. On the property comprising Town Center are a large YMCA, the Coppell Justice Center, and Coppell Town Center, the equivalent of a city hall, which houses city administration and government.

"This little piggy stayed home": No Sense of Place or Community?

Absent from promotional materials and most discussions about the city is mention of the activities and people that generate a sense of place. Talking with current and former Coppell residents and relatives of Coppell residents during the course of my research, I heard repeatedly about Coppell's

The formal design of the walled gateway to Coppell's Town Center does not communicate an air of welcome. The building behind this gate is the firehouse. (Photograph by author)

Coppell Town Center. The town hall was built in 1986. (Photograph by author)

rapid growth, about its central location in the Metroplex, and about property values. For example, one unmarried man commented that he lived in
Coppell, even though there were more young families than other single people, because he could get much more house for his money in Coppell than
he could closer to Dallas, and, because of the extensive highway network,
he was close enough to Dallas that he could visit friends and participate
in Dallas's vibrant cultural life. Conversations about Coppell offered little
indication of communal identity and pride of place among residents that is
apparent among locals of other small cities like Gilroy. Perhaps contributing
to the apparent lack of communal spirit is that many of those who work for
the betterment of the city do not live there. One city employee estimated
that less than 40 percent of city employees live in Coppell, not because
they do not want to but because they cannot afford it. More than one city
employee mentioned a prohibitively high cost of living as the reason for not
living in Coppell. While these people work to develop senses of place and
community for Coppell, they invest their leisure time and energy building
community elsewhere. These folks commute to work in a city that has built
its identity around the ease with which residents can commute away from
it for their work.

Coppell's recent development as a suburb, the commuter lifestyle of
many of its residents, and its automobile-centric design do much to inform
the absence of a connection among residents, and between residents and
the town they inhabit. Coppell exemplifies what New Urbanism labels classic suburban sprawl: "residential 'communities' utterly lacking in communal
life" serviced by businesses in strip shopping centers (Duany et al. 2000, x).

Because most Coppell residents moved to the area within the past twenty
years, there is no heritage of the meaning-ascribing and place-defining
lived experiences among past and present residents, what Anne Buttimer
(1980) describes as "the process of dwelling." Not only is a majority of the
population recently arrived, there is a sense among residents that people
do not stay long enough to invest in the community. Based on interviews
with thirty-nine community "stakeholders," including "homeowners, business representatives, church leaders, developers, and others with an interest
in the future of Coppell," the authors of a city planning report observe that,
"even though Coppell is principally a residential community, many residents
do not live here for very long (some just 3–5 years). Many move because of

company transfers. This may make it hard to encourage more resident participation on future plans" (Hellmuth 1996, 7, A-8).

Absent is a sense of shared past from which image makers spearhead-
ing citywide events can draw to distinguish their suburban oasis from other
nearby suburbs, the quest for place differentiation that David Harvey calls
"interplace competition" (1993, 8). Localities are defined in part by how their
inhabitants and image makers conceive of, present, and represent the physical space in comparison to other places. As previously mentioned, particularly noteworthy is the fact that Coppell developers define the city by its
geographic proximity to other cities, thus highlighting the mobile nature
of contemporary life and, by implication, of its residents. Their approach to
place-promotion is consistent with Doreen Massey's (1993) suggestion that
a locality's character can only be understood by linking it to places beyond
its borders; that is, localities are constituted by their economic, political,
and cultural links with the world beyond their borders. Approached with
this understanding of locality, Coppell is recognized as a somewhat typical,
developer-built, mid- to late twentieth-century American suburban city.

One of the consequences of a place being defined primarily in relation
to other places is that image makers and residents risk overlooking its *genius
loci*, the characteristics, features, or history that make it distinct. Eliminating
or suppressing distinctive places and standardizing landscapes can leave
residents and visitors nothing upon which to build a connection to place,
resulting in what Edward Relph (1976) calls "placelessness" or no sense of
place. That Coppell's planners created an area called Town Center suggests
they recognized the symbolic value of having a town center, though there
was no plan as to how to achieve it: the consultants who authored the 1996
Comprehensive Plan noted that

> Town Center needs to be the central focal point to create a community feel-
> ing. But it also needs a master plan. The Town Center should include public
> uses like City Hall, library, civic center, performing arts center, etc. Support
> uses, like the YMCA or restaurants, would also be appropriate (although
> most do not want a "fast-food restaurant row" in the Town Center). Almost
> one-third of the original area has been lost to development—should the City
> consider buying the undeveloped land? Most adjacent homeowners want
> Town Center to remain as open space. (Hellmuth, A-3)

As if to compensate for an absence of meaningful places in the present, image makers incorporate references to the past. This can be done by incorporating architectural styles meant to connect symbolically the new buildings to an idealized or generic past. Coppell city planners' determination to follow an "old world" architectural style as they established the city is an example of looking outward and to the past to create identity rather than cultivating that which might be distinctive to the place being inhabited. Coppell Director of Planning Gary Sieb explained to me that the City "doesn't have a formal definition of 'old world' but what we've put together from a variety of sources . . . is that masonry is the prevailing building material, it should be of darker tones, real brick (not fake), other masonry products—cast stone, SOME (less than 20%) stucco, wrought iron, rock, and traditional building materials are best. Proportion is important, gabled roofs are encouraged, small paned windows are recommended, and dark shingles with some texture all contribute to the [old world] theme." Despite their dedication to building according to an "old world" architectural style, evocative of a generic but established community and traditions, Town Center lacks features that invite residents to make it a communal gathering place and, consequently, a physical space around which residents develop senses of place and community.

Another way to evoke the past in the present is through the rhetorical strategy of referencing the past in place names. One of the planned subdivisions in Coppell, for example, is called "Old Coppell." The oxymoronic name rhetorically compartmentalizes place-history: it recalls by implication what once was, yet inside the small subdivision's ivy-covered walls there is evidence neither of anything old nor of anything unique to Coppell. The homes inside the Old Coppell subdivision are a style New Urbanists call the "North Dallas Special," a design common among homebuilders at the upper end of the market (Duany et al. 2000). Although not unique to North Dallas, the title is fitting since many of the homes in Coppell and other suburbs of Dallas are in this style. This single-family home style, Andrés Duany and his colleagues explain, "attempts to create a skyline of an entire village. It is meant to stand alone" (76). Colloquially known as McMansions because of their ubiquity and similarity, these homes are "the fast food version of the American dream" (ibid., 41), they emphasize privacy, maximize livable space for the lots on which they sit, are repetitive in their design, and minimize features that facilitate interaction with neighbors.

The entries to Old Coppell Estates subdivision are bordered by ivy-covered masonry walls. Standing on both sides of the road at each of the two entries are small, brick and stone structures that suggest a gate house. (Photograph by author)

Distinct from but adjacent to the late twentieth-century "Old Coppell" subdivision is an area called Old Coppell, the center of which for decades has been a traffic signal at a crossroads a couple of miles from Coppell's bustling commercial areas. Absent from historic Old Coppell are the McMansions that define most of Coppell's residential landscape. Instead, in addition to a few early twentieth-century clapboard buildings, there are mid-century one-story homes, a few small businesses, a senior center, a school, and a trailer park. Also there, at the head of Old Coppell's crossroads, is the Stringfellow home, circa 1890s, the oldest extant home in Coppell. Recognizing "citizens' desire for a mixed-use town center to provide a 'sense of place' that the community has been missing for years," a long-term Master Plan to redesign and redevelop Old Coppell as a place-defining focal point was formalized in 2001 (Looney Ricks Kiss 2002). In May 2005, an amendment to Coppell's City Zoning Ordinance designated Old Coppell a historic area. Coppell's Assistant Director of Planning Marcie Diamond explained that calling Old Coppell a historic district is local zoning nomenclature; the area does not have official state designation as a Historic District.

These houses, located in the Old Coppell subdivision, typify the North Dallas Special style. Note the proximity of the airplane in the lower image, a reminder how close Dallas–Ft. Worth International Airport is to Coppell. (Photographs by author)

The center of the "historic" Old Coppell is the intersection of South Coppell and Bethel Roads. At the head of South Coppell Road, behind the signs, stands the Stingfellow home. It was for sale at the time this photograph was taken, September 2005. (Photograph by author)

Kent C. Ryden (1993, 40) defines sense of place as constituted in part from meanings and associations a person ascribes to a place: "For those who have developed a sense of place, then, it is as though there is an unseen layer of usage, memory and significance . . . superimposed upon the geographical surface. . . ." The emotive associations that tie individuals to communal physical space come from residents sharing memories of the space as well as generating new ones through lived experiences in the place (Buttimer's "process of dwelling"), thereby endowing it with more significance. The challenge of creating a meaningful invisible landscape for a young city whose residents are new and do not have narratives of the landscape is significant. Traditional community building and nurturing institutions, such as extended family and neighborhoods, can be difficult to sustain in contemporary life's highly mobile society.

To facilitate a sense of familiarity and connection, city and civic leaders often turn to traditional forms of community affirmation. Local festivals are one strategy that can help facilitate communal identity among otherwise disconnected populations. Sharon Logan told me that the City Council "believes that community festivals and events help to foster the concept of 'a sense of community.'" The organizers and promoters of PigFest were similarly reflexive: they recognized, and in fact hoped, that through the festival frame they would facilitate a sense of communal identity among locals and within the larger Metroplex.

Coppell's image makers had good reason to think that a community festival was the appropriate medium for advancing their community-generating agenda. The U.S. Department of Housing and Urban Development (HUD) extols the virtues of hosting an annual festival as a way for a city to celebrate itself in a booklet titled "Urban Fairs: How Cities Celebrate Themselves" (Office of Public Affairs 1981). One of the primary features associated with community festivals is "the sharing of community character" (Getz 1989, 128). Coppell's image makers knew that other cities and towns used the festival format to secure place differentiation; they had heard of and witnessed successful food-place branding celebrated at annual festivals from places like faraway Gilroy and nearby Grapevine, Texas, home of the long-running and well-attended annual celebration of Texas wines, GrapeFest. They seemed to ascribe to a "Field of Dreams" philosophy: if they hold an annual festival, people will attend and, consequently, a sense of place would emerge.[5]

In the spirit of community building and place promotion, PigFest organizers hoped to celebrate the landscape's agrarian past within the constraints of an affluent suburban present in hopes of creating a sense of community for the future. This agenda seemed particularly important for the nascent upscale suburb of commuters. Rapid population expansion and associated residential and commercial growth left the new city of Coppell with few identity-distinguishing features to differentiate it from other nearby suburbs. PigFest organizers, who included primarily civic leaders and a few city employees, hoped to generate a successful place brand and a sense of collective identity for Coppell by creating a festive foodscape.

"This little piggy went to PigFest . . .":
The Birth and Demise of PigFest

Coppell Celebrates was a nonprofit organization formed in 1993 to "coordinate events that promote the benefits of living and working in Coppell,

Texas, and enhance the quality of life and work in Coppell."[6] Its ten-member Board of Directors was comprised of an appointed representative from the City, Coppell Chamber of Commerce, Coppell Independent School District and select community service organizations (Rotary Club of Coppell, Lions Club, Exchange Club, Women's Club), as well as three business leaders elected by the appointed directors.[7] Even though city employees sat on the Coppell Celebrates board, operating events under that organization diverted financial and organizational responsibilities away from city government. It also allowed the events to be considered community events because they were not, strictly speaking, organized by the city. Through their events, Coppell Celebrates became the image makers for the city.

In 1996 Coppell Celebrates transformed a struggling spring festival, Funfest, into PigFest. The three-day, porcine-themed event was intended primarily for Coppell families, with secondary and tertiary target audiences of residents in neighboring communities and pig enthusiasts. During its tenure, the Festival was heavily promoted in local media: paid advertisements on major network-affiliated local television stations, press releases sent to four major papers serving Coppell and the Metroplex, advertisements in direct mail pieces sent to all Coppell homes, inserts into the Money Mailer coupon/promotion envelopes delivered to Coppell and Las Colinas (a neighboring town) homes, and fliers handed out in all Coppell schools.

In anticipation of the first Festival, one newspaper reporter notes that the event "will pay homage to the city's widely unknown history" (Medigovich 1996). To acquaint residents with this little known heritage, a PigFest special section in the local paper included a short article about Coppell's agrarian past. The article, "Pigfest part of Coppell history," begins: "Considering that 845 acres of the present Coppell was once a pig farm, it's no wonder those behind this year's Pigfest decided to dedicate the festivities to the beloved fine-haired friend" (Hoyt 1996). The article continues with personal recollections from Coppell resident Bob Ottinger, whose family operated a pig, cattle, and grain farm for seventeen years on the site of what is now Coppell Town Center. As though this article was enough to familiarize residents with Coppell's history, no similar retrospective appeared in subsequent years. A short, pre-festival article the second year did incorporate one sentence reminding readers that "Pig Fest is named in honor of the affluent Metroplex community's heritage—much of the suburban sprawl that is Coppell formerly consisted of hog farms, including the land on which the city's Town Center now sits" (Sipos 1997). In reality, however, although much of the land that constitutes contemporary Coppell was farmland, and hogs often were among the animals kept on family farms, the land was not dedicated solely or primarily to hogs.

Festival organizers selected pigs as the theme not only because some of their city was built on farmland that had previously hosted pigs; they also regarded pigs as a novelty and thought novelty appeal would translate into visitorship. Sharon Logan reflected that "[t]rying to establish an event in the Metroplex is like trying to make a leaf on a tree stand out from the rest. There are so many events and so many opportunities for people to spend discretionary income that the competition for attendance, attention and media support is unbelievable. So, the 'pig theme' really made the festival stand out from the rest of the events [in the Metroplex]." Then City Manager Jim Witt summarized, "Pigs are a hot item. . . . I think it's a cute theme" (Medigovich 1996). Pigs, especially piglets, were a "hot item" in 1995 in large part because of the amazingly successful family movie *Babe, the Gallant Pig*. The pig theme that Coppell Celebrates chose combined a popular culture trend with a segment of Coppell's agricultural past.

To jump-start their new themed festival, Coppell Celebrates hired S. S. "Sparky" Sparks, a Dallas consultant with a reputation for coordinating unusual events. Sparks remembers accepting the job because it "sounded fun," and PigFest was "a promote-able concept for a festival that would get ink for Coppell and get people out." Subsequent to the first PigFest, Coppell Celebrates coordinated the event without him, but for the first year, organizers believed that his creativity and connections were essential. Coppell Celebrates also worked with the Metroplex Association of Potbellied Pig Enthusiasts (MAPPE), a North Texas nonprofit pig-rescue and educational organization.

PigFest took place at Andy Brown Park West, part of an expansive park with soccer fields, baseball diamonds, and open space hospitable to a festival. The inaugural PigFest contained several events customary of community festivals but modified for pig participation. Included among the "'Pig'Tivities" were a pig parade (so popular it was repeated several times during each Festival), a pig beauty pageant and fashion show, and competitive events organized under the title "Olym'Pig' Events." There were ample

PigFest Petting Farm, 1999. (Photograph by author)

opportunities for human involvement as well: people participated in competitive events such as the "Pig Out," a hot dog eating contest; a pork cook-
off; a Pigskin Punt, Pass and Kick contest; and a pig calling contest. Most
activities were run by volunteers from local nonprofit groups, groups that
used the Festival as an opportunity for fund-raising and information dis-
semination. Among the noncompetitive events for humans were a Harley-
Davidson "Road Hog" show, a community "Pig-nic," music performances by
local school groups, a small selection of arts and crafts, and carnival rides
and games. To attract adult attendees, organizers hired several regionally
recognized musical bands to perform throughout the Festival.

At the inaugural PigFest, young visitors were encouraged to visit the
"Pig Pen," where children could touch farm animals such as goats, sheep,
baby chicks, a calf, and ducks. Interestingly, for subsequent Festivals, "Pig
Pen" became the name of the children's area and the petting zoo was called
the "Petting Farm." In this small enclosed space suburban children were
introduced to animals that would have shared space with humans on the
family farms that stood where Coppell now stands.

Toddler feeding a pot-bellied pig, PigFest, 1999. (Photograph by author)

Although the area around Coppell was once primarily farmland, the cotton fields and animal barns have long since been replaced by paved roads and brick buildings, leaving festival organizers to look outside the city to source the festival's iconic pigs. Part of this duty for the inaugural PigFest went to Sparks, the hired Festival coordinator, who purchased or rented pigs to "staff" the competitive events at PigFest. For the first PigFest, Mr. Sparks also arranged for the petting zoo (then Pig Pen) animals. MAPPE provided the pigs that participated in the parade and beauty contests. The fact that the animals spectaclized for the Petting Farm and pig events were bought, hired, and borrowed reinforces how far removed Coppell was from the agricultural past that organizers intended PigFest to commemorate.

After the first year, MAPPE became the sole provider of pigs for PigFest. In addition to supplying pigs for all the "'Pig'Tivities," MAPPE representatives set up a display tent where PigFest attendees could learn about pot-bellied pigs as pets. For a small fee, anyone could pet and feed a pig (fifty cents for a child-size handful of feed), or have a picture taken with one of several young and adult pot-bellied pigs (three dollars). On Saturday afternoon of PigFest

1999, the MAPPE pig petting and photographing drew a larger crowd than did the puppies and dogs at the Humane Society's Adopt-a-Pet tent.

That same year, the Petting Farm and the MAPPE tent were well away from each other, separated by the "Food Court," where vendors offered ubiquitous festival foods like corn dogs, funnel cakes, nachos, hot dogs, and lemonade. The result of this festival-scape was a jumble of olfactory stimulation: barnyard smells emanating from the Petting Farm and pig pens mingled with the sweet, fry smell of funnel cakes and corn dogs. At each venue, humans were encouraged to interact with animals: the latter through literal consumption, and the former two through hands-on interaction.

The fact that pigs were not included in the Petting Farm after the inaugural PigFest—that those available for petting and feeding were situated in the educational/pet-rescue MAPPE tent—signals a shift in the event from celebrating Coppell's agricultural past, a past that included raising pigs, to regarding pigs as pets. This shift was notable in other areas as well, especially food-related activities. The pork cook-off of 1996 was not repeated in 1997. Its inclusion in the schedule for 1998, but not for 1999, is perhaps indicative of the confusion that underlay PigFest. Emblematic of the inherent ambivalence toward pig as pet or pig as provision was the inclusion in 1997 of a chili cook-off and Texas barbeque that featured beef rather than pork. In Texas, since chili and barbeque traditionally incorporate beef not pork, the inclusion of a pork cook-off was a bit unconventional for a Texas food competition.

Not all the diversions at PigFest involved pigs and farm animals. Coppell Celebrates contracted a carnival company to provide midway rides and amusements.[8] They included a midway in their community festival because it generates substantial profits, and it attracts people: the bright lights of carnival rides and games, set up a few days in advance of the actual festival, are what PigFest volunteer and Coppell resident Angelo Vaccaro calls an "immediate magnet" for attendees. PigFest organizers contracted for amusement that would appeal particularly to children, part of their effort to promote festival attendance of residents with young families. Among the attractions provided by the Kaiser carnival company in 1999 were a small Ferris wheel, the spinning tea cups ride, and the TITANIC Adventure Slide™, a thirty-three-foot-high inflatable slide that mimics the sinking *Titanic* cruise ship. The Titanic slide was so popular that the lines of children waiting to climb the ill-fated ship slide often interfered with other festival foot traffic.

Unbeknownst to organizers, the midway has long been both an alluring and a contested component of agricultural fairs and festivals. In his history of American agricultural fairs, Wayne Caldwell Neely (1935, 201) laments that modern carnival amusements, which are descended from sideshows of English fairs, are "yet another manifestation of the rise of commercialized entertainment." Ted Ownby (1995) notes that the midway and what was perceived as its scandalous or threatening popular culture was regarded as an assault on late nineteenth-century southern Evangelical sensibilities. In her history of the Minnesota state fair, Karal Ann Marling notes that, by the early 1890s, critics that regarded the midway as having "no legitimate place on a fairground" were "clearly in the minority among crowds of urbanites without the faintest interest in agricultural matters who came to the state fair to be diverted and delighted on the Midway" (1990, 187). More than a century later, long lines of eager children waiting to enjoy PigFest's midway suggest that the midway continues to capture the attention and affection of urbanites and suburbanites.

While midway amusements certainly distract from other festival events, thereby diluting the theme of the event, they often are instrumental to a festival's tangible (financial) and intangible (positive experience of festival visitors) success. They are part of what Marling describes as a symbiotic relationship in which the agricultural elements of a fair have a "natural complement in the trickery, bright lights, and illusions of the entertainment district" (ibid.). A vital component of the symbiosis is financial: "history also teaches that without the receipts from the Ferris wheel, Little Egypt, and the rest of the gaudy attractions, the Columbian Exposition would have finished its run in debt and disgrace" (ibid.).

The midway was, it turned out, an essential component of PigFest as well. In mid-March 2000, the contracted carnival company canceled. Coppell Celebrates contacted other carnival companies, but with just one month's lead time, they was unable to secure another company for their event. Fearing that families would not come to midway-less festival, Coppell Celebrates canceled PigFest rather than risk financial losses. For an event described as having "the air of an overgrown school carnival" (Simnacher 1999), the loss of the primary children's attraction and event money-maker was devastating. It was not the rides that would be missed by organizers, but the revenue generated by them, revenue that was necessary to keep the festival and its organizing body afloat. Without their percentage of the carnival company's take, I was told, perhaps $25,000 in festival expenses would have to be covered out of the City's general fund, even though it was not a city-sponsored event.

According to minutes from a March 20, 2000, Coppell Celebrates PigFest planning meeting, the absence of a carnival company was not the only reason behind the event's cancellation. During this meeting, members of the board outlined other concerns, among them, "the shortage of volunteers and community assistance from civic organizations." The Band Boosters had agreed to volunteer for the event, and a local Girl Scout troop was committed to having a booth in the children's area, but city workers who had volunteered in the past would not be available that year because of an employee banquet. As of the late-March date, there was only one entertainer under contract, no food vendors had signed contracts (although several verbally had agreed to be present), and no one had been contracted to supply the animals for the Petting Farm—the event was only one month away and there were many holes yet to be filled.

Another concern discussed by board members was the weather. Although spring in North Texas can be ideal for outdoor events, rain is always a possibility, and nothing dampens an outdoor fete faster than a Texas-sized storm. Rain-reduced attendance translates into reduced revenue and, especially for events with substantial entertainers' fees, the loss can be substantial. As if to reinforce that Coppell was not alone in having to consider the economic consequences of bad weather on festivals, Sharon Logan sent me an article (Morrison 2005) about the cancellation of Arbor Daze, a seventeen-year-old festival held in nearby Euless, canceled forever in 2005 because of weather-induced financial losses and fears of similar losses in the future. Without vendor fees and other event revenue, the musical entertainment contracted to perform at PigFest would have to be paid out of the Coppell Celebrates account, but funds in the account came from each year's PigFest income. No PigFest meant no funds in the bank. In 1999, severe rains required the event to close early on Saturday evening and prohibited events from ever starting on Sunday, cutting into the potential profit for Coppell Celebrates. Organizers anticipated criticism from residents if a weather-caused complete cancellation became the financial reality: "What do you tell the taxpayers (especially those who don't attend) that you're going to have to pay $20,000 worth of bills for an event that never happened," Sharon Logan hypothetically queried while reflecting on PigFest's cancellation. Coppell Celebrates would be responsible for unpaid expenses, but how would they pay expenses without sufficient revenues from the previous year's PigFest? She suggested that "it would be easier to drop a successful thing and move on than to run it into the ground and live with that negative legacy. . . . Plus the novelty of 'pigs' eventually wears off and it doesn't stand out as much. It garnered the attention we were seeking at the time."

Minutes from Coppell Celebrates' fateful March 20 meeting record that, in light of these problems, board member Bill Herries "entertained a motion to suspend PigFest and to close out all bank accounts for Coppell Celebrates with the money going to the city of Coppell Parks and Leisure Services Department, stipulating that the funds turned over from Coppell Celebrates would be used to implement a city-wide festival similar to PigFest." The motion was seconded and unanimously approved.

The event that replaced PigFest has since undergone further transformation. By 2003, Coppell's celebration of community spirit had evolved from the three-day PigFest to a three-day "Spirit of Coppell Family Days" festival to a "Spirit of Coppell July 4th Celebration" planned, funded, and operated by the Coppell's Parks and Recreation Department.

"And this little piggy had none": The Paradox of PigFest

Even though multiple considerations prompted cancellation of PigFest 2000, the primary reason offered by Coppell's image makers is the carnival company's short-notice cancellation. More significant than the event's cancellation is the fact that it was permanently removed from the calendar, that the communal-celebratory duties of Coppell Celebrates were turned over to a different organizing body, and that Coppell Celebrates—the organization charged with "enhancing the quality of life in Coppell"—ceased to exist. If the event had been successful at its intended goals of enhancing community spirit and providing positive exposure for Coppell, wouldn't organizers have found a way to continue the celebration in subsequent years, with or without carnival rides, despite the uncertainty of Mother Nature? While it is impossible to say what might have been, the fact remains that PigFest failed to create a food-place association; it was unable to brand Coppell a festive foodscape based on its agricultural past. Consideration of a combination of factors contributing to the demise of PigFest, in addition to the vagaries of weather and cancellation by the carnival company, sheds light on why PigFest did not achieve its desired goals. Notable among these contributing factors are the unsettling ambiguity of presenting pigs as both provision and pet, potentially inhibiting food taboos, and the variable and dynamic symbolic capacity of pigs.

• • •

The paradox of PigFest is grounded in the social semiotics of pigs. For centuries, pigs have been the object of both—and often simultaneous—revulsion and celebration (Bakhtin 1984 [1969], Stallybrass and White 1986). As Stallybrass and White (1986) explain, pigs have long been part of religious and social discourses in which they are associated with sin, evil, and the "low" discourses of the body and the fair. A generalized disgust, especially among Westerners, toward pigs stems in part from negative responses to what are perceived as gross behaviors, including pigs' ability to digest feces and what Westerners consider food waste or garbage, and their practice of wallowing in mud. Fraser Harrison (1982) suggests that pigs' association with rural, agricultural life made the urban bourgeoisie uncomfortable. Bringing pigs to market centers, however, muddled the dissociation between pigs and cities, and contributed to the association between pigs and transgression. Eventually, pigs' association in the popular imagination with the filth and danger of liminal or unfamiliar places like rural environments, slums, and carnivals was greater than their association with the bucolic.

Given pigs' heritage of negative association, and the profound disconnect between most contemporary Coppell residents and the agrarian world, it is no wonder that the idea of PigFest met with some resistance. Early on there were grumbles of discontent among some Coppell residents who did not favor iconizing pigs as the place brand. Even before the initial PigFest, then Mayor Tom Morton said he heard complaints about the event: "Those residents said they wanted Plato or Socrates read and didn't find our theme amusing" (Medigovich 1996). Among the dissenters was Coppell resident Madge Cruse. After several years on planning committees for previous festivals, she stepped down in protest over the pig theme. "I just don't think that Pigfest [*sic*] fits with the image that Coppell is trying to project," she told a newspaper reporter (Richter 1996). The disputation over Coppell's proposed place identity spread beyond Coppell's borders: Cruse's comments appeared not in the local Coppell newspaper but in the *Dallas Morning News*, which reaches a Metroplex-wide readership of more than one million people. Perhaps what Cruse felt was a lingering sentiment that demonized the pig "for its rustic boorishness from which polite citizens must dissociate themselves" (Stallybrass and White 1986, 51).

Consider, however, that in the late 1970s, some Gilroy residents, including the mayor, did not embrace garlic as a food or an industry worthy of celebrating, much less iconizing; they were hesitant about promoting what was perceived as negative and off-putting by many locals and passersby. As Rod Kauffman, then Vice President of Gentry Foods Corporation (now Gilroy Foods), commented, "The first year we claimed the [Garlic Capital] world title, I don't think people liked it much. It was like being called the Bad Breath Capital of the World. But it brings a lot of money in here—a lot" (Rebelloand 1986). Some Gilroy leaders doubted that the Festival would have a positive and lasting impact for the community. Festival cofounder Don Christopher told me that Gilroy's mayor had such low expectations that he did not attend the inaugural Garlic Festival, laughingly dismissing the Festival and suggesting that "the next thing you'll [Festival organizers] want is a prune festival."[9] But as Pat Anderson, then editor of the *Gilroy Dispatch*, opined in the days before the first Festival,

> It's easy to say, "We don't want to be known as the Garlic Capital of the World—it's degrading." How much more degrading would it be should the thousands of persons employed annually in fields and in shipping and processing plants hit the welfare rolls. The dust and aroma clinging to individuals and the town during the peak harvest and processing season should be a badge of honor, rather than of embarrassment. . . . Masses of machinery are sold in the area to aid [garlic] production. Thousands of workers take home a pay check after working in fields and plants. Trucking firms also share in the proceeds, not only plying back and forth to harvest fields, but subsequently transporting bulbs, powders, salts and liquid garlic to distant markets. . . Perhaps garlic does not have the sweet odor of the prune, in which early Gilroyans took such

pride, even though it, too, had some less than ideal aspects; but there are a great many pluses derived from the aromatic root. (1979a)

Garlic was and is vital to Gilroy's economy. Pigs and pig farming are neither part of contemporary Coppell nor a focal point of Coppell's agricultural history. Among Coppell residents there was no significant economic or symbolic reason to remain loyal to pigs. The absence of a connection between the realities of Coppell's recent or historic agricultural past and its suburban present left residents and visitors nothing with which to personally identify or connect. Even the lye soap making demonstration at PigFest 1996 given by Mabel Wells, whose family had run a dairy farm on what is now Coppell's Sandy Lake Road, did not represent the reality of modern pig farming. The demonstration would, as she said, "give people the chance to see what it was like back in the old days" (Hoyt 1996). The soap making component was not repeated in subsequent years.

Residents of Cincinnati, Ohio, like those in Gilroy and Coppell, also went through a process of contesting an icon meant to commemorate and celebrate one aspect of the city's historical identity. In the early and mid-nineteenth century, Cincinnati led the country in production and packing of pork products, earning it the appellation "Porkopolis." More than a century later, in the late 1980s, artist Andrew Leicester incorporated reference to Porkopolis into an art installation that would serve as the sculptural entrance to a recreational park near downtown Cincinnati. Reigning over Leicester's sculpture, *Cincinnati Gateway*, are four life-size (four foot tall), bronze, winged pigs standing atop twenty-two-foot columns. With the flying pigs, Leicester says he created "myth of Pigasus": "Like the Roman general after whom Cincinnati was named, who gave his all when asked to leave his farm and serve his country, Pigasus represents the millions of hogs after whom Cincinnati was nicknamed and who, likewise gave their all" (Doss 1995, 220). Incorporated into another less readily visible part of Leicester's *Gateway* is an image of a row of pigs on a slaughterhouse assembly line, also referring to Cincinnati's porcine production past.

The pigs were one of many visual references to Cincinnati's history incorporated into the iconographically rich piece, yet it was the flying pigs that caused a public debate, a debate Dolores Hayden (1995) analyzes as reflecting the potentially controversial and place-making capacity of animals as symbols. Citizens wondered aloud whether pigs would be interpreted as symbolic of the city's gruesome and greedy industrial past or of the city's entrepreneurial industrial spirit. Critics perceived the pigs as symbolizing greed and sloth, not characteristics by which they wanted their city to be known. Proponents regarded the pigs as whimsical, no less noble an icon than Michigan's wolverine or the National Park Service's Smokey the Bear. Because Leicester's plan for his sculptural entrance incorporated public participation in the development and maintenance of his piece, residents became invested in the project and, by extension, its symbols. Through the processes of public debate and civic engagement, over the period of a few months citizen contestation transitioned into consent: pigs were appropriated by residents as a positive symbol for their city.

The Cincinnati flying pigs episode is one example of pigs becoming emblematic of a place identity. A plethora of pig- and hog-themed places (e.g., Hog Island, Virginia; SPAM Museum, Minnesota) and commercial establishments (e.g., Hog's Breath Inn, California; Hog Wild Saloon, South Dakota; Pig-N-Whistle BBQ restaurants, Tennessee) throughout the country further indicate that swine are conducive to fetishization, iconization, and festivalization. According to S. Jonathan Bass (1995), the hog has become an enduring symbol of the American South. Not only did pigs in the South inspire the first self-service grocery store (Piggly Wiggly, founded by Clarence Saunders in 1916), they are the main ingredient in the region's barbecue pits. Many popular barbeque joints use images of pigs in their logos and on their business signs. Pigs also are the theme of many community festivals. Georgia, for example, is home to multiple successful events at which swine are celebrated and consumed as symbol and sustenance. Representative of the diversity of pig-centric events are Vienna's BIG PIG JIG®, Georgia's oldest, largest, and official barbecue competition (BIG PIG JIG 2005, Frazier 2005, Pascoe 2005); and the Ocmulgee Wild Hog Festival held in Abbeville, founded by the owner of a wild-hog-hunting camp. Texas also is home to feral pig festivals, including Sabinal's Wild Hog Festival and Bandera's Wild Hog Explosion.

That pigs as an organizing theme "works" in some cities but failed in Coppell suggests it was not only pigs' negative image that was the problem;

it was the process as well. The absence of pigs from contemporary Coppell economic life and repeatedly low levels of volunteer participation in PigFest contributed to a general lack of enthusiasm in supporting the annual Festival. Hesitation might have been assuaged by an event that, like the Gilroy Garlic Festival, engendered participation among many residents and brought positive notoriety to the city. Dolores Hayden notes that "Public history, architectural preservation, environmental protection, and public art can take on a special evocative role in helping to define a city's history if, and only if, they are complemented by a strong community process that establishes the context of social memory" (1995, 76).

Community engagement is as essential to the politics and processes of food-themed place construction as is the symbolic capacity of the iconized item or animal. Jane Adams attributes the ongoing success of the Cobden (Illinois) Peach Festival to the significant involvement of people within the community, from the Lions and Women's Clubs to grocery stores and residents who provide food for sale: "Mobilizing and organizing volunteer labor … draws people into close association with one another, validates the claims of community leaders, and contributes to the continued viability of a village that has been persistently under siege by larger social forces" (1990, 104).

Approximately seventy-five volunteers "staffed" PigFest in 1999, less than one-quarter of 1 percent of the population. Recall, in comparison, that nearly 10 percent of Gilroy's population actively participates in the Festival as volunteers. The festival format employed by the PigFest organizing committee did not inspire civic engagement on a personal level as does Gilroy's Festival.

Participation breeds loyalty to an event or to public art, as witnessed so strongly among the volunteers of Gilroy, who return year after year with great enthusiasm, and among the citizens of Cincinnati, whose participation in making a public art piece helped transform "a volatile civic controversy" into "a meaningful episode in community mobilization" (Doss 1995, 200). Volunteerism sustains the communal spirit generated through a festival beyond the festival days, and that contributes to a sense of community, a sense of place. While PigFest brought people together for a few hours over the course of a few days, it did not provide a venue for ongoing civic engagement—there was little tangible or intangible consequence of the event on which residents could reflect with collective or communal pride, and there was no outlet for the mediated communal identity promoted by the festival.[10]

• • •

Inherent in PigFest's organization and promotion were confusing and conflicting messages. Two different representations of pigs—pig as pet and pig as provision—collided at PigFest, without any accommodation for distancing the two. Together, they diluted the event's efficacy toward achieving its intended goals.

Edmund Leach's (1964) suggestion that human ambivalence toward pigs is based on the animal's proximity to how humans look and live continues to resonate, even among many who have never lived on a farm or worked with pigs. His contention that the pinkness of pigs, which resembles human flesh, problematizes the human/tame animal/wild animal binary helps explain some of the appeal of piglets as cartoon and movie characters, and advertising icons. That pigs traditionally were raised in close proximity to the house and fed household scraps, Leach asserts, further confounds the man-animal categories. Paralleling Leach's analysis, Claudine Fabre-Vassas (1997) observes that the bond-forming proximity of breeding necessitates some form of distancing between families raising pigs and pigs treated nearly as pets but being raised for slaughter. Such distance is attempted by associating pigs with insults, thus perpetuating a negative association of pigs.

The need to offset familial affection with distancing mechanisms illuminates an ambivalence that might be felt by others raising animals for slaughter but regarded as pets, particularly if the animals are few in number and raised in bond-forming proximity. The dissonance between farm animal as pet and farm animal as provision is very familiar to members of 4-H, a youth organization originally geared toward rural youth administered by the U.S. Department of Agriculture Cooperative Extension Service. Among the educational objectives of the 4-H are civic responsibility, agricultural technology, and animal husbandry. Showmanship of animals raised by 4-H'ers is a major component of 4-H animal husbandry, and 4-H'ers learn not to get too attached to the animals they raise and show because some of them will be sold for slaughter. Various mechanisms are available to help youngsters learn to cope with this emotional predicament, including short stories. In a children's book about raising pigs on a Pennsylvania farm, the young narrator Alisha Eberly, a member of 4-H, boldly confronts reality: "The saddest thing about being a pig farmer is that after we show our pigs we have to send some of them to market, where they are used as food" (Wolfman 2002, 43).

The ambivalence toward pigs was fundamental, though inadvertent, at PigFest, during which pigs concurrently were commemorated as farm animals, cooked in the cook-off, and spectaclized as playthings and pets. More specifically, the family farms commemorated by PigFest were farms raising pigs (among other animals) for human consumption, thus emphasizing pigs as food. Conversely, the nonprofit group that garnered attention from organizers, attendees, and media was the MAPPE, which supplied the pigs for events that framed pigs as playthings. Additionally, they disseminated information about their Adopt-a-Pig program (including pig-as-pet education) and their commitment to rescuing abandoned pet pigs.

The schizophrenic potential of representation complicates the capacity of domesticated farm animals for festivalization and commodification. Popular media personify pigs as cute, cuddly, or humorous. Consider, for example, the cartoon character "Porky the Pig," Warner Bros. lovable, naïve, stuttering pig. Consider also, the movie *Babe*, an empowering tale about a piglet that becomes a sheepherder alongside his sheepdog friends. While the movie did little for sheep farming, it catapulted piglets into popular culture one year before the inaugural PigFest.

Several food advertising campaigns humanize animals to use them as brand icons. In such campaigns, animals are anthropomorphized with voices and adorned with accessories, as is the case with Elsie the Cow, the spokescow for Borden Dairy products. Since 1939, a Brown Jersey cow wearing a necklace of yellow daisies has served as the corporate mascot, endearing customers to her and to the milk she markets. Personifications like this, intended to attract customers through product identification, problematize the iconization of domesticated animals as symbols of an agricultural heritage or food culture. Pigs at PigFest were dressed in human clothing and paraded around the festival site. Such spectacles challenged the image of pigs as farm animals bred for consumption. It was the latter conception of pigs that was the initial impetus for PigFest, but that message got muddled amid all the "'Pig'Tivities."

The ambiguity and contradictions inherent in pigs as symbol was present throughout PigFest, from Coppell Celebrates' selection of and residents' reactions to the pig theme, to the diverse pig and non-pig events and foods comprising the short-lived event, and to its rapid and complete erasure from the city's calendar. During PigFest, what was dirty (pig as farm animal) was dressed up and paraded, what was familiar (anthropomorphized pig) was cooked (pork cooking contest) and eaten (hot dogs), what was farm and fodder was repositioned as friend (pig as pet).

• • •

Food can function both to foster feelings of community and feelings of antagonism. Food taboos serve as a means of differentiating identity; how, when, where, or why something is eaten or not eaten becomes a marker of group membership or exclusion. Much is written about food avoidance, particularly religiously motivated, voluntary alimentary restrictions, and these are variously interpreted as encoded symbolic and metaphoric expressions (e.g., Douglas 1966, 1972), ecological and pragmatic strategies (e.g., Harris 1974, 1985, Simoons 1961), and part of a "multivalent nature of cultural patterns" (e.g., Laderman 1981).

An unanticipated problematic of PigFest was likely the implied and self-limiting inclusion-exclusion inherent in adopting pigs as the communal icon. Since Islamic and Judaic laws governing food preparation and consumption strictly prohibit contact with pork, a pig-themed event would likely alienate these groups or offend their sensibilities.[11] An event that features a pork cook-off and spectaclizes the forbidden would hold little or no attraction to populations practicing porcine taboo.

That Coppell Celebrates selected a pig theme suggests an absence of Jews and Muslims on the board of Coppell Celebrates, in Coppell's past, and in Coppell's current population. In all likelihood, the members of Coppell Celebrates were not aware of the potential problematic of pigs as taboo. Although the composition of Coppell's population changed rapidly in the late twentieth century, during the early 1990s, the population was relatively homogeneous. The city was not yet forced to concern itself with the multiculturalism of the wider metropolitan area. Yet other places that seem

homogeneous have confronted the potentially unsettling issue of pig symbolism with a firm hand. Despite pigs' value as a lucky symbol in China,
the government ordered a ban on advertising slogans or cartoons that use
images of pigs during the Chinese Year of the Pig. According to media
reports, the government instituted the ban to avoid insulting any of its ethnic minorities, especially the approximately twenty million Muslims who
comprise just 2 percent of the country's population (Lim 2007).

There is not a synagogue or temple in Coppell, but there are several
within the Metroplex, indicating that there are sizable Jewish and Muslim
populations in North Texas. The presence of kosher foods (albeit a very
small selection) at Coppell grocery stores suggests that some of the city's
residents follow these dietetic laws or choose to eat kosher foods.

Attending a pig-themed festival would not be against the religiously
based dietary laws but, since the proscription is to avoid contact with swine,
such an event may be interpreted as taboo, repulsive, or exclusionary by
implication. Although inadvertent, alienating a sector of the population was
likely a contributing factor to why PigFest failed to capture the attention of
a larger audience in the Metroplex.[12]

"And this little piggy went wee, wee, all the way home": Communities of Memory from the Inside Out

Coppell, in a critical way, is similar to Suffolk, Massachusetts, the town soci-
ologist Robert Bellah and his colleagues studied for their 1985 communitarian classic *Habits of the Heart: Individuals and Commitment in American
Life*. As in Bellah's Suffolk, many residents of Coppell work outside the city,
so their daily "work life" separates them from their place of residence. As is
the case with most of the individuals interviewed for Bellah's project, residents of Coppell are not rooted in communal traditions. "The community
of civic-minded, interlocking families rooted in two hundred fifty years of
tradition—does not really exist. Three-fourths of Suffolk's present population have moved in within the past twenty five years. Most of them are not
deeply involved with the town," notes Bellah (1986 [1985], 11). He emphasizes
the importance of traditions for ensuring that communities survive and

hopefully thrive. Through telling and retelling stories of collective history, individuals build "communities of memories," communal identity is maintained, and individuals within the community are rewarded with a sense of belonging.

The year following PigFest's demise, Coppell City officials and the Coppell Chamber of Commerce hosted what the promotional brochure described as a "spring event with a festival like atmosphere to bring out the SPIRIT OF COPPELL and bring its FAMILIES together to unite and celebrate together" (City of Coppell 2000, emphasis in original). In case previous years' vendors missed PigFest, the brochure for Spirit of Coppell Family Days 2001 reminded them that, "In years past, this city festival has been known as *PigFest*. With the changing of the date, location and structure, the name was changed to bring a sense of spirit and unity to this growing community festival." It is ironic that the text invokes the illusion of continuity while also acknowledging changes to all logistical and structural details. What was most important, it seems, was to capitalize on the community-generating capacity of the festival frame. That the event was not repeated indicates that the organizers, in their effort to strengthen a sense of community and a sense of place among residents, neglected to involve locals enough in identity-forming and identity-performing discourses that could generate communities of memory.

Leicester's public art sculpture in Cincinnati recalls the city's history, from pre–Anglo Native American settlement to twentieth-century industrial prosperity. A shared past that is recalled in the collective and enacted by individuals, as was the production of *Cincinnati Gateway*, connects the past with the future through the present, and, if successful, provides a fundamental link between people and the physical space constituting their locality. Such an intangible connection between people and landscape is what endears people to place, thus creating a sense of place.

By highlighting an agrarian past in a suburban present, from the outset PigFest planners had a potentially uncomfortable polarity: amid upscale subdivisions and manicured medians dividing six-lane roadways, they set out to commemorate the past by containing and commodifying it. Although the farm animals of Coppell's past were also contained, their confinement during PigFest was extreme. Petting Farm animals were confined to a pen. The Pony Rides had ponies tethered with chain to a central post so that

Tethered ponies, PigFest, 1999. (Photograph by author)

their and their riders' movement was limited to a small circle. The pigs were paraded on leashes, monitored during sporting events, and like the Petting Farm animals, confined to pens. Interacting with farm animals is a natural activity of children raised on a farm. At PigFest, however, pigs symbolized a narrow representation of Coppell's past and a novelty of the present were caged and commodified.

Despite PigFest's failure to generate long-lasting excitement about Coppell's agricultural past, it remains central to members of the Coppell Historical Society and City staff dedicated to generating a sense of place. Rather than focus on a particular farm animal, Historical Society member Jean Murph explained, community-building efforts now aim to evoke a more generalized agricultural past. A weekly Farmers Market, initiated by the Historical Society and administered by the City, is intended to remind residents of the importance of Coppell's agricultural history. The Farmers Market began in 2003 as a "conscious effort to show that part of Coppell's history was land, farming," Ms. Murph commented. Held on Saturdays late spring through late fall, the market attracts area residents who come to buy produce, fresh eggs, herb plants, or organic poultry and cheeses from

Coppell Farmers Market, August 2005. (Photograph by author)

among ten or so grower/producer vendors. During the 2005 season, on each of multiple visits I watched a small but steady stream of mostly adults walk through and make purchases at the Farmers Market. Those who advocated starting the Farmers Market had several good reasons to do so. Not only do such markets help people reconnect with their food supply, according to New Urbanists, they can also serve as "incubators" for ideas and involvement (Duany et al. 2000), in this case getting residents to interact, even if briefly and superficially, with other residents, and familiarizing residents with historic Old Coppell.

In addition to evoking Coppell's agricultural past, the Farmers Market is intended to emphasize the significance of the old downtown, and to generate more interest in and support for its redevelopment. For the time being the market is held on an empty lot in historic Old Coppell, but as that area's redevelopment as outlined in the Old Coppell Master Plan comes to fruition in the coming years, the Farmers Market will be relocated to another site.

Promotional text reflects the various goals organizers have for the market: "The City of Coppell initiated a revitalization Master Plan of Historic Old Town and the Coppell Farmers Market is proud to lead the way in bringing local growers/producers back to Coppell while fostering a sense of place for Old Town."[13] As Edward Relph notes, however, meaningful places cannot be designed: "places have to be made largely through the involvement and commitment of the people who live and work in them; places have to be made from the inside out" (1993, 34). Place making is affected by architectural design as well as the social relationships and patterns of activity among residents. Coppell is struggling with cultivating a sense of place not because it is a relatively new city, but because the character and design of its public buildings and spaces, roadways, and enclosed subdivisions do not facilitate casual interaction among residents. Planners and residents recognize this, and are no longer guided predominantly by the ethos of walled subdivisions. Instead, they realize, albeit a bit belatedly, that "Masonry walls around subdivisions often hurt Coppell's sense of community" (Hellmuth 1996). But it is not too late, and a small but vocal group of people is working to endow Coppell with community spirit. As the Master Plan for historic Old Coppell illustrates, Coppell's image makers continue to look toward the past to differentiate and brand their city, and to foster a sense of place among residents of Coppell and the wider Metroplex.

CHAPTER SEVEN

Festive Foodscapes

Food Symbolization and Place Making

E ntertainment, arts, and culture form what John Hannigan calls the "new economic grail" for cities hoping to secure a competitive edge in the commodity-driven modern world (2003, 352). Food should be included on that list as well. It is a potentially lucrative and tenacious subject matter for theming a locality, asserting differentiation through aggrandizement, securing a place brand, and concurrently generating senses of place and community. Calendars across the country illustrate the ubiquity of food as a theme for communal celebrations, from place-specific food festivals to "Taste of . . ." festivals to ethnicity or culturally specific food festivals, all indicating that image makers and event planners recognize the popular appeal of festivalizing food.

The process of place branding, like other cultural processes, is dynamic and multisensory. As this work illustrates, there are multiple dimensions to iconizing food as a strategy of place branding and community building, and the symbolic meaning associated with or attributed to food informs its use as iconic of collective identity. The stories of how Gilroy became a festive foodscape and of Coppell's image makers' attempt to create a festive foodscape illustrate how branded place identities are shaped by history, zeit-geist, imagination, perception, culinary curiosity, and a quest for differen-tiation. This ethnographic project was about how some people encounter place and try to invest it with significance. Following the path suggested during my research, I privileged the symbolic capacity of food to become emblematic of a place more than of a particular people, and to create a sense of place for locals and tourists that is celebrated rhetorically through claims of aggrandizement and literally through a festival.

. ♦ .

Food as a marker of identity and medium for communication is a particularly appetizing subject. Food is encoded with symbolic significance through fam-ily, religion, history, and festivity. Like all symbols, symbolized foods tran-scend the immediate situation in which they are used. Through fetishization, iconization, and festivalization, often a food item becomes denatured; it no longer is associated with the land and agricultural processes that transform it from crop to comestible. History, including in part agricultural heritage, is present by implication, as is the presence of those who work the land where the food is grown. As Don Mitchell notes, the "beautiful and the damned" coexist, though most often the former is given priority over the latter.[1] In the case of a foodscape, the food and its festivalization are the beautiful, and the implicated processes of production are the damned.

Consideration of the inherently dynamic symbolization of food illus-trates the mutually symbiotic relationship between globalization and local identity. This relationship can be brought into focus through a variety of lenses—one that focuses on the transformative forces of homogenization and heterogenization (e.g., Wilk 2002) or another that zeros in on the capacity of food to be a vehicle for appropriation and resistance (e.g., Ferrero 2002). Looking through multiple complementary lenses, and by focusing on food-themed place branding and aggrandizement, my work contributes food-centered, geographically oriented thick description to discourses of food symbolization, place, and identity.

Since food is a semantic vessel, its use as a symbol or icon of identity is never one-dimensional. In addition to bearing emotional, cultural, religious, or economic associations, food items and their strategic symbolization can evoke and even valorize history. What a society chooses to remember about the past influences the present: how it evokes a useable past also provides insight into the society's present and the future. Did the Coppell Celebrates Board of Directors envision pigs as part of Coppell's future? In their effort to provide their city with a sense of community and a place brand by looking to the past, they neglected to provide a vision for the future. Memorializing an agrarian past suggests a positive valuation of the family farm, which holds a significant place in the American imagination. It is evocative of an idyllic and sometimes nostalgic conception of the Jeffersonian yeoman farmer, a character with little in common with the upper-class families of Coppell. This evocation may work in Gilroy because, although Gilroy's agricultural landscape is dominated by agribusiness not small farmers, agriculture in general and garlic in particular are fundamental to the city's economy. Gilroy's garlic-themed food-place association is informed by the city's agricultural past, a past that informs the present, and, if the success of the Gilroy Garlic Capital of the World place brand is any indication, will continue to inform the future.

Many other towns and cities similarly capitalize on food's capacity to symbolize identity by drawing on a food-specific agricultural past as a strategy of place differentiation. Jacksonville, Texas, for example, holds an annual festival celebrating its former status as the "Tomato Capital of the World." By commemorating its former capitaldom, festival organizers evoke nostalgia for the area's agricultural past while also celebrating the vitality of farming to the city's current economy. Jacksonville perpetuates what Bellah et al. call a "community of memory" (Bellah et al. 1986 [1985]): through the Tomato Festival the Chamber of Commerce and residents retell their history as a way to make meaningful, affirm, and perpetuate residents' collective identity among themselves and to outsiders.

The theming of towns and cities is a coping strategy, that is, a locally practiced strategy employed to make sense of and cope with the economic and social pressures of our modern age (Jóhannesson et al. 2003). Among those pressures are the real or perceived needs to generate a sense of place and a sense of community among residents, and to differentiate the locality from other places to secure tourism and commerce. Locale aggrandizement, asserted through claims of capitaldom and performed through festivals, is an attempt to secure place differentiation through place branding.

Jacksonville, Texas, Chamber of Commerce Postcard. The text on the back of the postcard reads "Jacksonville was once known as the Tomato Capital of the World and celebrates Tomato Fest each year on the second Saturday in June." (Author's collection)

Aggrandizement is a complex neolocalist impulse comprising issues of authenticity, nostalgia, and a quest for personal and communal grounding—for rootedness, albeit ephemeral, in an uprooted world. The neolocalist impulse articulated in claims of aggrandizement is part of an ongoing quest for communal identity especially within locales whose traditional community-generating institutions are eroding as the result of suburbanization or rural decay. Terrence Haverluk asserts that neolocalism and heritage tourism "counter the homogenizing effects of globalization and the creation of faux landscapes" (2002, 45–46). While this may be true in some instances, the inherently selective nature of marking heritage and of neolocalist efforts may generate "faux" spaces or spaces with spurious connections to what is being commemorated. Aggrandizement that highlights a food-place association is a way to connect contemporary life with a real or fictive agricultural past. Iconizing a product of the land implicitly connects the food to the earth and the processes required to transform it from field to table. At the same time, however, a festive foodscape emphasizes the denaturing of food in the contemporary marketplace.

What is the reasoning behind the impulse to declare a place the capital of anything, and the impact of there being multiple localities that make similar, if not competing claims? I contend that food-themed capitaldom claims are part of image makers' desire to have localities recognized as distinctive, despite the reality that what they market as distinctive is, in fact, something they have in common with other localities. Indeed, commemoration based on neolocalism and heritage can produce landscapes or symbolic identities that are similar, as when more than one city asserts capitaldom of the same product. As unlikely as this may seem, there are three cities in the United States that each claim to be the Spinach Capital of the World: Alma, Arkansas; Crystal City, Texas; and Lenexa, Kansas.

No doubt image makers are seduced by Gilroy's successful example of food-place branding. The Capital of the World phenomenon is not limited to food, yet food is a common theme for aggrandizement. This is because not only do people need to eat, but also because people want to eat, and the festive foodscape frame affords license for everyone to play with their food.

Food, Recontextualization, and Commemoration

The people who image a place, and the self-inscribed texts created to promote place identity, must be integral to any study of that place. Furthermore, the specificity of any locale is constituted of natural, historical, and social influences, all of which must be taken into consideration as components of place making. Equally important is consideration of the reception among "outsiders" to the locality as a festive foodscape, for it is the acceptance and support of nonresidents as well as residents that make the foodscape place brand a success. The preceding ethnography illustrates such a multilayered and multidisciplinary approach to appreciating how and why image makers chose a particular food, and how the place-specific food festival celebrating that food can become an integral part of a city's identity as a foodscape.

Through food-themed place branding, image makers provide residents and visitors links to the physical landscape, albeit rather obtuse or abstracted links. If successful, the iconic food, now symbolizing the locality, provides connections to the place that can be absorbed, such as an intangible but palpable sense of place and sense of community, or literally carried away, like garlic ice cream purchased during the Gilroy Garlic Festival or at the Garlic Shoppe during non-Festival days. If buying a souvenir condenses a tourism experience, consumption of an iconized food is ingestion of the symbolic identity of a foodscape.

Once created, an invented tradition can take on a life of its own, despite an absence of an authentic antiquity (Hobsbawn 1983). While this can be and often is the case, for a tradition to continue, for it to remain vital to the practicing group, it must resonate with some level of meaning. The polysemic festival frame affords ample opportunities to deliver multiple messages and meanings, thus a festival can affect many people differently. The ambiguity inherent in the performative genre of festival is part of its appeal, and part of its danger. Secular rituals like annual festivals are "dramas of persuasion" (Myerhoff 1977); the success of what is intended to be a community affirming event, like any drama, must resonate among community members in order to be convincing. The immediate and continued success of the Gilroy Garlic Festival, and the repeated involvement of locals as volunteers, indicate that organizers successfully "persuaded" community members to believe in— and invest in—their drama. PigFest, despite organizers' best efforts, failed to persuade the citizens of Coppell: the multiple contradictory messages enacted during the event, and an organizational format that did not facilitate enough volunteer involvement for residents to become invested, were unable to convince residents that the theme or the event was apposite for their city.

In their efforts to impose legitimacy on PigFest, organizers dubbed the inaugural Festival the first "annual." Incorporating "annual" into an event's name evokes the legitimacy and authority of history: the word suggests continuity of an implied link to the past and the future. PigFest exemplifies "nonce rituals," awkward and self-conscious secular events "laboring under their obvious contrivance, and the often touchingly transparent hopes and intentions of the participants."[2] These events lack the consensual, "self-evident" basic symbols that convey "the rightness which endows authenticity and conviction to any circumstance where they occur" (Myerhoff 1977, 201).

Through place branding, food commemorates the landscape by an implied reference to food as an agricultural product. Because place-specific food festivals are a modern articulation of traditional agricultural fairs and harvest festivals, their discourse implicates a degree of nostalgia for an agrarian past or present. Inherent in commemorations of landscape are a lingering infatuation with a rural ideal, nostalgia for a falsely remembered simpler past, and nostalgia for the present. Nostalgia for the present, the practice of bracketing and historicizing the present as if it has already slipped away (Jameson 1989, 1990), may be particularly resonant with urbanites who venture into the suburbs or a rural locale to commemorate the food-land connection. Along a similar vein, the increased use of four-wheel-drive vehicles for urban transportation may indicate the continued power of a rural ideal (Thrift 1989), or at least an attraction to the perceived idyllic rural. Readily noticeable names of SUVs, such as Explorer, Expedition, Trail Blazer, and Yukon, evoke a lingering infatuation with a mythologized spirit of frontier exploration and the open spaces of the American West. Similarly, people retreating to rural homes, be they condominiums along the shore or log cabins in the mountains, suggests a continued desire to escape temporarily the trappings of urban life, a sentiment anticipated in the nineteenth century by Frederick Law Olmsted, Calvert Vaux, and the urban officials who hired them to create parks as pastoral oases in emerging American cities. The actions of iconizing and festivalizing an agricultural product are strategies of differentiation enacted in the present that are gestures toward the past in hopes of contributing to the future.

Food festivals can transcend social, religious, and cultural differences that might otherwise be divisive within a locality. George Lewis asserts that because festival organizers in Stockton, California, chose asparagus, what he suggests is an "ethnically and culturally neutral food symbol," as their place icon, "all community subgroups could feel equally included, likely a significant point in the success of this festival" (1997, 75).[3] Gilroy and Coppell image makers each chose a food that was not symbolically or culturally neutral as the theme around which to organize a community generating festival. Coppell's image makers' attempt at iconizing pigs implicated several potentially limiting and conflicting messages, all of which contributed to the collective rejection of the porcine-themed event.

Gilroy Festival organizers also were vulnerable to collective rejection of the proposed festivalization of their foodscape identity by choosing to celebrate symbolically charged garlic. Negative associations included lingering dietary reform ideology and anti-immigrant prejudices, and what many

perceived as garlic's off-putting smell. But timing, marketing, Gilroy's location in a culturally progressive area, and recontextualization tilted a liminal situation in favor of organizers. The garlic-Gilroy connection promoted
initially by garlic growers, and subsequently by the Festival Association,
abstracted garlic from its agricultural and cultural contexts, thereby avoid-
ing the hot issues of labor and ethnic associations. Although the foods
prepared at Gourmet Alley are Americanized versions of Italian foodways,
garlic is presented in an atmosphere devoid of any ethnic markers. The
focus of Gilroy's identity as a foodscape is based on garlic as a festivalized,
consumable commodity.

Foodscapes and Contemporary Food Discourse

Food-themed aggrandizement and place-specific food festivals are articulations of contemporary food discourses that inform individual and collective
identities. I contend that the widespread popularity in the last quarter of the
twentieth century among organizers and attendees of food-themed festivals
is part of contemporary food discourse; that is, the visual, textual, symbolic,
literal and metaphorical conversations Americans, as a culture, have about
food. Sharon Zukin argues that "Both gentrification and new cuisine represent a new organization of consumption that developed during the 1970s.
Both imply a new landscape of economic power based, in turn, on changing
patterns of capital investment, production, and consumption" (1991, 214). A
"new cuisine" or a new approach to food is part of a larger societal shift in
food systems and in social landscape, and constitutes contemporary social
discourses of food. Among the changes in social landscape, and part of this
new cuisine, is the increased popularity of food as organizing theme for
festivity. The resulting festive foodscapes have become familiar features on
civic and social calendars across the country and indicate acceptance within
the popular imagination of food-place associations. Community leaders and
image makers recognize food festivals as a way to promote local commodities and facilitate more interaction between the tourist and the host culture
(Çela et al. 2007). Particularly among rural communities, food festivals celebrating a local product accentuate the distinction between the pastoral and
contemporary urban life.

Fetishizing food—recontextualizing it so that references to it are devoid of past or present negative associations—mirrors how most commodities are presented in contemporary consumer culture. No marker of identity is neutral, and a foodscape is no exception: it is inscribed with social and symbolic subtexts. To control how subtexts are read, most often the foods presented at place-specific food festivals are denatured, just as many food items are by the time they get to the grocery store, and dissociated from cultural associations.

I opened posing this question: "Why do some community leaders select a food item around which to build and maintain a collective identity?" The transactional character of food—its multivalence and malleability as a symbol—makes it an attractive focus for image makers charged with community building and place differentiation. People with discretionary income are willing to play, literally and figuratively, with their food, adding to its appeal as a commodity for symbolization, fetishization, and festivalization. Consumption of place and consumption of identity are made palatable in a festive foodscape.

APPENDIX A

Coppell, Texas, and Area Data

Table A.1.
North Texas Suburban and Urban Cities' Population Growth, 1990–2000

City	% change
Carrollton	+32.7
Coppell	**+109.8**
Grapevine	+42.4
Irving	+23.5
Lewisville	+67.6
Dallas (city)	+18.1
Ft. Worth (city)	+19.3
Texas (state)	+22.8

Sources: U.S. Census Bureau, State and County QuickFacts, "'Carrollton (city), Texas,''Coppell (city), Texas,' 'Grapevine (city), Texas,''Irving (city), Texas,''Lewisville (city), Texas,''Dallas (city), Texas,''Ft. Worth (city), Texas'" (U.S. Census Bureau web site), available from http://quickfacts.census.gov, accessed August 16, 2005.

Table A.2.
Coppell, Texas, 2000 Racial Demographics

Race	Number of people	% of population
One Race	35,251	98.0
White	*29,929*	*83.2*
Black or African American	*1,174*	*3.3*
American Indian, Alaska Native	*122*	*0.3*
Asian and other Pacific Islander	*3,343*	*9.3*
Some other race	*675*	*1.9*
Two or more races	707	2.0
Total 2000 population	35,958	100

Sources: U.S. Census Bureau, "Fact Sheet Coppell city, Texas" (U.S. Census Bureau 2000b), available from http://factfinder.census.gov, accessed August 16, 2005.

Table A.3.
North Texas Suburban and Urban Cities' Median Income (1999) and Owner-Occupied Home Values (2000)

City	Median household income, 1999	Median value owner-occupied single-family homes, 2000
Carrollton	$62,406	$125,900
Coppell	**$96,935**	**$210,700**
Grapevine	$71,680	$157,100
Irving	$44,956	$94,200
Lewisville	$54,771	$116,700
Dallas (city)	$37,628	$89,800
Ft. Worth (city)	$37,074	$71,100
Texas (state)	$39,927	$82,500

Sources: U.S. Census Bureau, "Fact Sheet Coppell city, Texas" (U.S. Census Bureau 2000b), available from http://factfinder.census.gov, accessed August 16, 2005.

Note: Coppell is not without poverty. According to the 2000 census, 680 individuals were below the poverty level. That is 1.9% of the city's population. By comparison, 15.4% of Texas's population is below poverty level, only slightly higher than the national average of 12.4%. U.S. Census Bureau, "Coppell (city), Texas" (U.S. Census Bureau 2000a), available from http://quickfacts.census.gov/qfd/states/48/4816612.html, accessed August 16, 2005.

APPENDIX B

Contributing Individuals

Many people contributed to my research, enhancing my ethnography with local knowledge, personal experience narratives, and historical fact. Over my years of research I engaged in innumerable formal and informal conversations with individuals interested in and willing to talk with me about food, festival, and community identity. My observations and analyses are informed by the people with whom I had casual conversations as well as those with whom I had more formal and/or repeated interactions. Listed below in alphabetical order are some of the people who shared significant time and information with me.

Andrea Adema, Buffalo, New York
Julia Adema, Tiburon, California
Ty Ash, Gilroy, California
Lauren Bevilacqua, Gilroy California
Kristen Carr, Gilroy, California
Robert T. Chomiak, Coppell, Texas
Bill Christopher, Gilroy, California
Don Christopher, Gilroy, California
Marcie Diamond, Coppell, Texas
Elizabeth Engelhardt, Austin, Texas
Chris Filice, Gilroy, California
Val Filice, Gilroy, California
Patti Hale, Gilroy, California
Jodi Heinzen, Gilroy, California

Bill Lindsteadt, Gilroy, California
Chris Hinterman, Ennis, Texas
Tom Howard, Gilroy, California
Eve Jochnowitz, New York, New York
Beth Johnston, Delray Beach, Florida
Ruth Kendrick, Ogden, Utah
Joann Kessler, Gilroy, California
Doug Kuczynski, Sacrmento, California
Karen LaCorte, Gilroy, California
Thom Lapworth, Quartz Hill, California
Janie Liebich, Gilroy, California
Sharon Logan, Coppell, Texas
Bill Lynch, San Francisco, California
Jean Murph, Coppell, Texas
Melanie Newby, Bradenton, Florida
Melissa Noto, Gilroy, California
Rhonda Pellin, Gilroy, California
Patsy Ross, Gilroy, California
Beth Royals, Richmond, Virginia
Adam Sanchez, Gilroy, California
Dan Shoemaker, Bowling Green, Ohio
Jennifer Shropshire, Philadelphia, Pennsylvania
Gary Sieb, Coppell, Texas
Bill Smothermon, Coppell Texas
Brian H. Smith, Kingston, New York
Lucy Solorzano, Gilroy, California
S. S. "Sparky" Sparks, Wills Point, Texas
Diane Sparrow, Osage, Iowa
Elaine Sweet, Dallas, Texas
Carole Thomson, Gilroy, California
Angelo J. Vaccaro, Coppell, Texas
Lani D. Yoshimura, Gilroy, California

NOTES

1. Throughout this work, I use the term *image makers* to refer to community and business leaders, residents and nonresidents of a locality, city officials, and/or public relations/media professionals engaged in the processes of creating and marketing a community's image or identity. Often at the other end of the image-production spectrum are those who toil behind the scenes creating the physical spaces being marketed. In his labor theory of landscape production, Don Mitchell stressed the importance of incorporating histories of the people who work to create imagined and physical landscapes. In the chapters that explore Gilroy, California, these often quiet workers are recognized. Don Mitchell, *The Lie of the Land: Migrant Workers and the California Landscape* (Minneapolis: University of Minnesota Press, 1996).

2. Globalization is not a modern process; what is modern is the scale and speed with which information and people flow around the world. Globalism and globalization are, like other concepts being explored in this section, ambiguous yet prolific terms readily incorporated into contemporary social and cultural theory. Globalization has been embraced as a conceptual paradigm since the early 1990s. Mike Featherstone suggested it is the theoretical successor to "modernity" and "postmodernity." Although thankfully the debate between the latter two concepts has faded from the spotlight of social theory, it continues as a thematic framework with the added element of globalism. My perspective on globalization and globalism is informed by theorists like Featherstone, who eschewed the binaries of heterogeneity/homogeneity and cultural integration/disintegration in favor of conceiving of global exchanges as "generative processes." Like geographers who situate their subject matter, Featherstone and I advocate appreciation of spatialized global modernities. See Mike Featherstone, "Global Culture: An

Introduction," in *Global Culture: Nationalism, Globalization and Modernity*, ed. Mike
Featherstone (London: Sage Publications, 1990); Mike Featherstone and Scott Lash,
"Globalization, Modernity and the Spatialization of Social Theory: An Introduction," in
Global Modernities, ed. Mike Featherstone, Scott Lash, and Roland Robertson (London:
Sage Publications, 1995).

   3. Nicholas W. Jankowski, "Creating Community with Media: History, Theories and
Scientific Investigations," in *Handbook of New Media: Social Shaping and Consequences
of ICTs*, ed. Leah A. Lievrouw and Sonia Livingstone (London: Sage Publications, 2002).
For an introduction to media-centered community studies, see Paul Adams, "Television
as Gathering Place," *Annals of the Association of American Geographers* 82, no. 1 (1992):
117–135; Wayne McIntosh and Paul Harwood, "The Internet and America's Changing
Sense of Community," *The Good Society* 11, no. 3 (2002): 25–28.

   4. The sense of community advocated by New Urbanism, though rarely defined,
seems to expand on the definition put forth by David McMillan and David Chavis.
Their theory outlined four constitutive dimensions of a sense of community: membership, mutual influence, needs fulfillment, and emotional connection. These four
aspects contribute to what I regard as the experiential essence of sense of community
and sense of place. See David W. McMillan and David Chavis, "Sense of Community:
A Definition and Theory," *Journal of Community Psychology* 14 (1986): 6–23. Although
David McMillan revisited the theory a decade later, his later thoughts have not been
absorbed by empirical researchers as readily as were the earlier definition and theory
(David W. McMillan, "Sense of Community," *Journal of Community Psychology* 24, no. 4
[1996]: 315–325). David Harvey's critique of New Urbanism's "nostalgic appeal to 'community'" echoes the skeptical caution with which I approach New Urbanism, which
seems inclined to embrace the ideal or image of community without critically evaluating
the complexity and implications of the concept. David Harvey, "The New Urbanism and
the Communitarian Trap," *Harvard Design Magazine*, Winter/Spring 1997, 3.

   5. "New Urbanism" (New Urbanism web site).

CHAPTER ONE.
MAKING A FOODSCAPE: GILROY AND THE ICONIZATION OF GARLIC

   1. Gary Walker, *Vichy, Capital of Free France Compared to Gilroy, Garlic Capital
of the World, 20-Sept-2003* (Trekshare web site, [cited March 15, 2004]), available from
http://www.trekshare.com/index.cfm?p1=48&journalid=7657. Another oft-repeated
item of local lore about Gilroy's heavily perfumed air is that humorist Will Rogers once
said that Gilroy is the only place in America where you can marinate a steak by hang-
ing it on a clothesline. Whether or not Rogers ever breathed Gilroy's garlicky perfume,
and whether or not he actually uttered the comment about marinating steaks is not
discussed among locals, who prefer to perpetuate Gilroy's odoriferous reputation with
good-natured humor.

2. My observations and analysis of Gilroy are based on multiple visits to the city between 1999 and 2005, formal interviews and informal conversations with residents of and visitors to Gilroy, archival research, and annual attendance at the Gilroy Garlic Festival. For clarity, when referring specifically to the Gilroy Garlic Festival throughout the book, I use a capital *F*—Festival.

3. Like *foodways*, a term employed by folklorists, anthropologists, nutritionists, food studies scholars, and others, *foodscape* encompasses multiple facets of procuring, manipulating, and consuming food. These terms also represent the potentiality and significance of food symbolism. *Foodscape* connotes a situatedness more than *foodways* does, privileging the real or imagined physicality of food-place relationships. For comparison, see Pauline Adema, "Foodways," in *The Oxford Companion to American Food and Drink*, ed. Andrew F. Smith (New York: Oxford University Press, 2007b), 232–233.

4. Graham M. S. Dann and Jens Kristian Steen Jacobsen, "Tourism Smellscapes," *Tourism Geographies* 5, no. 1 (2003): 3–25; Douglas Pocock, "The Senses in Focus," *Area* 25 (1995): 11–16; J. Douglas Porteous, "Smellscape," *Progress in Human Geography* 9, no. 3 (1985): 356–378, and *Landscapes of the Mind: Worlds of Sense and Metaphor* (Toronto: University of Toronto Press, 1990); Richard Cullen Rath, *How Early America Sounded* (Ithaca: Cornell University Press, 2003); Paul Rodaway, *Sensuous Geographies: Body, Sense and Place* (London: Routledge, 1994).

5. Silicon Valley is the colloquial nickname for San Jose and the surrounding area, so assigned because the city is a center for high-technology innovation and industries. Silicon in the name refers to an ingredient used in making the semiconductors that are used in computers.

6. Throughout most of the nineteenth and twentieth centuries, Gilroy's economy was dominated by agriculture and agricultural processing. The primary crops changed with time, as did agricultural technology, and consumer demands and desires. Condensed versions of the town's agricultural and settlement histories are found in "City of Gilroy Consolidated Plan July 1, 1995 to June 30, 2000" (City of Gilroy, 1995); Patricia Baldwin Escamilla, *Gilroy, California: A Short History* (Gilroy: Gilroy Historical Museum, 1997). My overview of Gilroy's history is drawn from these sources, newspaper articles and other materials in the Gilroy Historical Museum, and interviews of Gilroyans during the course of my field research.

7. Although Gilroy, with a population of just over three hundred people, was established by 1867, it was not until February 18, 1868, that the Town of Gilroy was incorporated by the Santa Clara County Board of Supervisors. On March 12, 1870, the City of Gilroy was incorporated by the California State Legislature. By this time the young city had grown to three thousand residents.

8. Mark Gottdiener differentiates between "consumption of space" for business or residential or tourism purposes, and "spaces of consumption," which are engineered, themed spaces. See Mark Gottdiener, "The Consumption of Space and the Spaces of Consumption," in *New Forms of Consumption: Consumers, Culture, and Commodification*, ed. Mark Gottdiener (Lanham: Rowman and Littlefield, 2000b), 265–285.

9. These calculations exclude retail, government, and health services, which would be substantial. Gilroy's Economic Development Corporation (EDC) chooses to promote employment figures for private, nongovernment entities, consistent with economic development materials published by many other cities. Gilroy Economic Development Corporation, *Local Business, Economy* (Gilroy Economic Development Corporation web site, 2004b [cited July 21, 2004]), available from www.gilroyedc.com/localbusiness.htm. Because that is how city leaders choose to represent themselves, these are the numbers I use as well. Prior to the opening of Bonfante Gardens Theme Park in 2001, Christopher Ranch and Gilroy Foods were the area's two largest employers. They are now ranked numbers two and three, respectively, but their employee numbers combine to secure the garlic industry's place as the largest employer in Gilroy. According to Bill Christopher, Christopher Ranch has about 450 full-time, year-round employees and about 2,000 seasonal (approximately June, July, August) workers. These numbers total well over the 538 employees recorded in EDC documents and on the EDC web site. Gilroy Foods processes garlic, among other vegetables; Christopher Ranch grows as well as processes garlic in Gilroy. The dramatic seasonal increase in Christopher Ranch's employee numbers reflects their need for field labor, sorters, and braiders during the annual harvest.

10. These two characteristics of Gilroy were mentioned often in newspaper articles during the Festival's first years, and they are recounted by locals and nonlocals who experienced them firsthand. Former Bay area resident Dan Shoemaker recalled the city's reputation as a speed trap. Dan Shoemaker, October 14, 2004. The speed trap anecdote also is recounted by Festival cofounder Don Christopher in Amy Sutherland, *Cookoff: Recipe Fever in America* (New York: Viking, 2003).

11. Tom Gallards, a former dehydration production manager, quoted in Kathryn McKenzie Nichols, *Smell It Like It Is: Tales from the Garlic Capital of the World* (Santa Barbara: Fithian Press, 1991). Narratives of Gilroy's traveling distinctive scent abound. A former resident of Santa Cruz, some forty miles west of Gilroy, who I met in July 2005, recalled with good humor smelling garlic in Santa Cruz during the summer months.

12. The discouraging state of downtown as a commercial center was the topic of conversation on several occasions during my visits to Gilroy and has been high on the list of City Council concerns for several years. See, for example, Nicole, *Smell It Like It Is*, 9–10; Serdar Tumgoren, *The Top 10 Stories of 2004* (Gilroy Dispatch web site, article dated January 3, 2005, [cited March 14, 2005], available from www.gilroydispatch.com/article.asp?c=137978).

13. Thanks to Jennifer Shropshire for bringing this festival to my attention. Information about the Pocono Garlic Festival is available at www.poconogarlic.com.

14. On distinction as status and identity marker, see Pierre Bourdieu, *Distinction: A Social Critique of the Judgement of Taste* (London: Routledge and Kegan Paul, 1984). On perceiving and representing a thing or a cultural Other as exotic, see Edward W. Said, *Orientalism* (New York: Pantheon Books, 1978). On the production of distinction in the name of heritage tourism, see Barbara Kirshenblatt-Gimblett, *Destination Culture: Tourism, Museums, and Heritage* (Berkeley: University of California Press, 1998).

15. For more detailed consideration of such forces and consequences see, for example, Gerry Kearns and Chris Philo, "Culture, History, Capital: A Critical Introduction to the Selling of Places," in *Selling Places: The City as Cultural Capital, Past and Present*, ed. Gerry Kearns and Chris Philo (Oxford: Pergamon Press, 1993a), 1–32; Hal K. Rothman, *Devil's Bargain: Tourism in the 20th Century American West* (Lawrence: University of Kansas Press, 1998); Chris Wilson, *The Myth of Santa Fe: Creating a Regional Tradition* (Albuquerque: University of New Mexico Press, 1997).

16. Pauline Rosenau argues that Americans have a "taken-for-granted enchantment with competition." A competition paradigm, she asserts, is part of America's legacy of rugged individualism and is the basis of the American political system and economy; it is also the organizational paradigm of children's after-school undertakings, such as little league baseball, and some sectors of entertainment, such as gambling, reality television, and game shows. Indeed, the competitive paradigm is ingrained into contemporary American culture. Pauline Vaillancourt Rosenau, *The Competition Paradigm: America's Romance with Conflict, Contest, and Commerce* (Lanham: Rowman and Littlefield, 2003).

17. For a discussion of how ethnicity and articulations of ethnic heritage were parts of the identity-making process for Norwegian Americans, and a discussion of how cultural heritage can be employed not only for communal affirmation but also for the invention of an "ethnic place," see Steven D. Hoelscher, *Heritage on Stage: The Invention of Ethnic Place in America's Little Switzerland* (Madison: University of Wisconsin Press, 1998); April R. Schultz, *Ethnicity on Parade: Inventing the Norwegian-American through Celebration* (Amherst: University of Massachusetts Press, 1994).

18. The web-based "Fact Index" maintains a list of more than 160 self-proclaimed capitals of the world of something. Their admittedly incomplete list can be viewed at *Self-Proclaimed Capitals of the World* (Fact Index web site, [cited September 13, 2004]), available from http://www.fact-index.com/s/se/self_proclaimed_capitals_of_the_world. html. There are so many places promoted through aggrandizement that ePodunk organizes its "Claims to Fame" section by "Boasts by topics." Categories include Agriculture, Clothing, Food (not to be confused with agriculture), and weather. See *Claims to Fame* (ePodunk, Inc., web site, [cited September 13, 2004]), available from http://www .epodunk.com.

CHAPTER TWO.
THE FESTIVALIZATION OF GARLIC:
CREATING AND CELEBRATING COMMUNITY IN GILROY

1. Nino Lo Bello, "Breathtaking Possibilities, the World's Garlic Capital," *San Francisco Examiner and Chronicle*, September 10, 1978, 49. To this day Arleux celebrates its garlic production with a festival each September, distinguishing itself as the "*capitale de l'ail fumé*," the capital of smoked garlic. The festival of Arleux dates back to 1961. See

Arleux (Arleux, France, web site, [cited March 16, 2004]), available from http://www. arleux.com/index.html.

2. As performance theory gained popularity among folklorists and other observers of culture, Roger Abrahams advised caution and encouraged the use of an enactment-centered approach to performative display events. He argued that performance theory and the metaphor of performance are not applicable to all cultural displays. Instead he encouraged folklorists to adopt the trope of enactment which, as he explained, includes performative dramas and other cultural displays, and allows for critical analysis of those displays without forcing them to fit the metaphor of performance. My approach to reading cultural displays, including mediated food-themed identities and community festivals, combines Abrahams's enactment-centered theory and folklore's performance theory, adapted from Richard Bauman's groundbreaking work on verbal art. See Roger Abrahams, "Toward an Enactment-Centered Theory of Folklore," in *Frontiers in Folklore*, ed. William R. Bascom (Boulder: Westview Press for the American Association for the Advancement of Science, 1977), 79–120; Richard Bauman, *Verbal Art as Performance* (Prospect Heights: Waveland Press, 1977).

3. My use of the concepts "frame" and "key" are drawn from the seminal work, Erving Goffman, *Frame Analysis: An Essay on the Organization of Experience* (New York: Harper & Row, 1974). My conception of the festival frame as situated play expands on the ideas presented in Gregory Bateson, *Steps to an Ecology of Mind* (New York: Ballantine Books, 1972). Additionally, my take on festivals supports John MacAloon's attribution of the "joyous mood" of festival to its Latin etymological: *festivus* ("gay, merry, lighthearted") and *festum* ("festival" or "festival time"). See John J. MacAloon, "Olympic Games and the Theory of Spectacle in Modern Societies," in *Rite, Drama, Festival, Spectacle: Rehearsals toward a Theory of Cultural Performance*, ed. John J. MacAloon (Philadelphia: Institute for the Study of Human Issues, 1984b), 246.

4. Examples abound within anthropological literature that demonstrate such a Goffmanesque approach to framed experience. The quotation is from Sally F. Moore and Barbara G. Myerhoff, "Introduction: Secular Ritual: Forms and Meaning," in *Secular Ritual*, ed. Sally F. Moore and Barbara G. Myerhoff (Assen/Amsterdam: Van Gorcum, 1977), 19.

5. Giovanna Del Negro and Harris Berger argue that there is no essential "everyday," that the notion is an interpretive framework rather than a structural feature defined by dialectical opposition to special events. I concur that it is an interpretive framework and suspect they would agree with my contention that the two modes of classifying time and events are not mutually exclusive. In comparison, David Sutton encourages differentiation between everyday and ritual events, though he argues for inclusion of both in ethnographic studies. See Giovanna P. Del Negro and Harris M. Berger, "New Directions in the Study of Everyday Life: Expressive Culture and the Interpretation of Practice," in *Identity and Everyday Life: Essays in the Study of Folklore, Music, and Popular Culture*, ed. Harris M. Berger and Giovanna P. Del Negro (Middletown: Wesleyan University

Press, 2004); David E. Sutton, *Remembrance of Repasts: An Anthropology of Food and Memory* (Oxford: Berg, 2001).

6. For more detailed discussions and examples, see Barbara A. Babcock, "Reflexivity: Definitions and Discriminations," *Semiotica* 30, no. 1/2 (1980): 1–14; Bateson, *Steps to an Ecology of Mind*; Bauman, *Verbal Art as Performance*; Richard Bauman and Charles L. Briggs, "Poetics and Performance as Critical Perspectives on Language and Social Life," *Annual Review of Anthropology* 19 (1990): 59–88; Goffman, *Frame Analysis: An Essay on the Organization of Experience*; Dell Hymes, "Competence and Performance in Linguistic Theory," in *Language Acquisition: Models and Methods*, ed. Renira Huxley and Elisabeth Ingram (London: Academic Press, 1971), 3–24, and "Breakthrough into Performance," in *Folklore: Performance and Communication*, ed. Dan Ben-Amos and Kenneth Goldstein (The Hague: Mouton, 1975); Deborah A. Kapchan, "Performance," *Journal of American Folklore* (1995): 479–508, and *Gender on the Market: Moroccan Women and the Revoicing of Tradition* (Philadelphia: University of Pennsylvania Press, 1996); Frank Manning, ed., *The Celebration of Society: Perspectives on Contemporary Cultural Performance* (Bowling Green: Bowling Green University Popular Press, 1983); Américo Paredes and Richard Bauman, eds., *Toward New Perspectives in Folklore* (Austin: University of Texas Press for the American Folklore Society, 1972); Milton B. Singer, *When a Great Tradition Modernizes* (New York: Praeger, 1972); Victor Turner, *Schism and Continuity in an African Society: A Study of Ndembu Village Life* (Manchester, England: Manchester University Press, for the Rhodes-Livingstone Institute, 1957), and *The Ritual Process: Structure and Anti-Structure* (Ithaca: Cornell University Press, 1979 [1969]).

7. Examples abound of how spaces become meaningful places. For a historical example of how immigrants develop an attachment to place, see Robin W. Doughty, *At Home in Texas: Early Views of the Land* (College Station: Texas A&M University Press, 1987). For examples of various spaces becoming valued public places, see Erika Doss, *Spirit Poles and Flying Pigs: Public Art and Cultural Democracy in American Communities* (Washington, D.C.: Smithsonian Institution Press, 1995); Dolores Hayden, *The Power of Place: Urban Landscape as Public History* (Cambridge: MIT Press, 1995).

CHAPTER THREE.
FROM FOREIGN TO FAD: GARLIC'S TWENTIETH-CENTURY TRANSITION

1. Sacvan Bercovitch, *The Puritan Origins of the American Self* (New Haven: Yale University Press, 1975). Robert Crunden asserts that it was John Winthrop's 1630 speech, delivered on board a ship bound for the New World, in which he used the phrase "city on the hill," that was the beginning of American exceptionalism, even before America existed. Robert M. Crunden, *A Brief History of American Culture* (Armonk, N.Y.: North Castle Books, 1996 [1990]).

2. On American cooking at the turn of the century and, more specifically, the rise of the domestic science movement, see Laura Shapiro, *Perfection Salad: Women and Cooking at the Turn of the Century* (New York: Farrar, Straus and Giroux, 1986). On general attitudes within American society toward food, see Harvey Levenstein, *Revolution at the Table: The Transformation of the American Diet* (Berkeley: University of California Press, 2003). On the growth and impact of national advertising, see Frank Presbrey, *The History and Development of Advertising* (New York: Greenwood Press, 1968 [1929]).

3. Hasia R. Diner, *Hungering for America: Italians, Irish, and Jewish Foodways in the Age of Migration* (Cambridge: Harvard University Press, 2001), 78. See also Michael J. Eula, "Failure of American Food Reformers among Italian Immigrants in New York City, 1891–1897," *Italian Americana* (2000): 86–99; Virginia Yans-McLaughlin, *Family and Community: Italian Immigrants in Buffalo, 1830–1930* (Ithaca: Cornell University Press, 1977).

4. The pairing of meatballs with spaghetti was not part of the traditional Italian service of pasta, at least not among peasants, reflecting the two-way relationship of Americanization and dietary reform efforts. Italian immigrants who came from rural areas, most of whom were peasants, had access to more foods in America than they had in Italy. They took advantage of America's abundance, ate foods that had previously been unavailable to them, and added elements to traditional dishes. "Traditional dishes following original recipes are still prepared in Italian-American homes, with the important exception that most of them contain a much larger quantity of dressing and additional ingredients." Among the dishes to which additional ingredients were added were "all varieties of the so-called Italian spaghetti with meatballs." Carla Bianco, "Migration and Urbanization of a Traditional Culture: An Italian Experience," in *Folklore in the Modern World*, ed. Richard M. Dorson (The Hague: Mouton, 1978), 61.

5. Warren J. Belasco, *Appetite for Change: How the Counter Culture Took on the Food Industry 1966–88* (New York: Pantheon Books, 1989); Harvey Levenstein, *Paradox of Plenty: A Social History of Eating in Modern America* (Berkeley: University of California Press, 2003 [1993]); Laura Shapiro, *Something from the Oven: Reinventing Dinner in 1950s America* (New York: Viking, 2004). In fact, historians and other writers position mid-century as pivotal for food cultures not only in the United States but throughout the world, simultaneously triggering more interest in and availability of gourmet as well as more industrialized foods. See, for example, Barbara Keen, "Lost Food, Lost Connections" (paper presented at the Proceedings of the Wellington Symposium of Gastronomy, March 16–18, 2001, Wellington, March 2001); Anneke van Otterloo, "The Riddle of Dutch Cuisine: National Taste and Global Trends," *Petits Propos Culinaires* 78 (2005): 39–51; Michael Symons, *One Continuous Picnic: A History of Eating in Australia* (Adelaide: Duck Press, 1982). Increasing national and international travel and tourism also contribute to rapid changes in local and national food

cultures. See for example David Burton, "Two Hundred Years of New Zealand Food and Cookery," *New Zealand Geographic* (1992): 18–39.

6. Among Beard's recommended breakfast dishes that embraced garlic were "Tiny Peppers Stuffed with Sausage," which called for two cloves of garlic for two pounds of ground pork, and "Codfish Provençale," which called for three cloves of garlic for one-and-one-half pounds of salt cod.

7. Other garlic-themed cookbooks include Susan Belsinger and Carolyn Dille, *The Garlic Book: A Garland of Simple, Savory, Robust Recipes* (Loveland: Interweave Press, 1993); Linda Griffith and Fred Griffith, *Garlic, Garlic, Garlic: Exceptional Recipes from the World's Most Indispensable Ingredient* (Boston: Houghton Mifflin, 1998); Victoria Renoux, *For the Love of—Garlic: The Complete Guide to Garlic Cuisine* (Garden City Park: Square One Publishers, 2005). Garlic's popularity as an ingredient continues into the twenty-first century. A March 2003 search for "garlic" in the recipe database of a CondèNet Inc. food-themed web site, www.epicurious.com, produced 4,690 recipes.

8. Philip Gleason suggests that several factors contributed to the post-1920s decline of attention to the "ethnic dimension" of American identity. In addition to immigration restrictions and the Great Depression, he notes the wide-reaching impact that a paradigm shift within the social sciences had on conceptions of race and identity. More specifically, a post-Depression reassessment of the concept of race discredited racialism, privileging instead the notion of culture and socialization as formative influences on individual and national identity. For a more extensive discussion of these ideological shifts, see Philip Gleason, "American Identity and Americanization," in *Harvard Encyclopedia of American Ethnic Groups*, ed. Stephen Thernstrom (Cambridge: Belknap Press of Harvard University, 1980), 31–58, and "Americans All: World War II and the Shaping of American Identity," *Review of Politics* 43 (1981): 483–518.

9. For consideration of the many forces behind changes in the American diet, see especially Levenstein, *Revolution at the Table: The Transformation of the American Diet*, and *Paradox of Plenty: A Social History of Eating in Modern America*.

10. For a brief discussion about how the 1970s ethnic revival facilitated new ways of thinking about race, see Matthew Frye Jacobson, *Whiteness of a Different Color: European Immigrants and the Alchemy of Race* (Cambridge: Harvard University Press, 1998).

11. *Pesto* is the name for the uncooked garlic-basil-pine nut-cheese-olive oil sauce that originated in Genoa, Italy. As with many other culinary words, the term pesto has become generic and now refers to any number of uncooked sauces made from a fresh herb or vegetable, nuts, cheese, and garlic. The fact that the Italian word has been incorporated into the English language indicates how widely embraced are the term and the sauce to which it refers.

CHAPTER FOUR.
GARLIC GALORE: FESTIVAL INVERSION, SUBVERSION,
AND THE ENACTMENT OF LABOR RELATIONS

1. Leslie Prosterman similarly notes that young twins and freckle contests at county fairs are "a formal presentation of the community to itself." Leslie Prosterman, *Ordinary Life, Festival Days: Aesthetics in the Midwestern County Fair* (Washington, D.C.: Smithsonian Institution Press, 1995), 18. Contests involving babies and children have long been components of fairs and festivals, as noted in Wayne Caldwell Neely's classic text on American agricultural fairs, Wayne Caldwell Neely, *The Agricultural Fair* (New York: Columbia University Press, 1935). Rodger Lyle Brown considers a festival baby-crawling contest, expansively reading it as "a legacy of master-race eugenics." Rodger Lyle Brown, *Ghost Dancing on the Cracker Circuit: The Culture of Festivals in the American South* (Jackson: University Press of Mississippi, 1997), 50. Robert Lavenda considers the sometimes contested nature of festival pageantry and social order at festivals intended to affirm community solidarity. Robert H. Lavenda, "Festivals and the Creation of Public Culture: Whose Voice(s)?" in *Museums and Communities: The Politics of Public Culture*, ed. Ivan Karp, Christine Mullen Kraemer, and Steven D. Lavine (Washington, D.C.: Smithsonian Institution Press, 1992), 76–104. Although Gilroy is a small city, it retains a rural feeling, perhaps in part because of the centrality of agriculture and agribusiness in the city's economy and defining the landscape, the casual friendliness of its residents, and the genuine communal pride communicated by residents.

2. Chris Filice, May 6, 2005. She made the comment while outlining the judging criteria to me just before the 2005 Gilroy Garlic Queen Pageant began. That Robert Lavenda has an article titled with the same phrase suggests that it is a common and potentially controversial undercurrent of community queen pageants. See Robert H. Lavenda, "'It's Not a Beauty Pageant!' Hybrid Ideology in Minnesota Community Queen Pageants," in *Beauty Queens on the Global Stage: Gender, Contests, and Power*, ed. Colleen Ballerino Cohen, Richard Wilk, and Beverly Stoeltje (New York: Routledge, 1996), 31–46.

3. For exemplary work on queen and beauty contests, see Sarah Banet-Weiser, *The Most Beautiful Girl in the World: Beauty Pageants and National Identity* (Berkeley: University of California Press, 1999); Lois W. Banner, *American Beauty* (New York: Alfred A. Knopf, 1983); Colleen Ballerino Cohen, Richard Wilk, and Beverly Stoeltje, eds., *Beauty Queens on the Global Stage: Gender, Contests, and Power* (New York: Routledge, 1996).

4. Over the years the frequency of the braiding demonstrations has varied. Schedules in each year's program booklet indicate that they were held once a day in 1982, thrice daily in 1983, twice daily between 1984 and 1993, and once daily between 1994 and 2001. Since 2002, they have been held twice each day.

5. "Garlic Braiding," Gilroy Garlic Festival Programs 1986–1992, documents of Gilroy Garlic Festival Association. For many years Bonnie Gillio led the braiding demonstrations and her farm donated the garlic for them. In 2001 Elaine Bonino took over the braiding demonstrations.

6. Bill Christopher recalls that in 1979, it was a woman who represented the Joseph Gubser Garlic Company and a man who represented Christopher Ranch. The female competitor caused quite a commotion when she won. There was no additional mention of gender for the following years when this format was followed, 1979 to the early 1980s, most likely 1982.

7. Outlining how the event was conducted in the past from the program booklets is problematic because the text in the program booklets is potentially misleading. In the years I attended the Festival, only professional toppers participated in the topping contest, but the text in the program booklet implied that anyone could try their hand at topping garlic. The text has changed very little year to year even though the event's format has changed. Bill Christopher thought that the open-participation format was followed for four to five years.

8. From 1979 to 1982, the topping contest was held once daily. Since 1983, contests have taken place twice daily, and since 1985 Festival program schedules indicate that there were separate contests for men and for women.

9. Mr. Christopher has organized the topping contest since the inaugural Festival. Assisting Mr. Christopher is Alfredo Franco, who has helped with the topping contest for fourteen years. During the Festival days, he is busy setting up each round of the contest, assisting with weighing the topped garlic to determine the winners, transporting the contestants to and from the Festival site, and escorting them to the Hospitality Area for pre- or post-contest meals.

10. Inevitably my conversations took place with other audience members who did not participate in the post-contest mayhem, making my pool of interviewees not completely random.

11. The account of meetings between Mr. Melone and Mr. Ganz is drawn from a legal document in which Mr. Melone outlined his pre-Festival meetings with Mr. Ganz. "Declaration of Rudy Melone," August 1, 1980, 1980 Festival box, documents of Gilroy Garlic Festival Association.

12. Among the legal documents prepared and apparently filed in the county court system was a "Complaint for Injunction and Damages." *Gilroy Garlic Festival Association, Inc., v United Farm Workers of America, AFL-CIO, and DOES I through CCC,* "Complaint for Injunction and Damages," August 1, 1980, 1980 Festival box, Gilroy Garlic Festival Office, documents of Gilroy Garlic Festival Office. A post-Festival letter to Mr. Melone from the attorney with whom the Festival Association had been working indicated that court action had not been pursued. That suggests that the picketing demonstration was nonviolent and caused no damage to property or reputation. Personal

letter from Attorney to Melone, August 11, 1980, 1980 Festival box, documents of Gilroy Garlic Festival Association.

13. Meeting Minutes, Gilroy Garlic Festival Association, July 29, 1980; Meeting Minutes, Board of Directors, July 29, 1980, 1980 Festival box, documents of Gilroy Garlic Festival Association.

14. Although the signature is illegible, the return address indicates the letter was sent from Carmel, California, a small city about an hour's drive southwest of Gilroy. Letter to the Garlic Festival, August 2, 1980, 1980 Festival box, documents of Gilroy Garlic Festival Association.

CHAPTER FIVE.
PLACE BRANDING AND SELLING PLACE:
CREATING AND MARKETING IDENTITY CAPITAL

1. These and other headlines are listed on a two-page document compiled by some-one associated with the Festival, presumably recording Festival publicity from newspa-pers and magazines across the county. The headlines quoted are from the *Washington Post*, August 1979, and the *New York Times*, August 1980. "Gilroy Garlic Festival Banner Headlines and Quotes," [1981?] 1981 Festival box, Gilroy Garlic Festival Association.

2. The term identity capital expands upon the concepts "symbolic capital" and "cul-tural capital" developed by Pierre Bourdieu and widely incorporated into social theory. Each of these forms of capital is a means of asserting distinction. For an exegesis on the relationship between capital and distinction, see Bourdieu, *Distinction: A Social Critique of the Judgement of Taste*.

3. My use of commodity fetishism, a concept from Karl Marx and filtered through many social theorists, recognizes that the action of fetishization removes a commod-ity from the context of its production. Harvey argues that the fragmentation of post-modernism is celebrating "fetishisms of locality" while also "ghettoizing" them with "an opaque otherness." As places become commodities, and particular foods become iconic of those places, the foods and representations of the foods exemplify commod-ity fetishism. Garlicabelia, especially items bearing the "Garlic Capital of the World" moniker, are tangible expressions of foodscape commodity fetishism. David Harvey, *The Condition of Postmodernity: An Enquiry into the Origins of Cultural Change* (Oxford: Blackwell, 1989a).

4. In 2003, *All American Festivals* Episode FE1A01 featured the Gilroy Garlic Festival for the first time. It has been replayed several times since then. An informa-tional web page on the Food Network web site provides recipes as well as a link to the Gilroy Garlic Festival Association web site. Food Network, *All American Festivals Episode Fe1a01* (Food Network web site, [cited March 15, 2004]), available from http://www.foodtv.com/food/show_fe/episode/0,1976,FOOD_9961_20517 ,00.html.

5. Scholars and practitioners of place marketing draw heavily from social theory, geography, tourism studies, and urban studies in their quest to brand localities. Included among the more influential voices articulating and informing place branding are Benedict Anderson, Mark Gottdiener, John Hannigan, David Harvey, Henri Lefebvre, and Sharon Zukin. See Benedict R. Anderson, *Imagined Communities: Reflections on the Origins and Spread of Nationalism* (London: Verso, 1983); Mark Gottdiener, *The Theming of America: Dreams, Visions and Commercial Spaces* (Boulder: Westview Press, 1997); John Hannigan, *Fantasy City: Pleasure and Profit in the Postmodern Metropolis* (London: Routledge, 1998); David Harvey, "From Space to Place and Back Again: Reflections on the Condition of Postmodernity," in *Mapping the Futures: Local Cultures, Global Change*, ed. Jon Bird et al. (London: Routledge, 1993), 3–29; Henri Lefebvre, *The Production of Space* (Oxford: Blackwell, 1991); Sharon Zukin, *Landscapes of Power: From Detroit to Disney World* (Berkeley: University of California Press, 1991), and *The Cultures of Cities* (Cambridge: Blackwell, 1995). See also Dennis R. Judd and Susan Fainstein, eds., *The Tourist City* (New Haven: Yale University Press, 1999); Gerry Kearns and Chris Philo, eds., *Selling Places: The City as Cultural Capital, Past and Present* (Oxford: Pergamon Press, 1993b); Michael Sorkin, ed., *Variations on a Theme Park: Scenes from the New American City and the End of Public Space* (New York: Hill and Wang, 1992).

6. For a discussion on the shifting connotations of *gourmet* see Carol M. Newman, "What Is Gourmet?" *Art Culinaire*, no. 75 (2004): 32–71; Carolyn M. Voight, "You Are What You Eat: Contemplations on the Civilizing the Palate with 'Gourmet'" (master's thesis, McGill University, 1997).

CHAPTER SIX.
"THIS LITTLE PIGGY WENT TO PIGFEST . . .": THE PARADOX OF PIGFEST

1. The festival is variously written as PigFest, Pig Fest, or Pigfest in different printed sources. I use PigFest because that is how it appeared in newsprint advertisements paid for by Coppell Celebrates, the group that organized the Festival. Also, that is the preferred spelling of Sharon Logan, Coppell's Community Information Officer and former Coppell Celebrates member. When asked about the different spellings, she commented, "I thought that the one word with two capitals was a novel way to do something. I thought it was a little catchier than Pig Fest or Pigfest." Since novelty was a secondary reason why pigs were the chosen theme for communal celebration, I adopted that spelling. Sharon Logan, Community Information Officer, City of Coppell. It is noteworthy, however, that the nearby suburb Grapevine, Texas, spells its annual celebration of Texas wines GrapeFest, thus PigFest's spelling is not novel or unique.

A caveat applicable to this work on PigFest is inherent in researching other short-lived festivals or community events: because they no longer occur, they are challenging

to document. As events vanish from calendars, they tend to disappear from conversation and, subsequently, from communal memory. In fact, during the years I worked
on this project after PigFest ceased, most people in the Dallas area, including Coppell
residents, to whom I mentioned the event had either a very faint memory of the event
or no recollection of PigFest. The difficulty of locating original PigFest event files and
documents was complicated because the organizing agency no longer existed. Whatever
files there were from PigFest 1996, 1997, and 1998 had been moved, misplaced, and pos-
sibly discarded. Newspaper articles provide a glimpse into what organizers put into their
press releases and, when reporters were curious, provide insight into the event's reception among attendees. Coppell and PigFest data presented in this chapter are drawn
from multiple visits to the city between 1999, when I had the good fortune of attending
what turned out to be the last PigFest, and 2006; formal interviews and informal conversations with city employees and area residents; archival and library research with
special attention to extant promotional materials, newspaper advertisements, and contemporaneous articles; files from PigFest 1999 and 2000; and personal recollections of
Coppell residents filtered through the fuzzy lens of time. One of the few works that documents another failed community-building festival is Anthony T. Rauche, "Festa Italiana
in Hartford, Connecticut: The Pastries, the Pizza, and the People Who 'Parla Italiano,"
in *We Gather Together: Food and Festival in American Life*, ed. Theodore C. Humphrey
and Lin T. Humphrey (Ann Arbor: UMI Research Press, 1988), 205–217.

   2. U.S. Census Bureau, *Phc-T-2 Ranking Tables for Metropolitan Areas, Table 3:
Metropolitan Areas Ranked by Population: 2000* (U.S. Census Bureau web site, [cited
August 16, 2005]), available from http://www.census.gov. Historical information
about Coppell and city data are compiled from multiple sources, including interviews
with residents and civic leaders; documents in the "History of Coppell," "Old Coppell
(Downtown)," and "Coppell from 1980–1990" folders at the Coppell Public Library
(sources cited individually where appropriate); Roy Barkley, ed., *The New Handbook of
Texas, Volume 2* (Austin: The Texas State Historical Association, 1996); Lou Duggan and
Jean Murph, eds., *The Citizens' Advocate Journal of Coppell History, Book I Centennial
Edition 1880–1990* (Coppell: Citizens' Advocate, 1990); Samuel L. Wyse Associates, and
Rady and Associates Inc., *City of Coppell, Texas, Comprehensive Plan, 1972–1992* (Dallas:
Samuel L. Wyse Associates, 1973); Charles H. Young, ed., *Grapevine Area History*
(Dallas: Taylor Publishing Company, 1979).

   3. Because Coppell was not incorporated as a city until 1955, there are no official
population numbers available. Population statistics for all unincorporated areas of
Dallas County prior to Coppell's incorporation include far more than the area comprising Coppell, so are of no use for determining with any certainty Coppell's pre-
incorporation population. Church rosters give some indication of the area's population,
but they do not provide accurate estimates, particularly for a rural farming community.
Prior to incorporation, and especially during the late nineteenth century, the population around Coppell consisted primarily of dispersed single-family farms with some

families living and working in the town itself. By all accounts it was a low-density population.

4. Grapevine Springs Park is quite significant in Texas history. According to most accounts, it was the site where, in 1843, Sam Houston, then President of the Republic of Texas, camped while waiting to sign a treaty with Indians that would allow white settlers to move into the region with less fear of Indian attacks. Although Houston left before signing the treaty, many similar treaties were negotiated and signed by native tribal leaders and Anglo officials in the area, thus clearing the way for contested but eventual white settlement of North Texas. For a history of the park, see Dave Garrett, "Grapevine Springs Park," in *The Citizens' Advocate Journal of Coppell History, Book I, Centennial Edition 1880–1990* (Coppell: Citizens' Advocate, 1990).

5. In the movie *Field of Dreams* (1989), a man builds a baseball diamond on his Iowa farm, believing that if he builds it, ball players from the past will come and play. They do. This philosophy is an articulation of sociology's self-fulfilling prophecy, developed by Robert Merton, which dictates that assigning a label to something or someone affects how that thing or person is regarded, thus affecting the outcome of events; that is, behavior is determined in part by meaning assigned to a situation. Robert A. Merton, *Social Theory and Social Structure* (Glencoe: Free Press, 1957).

6. "Mission," Bylaws of Coppell Celebrates, document dated January 14, 1993, Documents of Coppell City Information Office.

7. Angelo Vaccaro, former Coppell Celebrates Board member, commented that Coppell Celebrates "brought people together, to work together, who wouldn't normally work together." Apparently these various civic organizations had an ongoing rivalry and Coppell Celebrates was among the first times the groups, through their representatives, worked in unity.

8. During the first three years of PigFest, the Rotary Club contracted a different carnival company each year. Revenue from carnival amusements remained with the Rotary as part of their fund-raising efforts. Safety concerns raised in 1998 added to existing frustration among Coppell Celebrates members that the Rotary retained carnival proceeds. It also energized interest among Coppell Celebrates members in having carnival revenue directed toward general festival expenses rather than remain with a single group. For PigFest 1999, Coppell Celebrates assumed control of contracting the carnival company and revenues went toward the event's operating budget. Coppell Celebrates was charged with securing the carnival provider for 2000.

9. Recall that earlier in the twentieth century, Gilroy had a prolific pitted fruit industry, including growing plums and dehydrating them into prunes. Although prunes are not as pungent as garlic, they similarly have a less-than-positive association.

10. Ideally residents would have benefited from funds raised during PigFest since the profit was split between community service organizations, the "nonprofit partners" that facilitate the festival. According to the PigFest 1999 budget reconciliation report, the Rotary Club, Lions Club, and Chamber of Commerce split $3,829.66, the profit left

after vendors and other expenses were paid, and $2,000 was set aside in the Coppell Celebrates account as seed money for the following year.

11. Proscription against pork also is among the teachings of the Nation of Islam (NOI). For insight into the complexity of NOI's asceticism, in particular the rigidly controlled diet, see Doris Witt, *Black Hunger: Food and the Politics of U.S. Identity* (New York: Oxford University Press, 1999).

12. Public Law 94-521 prohibits the U.S. Census Bureau, and other demographic-collecting projects, from asking questions about religious affiliation on a mandatory basis, making it difficult to accurately assess a city's religious profile. Some information about religious practices is collected on a voluntary basis but it is very general in geographic and sectarian scopes. According to the Statistical Abstract of the United States 2002, in 1995, 73 percent of respondents said they were Protestant or Christian, 2 percent Jewish, 1 percent Orthodox, 1 percent Mormon, 5 percent "Other specific," and 8 percent "None" or non-designating. These generalized statistics support the apparent religious breakdown of North Texas; that is, it is predominantly Protestant and Christian, with a small percentage of the population pursuing Judaism and an even smaller percentage pursuing "other" faiths. U.S. Census Bureau, *Table 66. Religious Preference, Church Membership 1980 to 2000* (U.S. Census Bureau web site, [cited August 23, 2005]), available from http:www.census.gov.

13. *Coppell Farmers Market* (Local Harvest $_{SM}$ web site, [cited January 3, 2006]), available from http://www.localharvest.org/farmers-markets/M5795. Among the features of the Farmers Market itemized on the City's official web site is that it is "A Place with a Sense of Community." City of Coppell, *Coppell Farmers Market* (City of Coppell web site, [cited January 3, 2006]), available from http://www.ci.coppell.tx.us/.

CHAPTER SEVEN.
FESTIVE FOODSCAPES: FOOD SYMBOLIZATION AND PLACE MAKING

1. Mitchell considered "the connection between the material production of landscape [the damned] and the production of landscape representations [the beauty]" in the making of the California landscape. Mitchell, *The Lie of the Land: Migrant Workers and the California Landscape*, 1.

2. Barbara G. Myerhoff, "We Don't Wrap Herring in a Printed Page: Fusion, Fiction and Continuity in Secular Ritual," in *Secular Ritual*, ed. Sally F. Moore and Barbara G. Myerhoff (Assen/Amsterdam: Van Gorcum, 1977), 201. I understand Myerhoff's term "nonce rituals" to be a modification of "nonce word," which refers to a word invented or used for a specific occasion. As applied to secular ritual, nonce would similarly imply that the event was invented for a particular occasion or commemoration.

3. Lewis says that although asparagus "has never been exclusively claimed by any one ethnic group," in contemporary America it has "often been associated with the

upper class" (76). I contend this association is more than noteworthy and warrants further consideration: since food readily is used as cultural capital, consideration of the upper-class association may inform festival organizers' and/or potential attendees' expectations. Although they did not frame their festival this way, Stockton image makers could have promoted the asparagus festival, and through it Stockton's sense of place, as a "positional good." See James S. Duncan and Nancy G. Duncan, "Sense of Place as a Positional Good: Locating Bedford in Space and Time," in *Textures of Place: Exploring Humanist Geography*, ed. Paul Adams, Steven D. Hoelscher, and Karen E. Till (Minneapolis: University of Minnesota Press, 2001).

BIBLIOGRAPHY

[n.a.]. *Souvenir Magazine of Gilroy, Santa Clara County, California*. San Jose: George H. Chrisman, 1905.

[news services]. "Settlement in Garlic Strike." *Washington Post*, August 9, 1980, A11.

Abrahams, Roger. "Toward an Enactment-Centered Theory of Folklore." In *Frontiers in Folklore*, edited by William R. Bascom, 79–120. Boulder: Westview Press for the American Association for the Advancement of Science, 1977.

———. "The Language of Festivals: Celebrating the Economy." In *Celebration: Studies in Festivity and Ritual*, edited by Victor Turner, 161–177. Washington, D.C.: Smithsonian Institution Press, 1982.

———. "An American Vocabulary of Celebration." In *Time Out of Time: Essays on the Festival*, edited by Alessandro Falassi, 173–183. Albuquerque: University of New Mexico Press, 1987.

Abrahams, Roger, and Richard Bauman. "Ranges of Festival Behavior." In *The Reversible World: Symbolic Inversions on Art and Society*, edited by Barbara Babcock, 193–208. Ithaca: Cornell University Press, 1978.

Adams, Jane. "Creating Community in a Midwestern Village: Fifty Years of the Cobden Peach Festival." *Illinois Historical Journal* 83 (1990): 97–108.

Adams, Paul. "Television as Gathering Place." *Annals of the Association of American Geographers* 82, no. 1 (1992): 117–135.

Adema, Pauline. "Vicarious Consumption: Food Television and the Ambiguities of Modernity." *Journal of American and Comparative Cultures* 23, no. 3 (2000): 113–123.

———. "*Foodscape*: An Emulsion of Food and Landscape." *Gastronomica: The Journal of Food and Culture* 7, no. 1 (2007a): 3.

———. "Foodways." In *The Oxford Companion to American Food and Drink*, edited by Andrew F. Smith, 232–233. New York: Oxford University Press, 2007b.

Anbinder, Tyler. *Nativism and Slavery: The Northern Know Nothings and the Politics of the 1850's*. New York: Oxford University Press, 1992.

Anderson, Benedict R. *Imagined Communities: Reflections on the Origins and Spread of Nationalism*. London: Verso, 1983.

Anderson, Pat. "Gilroy Garlic Festival [Editorial]." *Gilroy Dispatch*, August 3, 1979a, 2.

———. "Sweet Smell of Success." *Gilroy Dispatch*, August 22, 1979b, 2.

Appadurai, Arjun. "Disjuncture and Difference in the Global Cultural Economy." *Theory, Culture and Society* 7 (1990): 295–310.

———. *Modernity at Large: Cultural Dimensions of Globalization*. Minneapolis: University of Minnesota Press, 1996.

Arleux. In, Arleux, France, web site, http://www.arleux.com/index.html (accessed March 16, 2004).

Ashworth, Gregory John, and Henk Voogd. *Selling the City: Marketing Approaches in Public Sector Urban Planning*. New York: Belhaven Press, 1990.

Ayer, Bill. Festival section, *Gilroy Dispatch*, July 2003, A7.

Babcock, Barbara, ed. *The Reversible World: Symbolic Inversion in Art and Society*. Ithaca: Cornell University Press, 1978.

Babcock, Barbara A. "Reflexivity: Definitions and Discriminations." *Semiotica* 30, no. 1/2 (1980): 1–14.

Bakhtin, Mikhail M. *Rabelais and His World*. Translated by Helene Iswolsky. Bloomington: Indiana University Press, 1984 [1969].

Banet-Weiser, Sarah. *The Most Beautiful Girl in the World: Beauty Pageants and National Identity*. Berkeley: University of California Press, 1999.

Banner, Lois W. *American Beauty*. New York: Alfred A. Knopf, 1983.

Barkley, Roy, ed. *The New Handbook of Texas, volume 2*. Austin: The Texas State Historical Association, 1996.

Bass, S. Jonathan. "'How 'bout a Hand for the Hog': The Enduring Nature of the Swine as a Cultural Symbol in the South." *Southern Cultures* 1, no. 3 (1995): 301–320.

Bateson, Gregory. *Steps to an Ecology of Mind*. New York: Ballantine Books, 1972.

Bauman, Richard. *Verbal Art as Performance*. Prospect Heights: Waveland Press, 1977.

Bauman, Richard, and Charles L. Briggs. "Poetics and Performance as Critical Perspectives on Language and Social Life." *Annual Review of Anthropology* 19 (1990): 59–88.

Bauman, Zygmunt. *Community: Seeking Safety in an Insecure World*. Cambridge: Polity Press, 2001.

"Before Garlic, Cigars Ruled." *Gilroy Dispatch*, November 1, 1996, D1, D2.

Belasco, Warren J. *Appetite for Change: How the Counter Culture Took on the Food Industry 1966–88*. New York: Pantheon Books, 1989.

Belasco, Warren J., and Philip Scranton, eds. *Food Nations: Selling Taste in Consumer Societies*. New York: Routledge, 2002.

Bellah, Robert, Richard Madsen, William M. Sullivan, Ann Swidler, and Steven M. Tipton. *Habits of the Heart: Individualism and Commitment in American Life*. New York: Harper & Row, 1986 [1985].

Belsinger, Susan, and Carolyn Dille. *The Garlic Book: A Garland of Simple, Savory, Robust Recipes*. Loveland: Interweave Press, 1993.

Bendix, Regina. "Tourism and Cultural Displays: Inventing Tradition for Whom?" *Journal of American Folklore* 102, no. 404 (1989): 131–146.

———. *In Search of Authenticity: The Formation of Folklore Studies*. Madison: University of Wisconsin Press, 1997.

Bentley, Amy. "From Culinary Other to Mainstream America: Meanings and Uses of Southwestern Cuisine." In *Culinary Tourism*, edited by Lucy Long, 209–225. Lexington: University Press of Kentucky, 2004.

Bercovitch, Sacvan. *The Puritan Origins of the American Self*. New Haven: Yale University Press, 1975.

Berman, Marshall. *All That Is Solid Melts into Air: The Experience of Modernity*. New York: Simon and Schuster, 1982.

Berry, Wendell. "The Pleasures of Eating." In *Cooking, Eating, Thinking*, edited by Deanne W. Curtin and Lisa M. Heldke, 374–379. Bloomington: Indiana University Press, 1992.

Bianco, Carla. "Migration and Urbanization of a Traditional Culture: An Italian Experience." In *Folklore in the Modern World*, edited by Richard M. Dorson, 56–63. The Hague: Mouton, 1978.

BIG PIG JIG. 2005. History. In, BIG PIG JIG® web site, http://www.bigpigjig.com/history.htm (accessed October 30, 2005).

Billington, Ray Allen. *The Origins of Nativism in the United States*. New York: Arno Press, 1974.

Bodnar, John. *Remaking America: Public Memory, Commemoration, and Patriotism in the Twentieth Century*. Princeton: Princeton University Press, 1991.

Boorstin, Daniel J. *The Americans: The National Experience*. New York: Random House, 1965.

Borish, Linda J. "'A Fair, Without *the* Fair, Is No Fair at All': Women and the New England Agricultural Fair in the Mid-Nineteenth Century." *Journal of Sport History* 24, no. 2 (1997): 155–176.

Bourdieu, Pierre. *Distinction: A Social Critique of the Judgement of Taste*. London: Routledge and Kegan Paul, 1984.

Brandes, Stanley H. *Power and Persuasion: Fiestas and Social Control in Rural Mexico*. Philadelphia: University of Pennsylvania Press, 1988.

Brown, Doug. "Haute Cuisine." *American Journalism Review* 26, no. 1 (2004): 50–55.

Brown, Linda Keller, and Kay Mussell. "Introduction." In *Ethnic and Regional Foodways in the United States: The Performance of Group Identity*, edited by Linda Keller Brown and Kay Mussell, 3–15. Knoxville: University of Tennessee Press, 1984.

Brown, Rodger Lyle. *Ghost Dancing on the Cracker Circuit: The Culture of Festivals in the American South*. Jackson: University Press of Mississippi, 1997.

Bunch, Noel. "Joe Dimaggio." *Life*, May 1, 1939, 62–69.

Burton, David. "Two Hundred Years of New Zealand Food and Cookery." *New Zealand Geographic* (1992): 18–39.

Buttimer, Anne. "Home, Reach, and the Sense of Place." In *The Human Experience of Space and Place*, edited by Anne Buttimer and David Seamon, 166–187. New York: St. Martin's Press, 1980.

Carson, Gerald. *Cornflake Crusade*. New York: Arno Press, 1976 [1957].

Çela, Ariana, Jill Knowles-Lankford, and Sam Lankford. "Local Food Festivals in Northeast Iowa Communities: A Visitor and Economic Impact Study." *Managing Leisure* 12 (2007): 171–186.

Chacon, Kurt. "President's Message." *24th Gilroy Garlic Festival Program* 2002, [unpaginated].

Chang, T. C. "Geographical Imaginations of 'New Asia-Singapore.'" *Geografiska Annaler Series B: Human Geography* 86, no. 3 (2004): 165–185.

Charles, Jeffrey. "Searching for Gold in Guacamole: California Growers Market the Avocado, 1910–1994." In *Food Nations: Selling Taste in Consumer Societies*, edited by Warren Belasco and Philip Scranton, 131–154. New York: Routledge, 2002.

City of Coppell. Coppell Farmers Market. In, City of Coppell web site, http://www.ci.coppell.tx.us/ (accessed January 3, 2006).

———. "Spirit of Coppell Family Days Vendor Application brochure." Author's files, 2000.

City of Gilroy. "City of Gilroy Consolidated Plan July 1, 1995 to June 30, 2000." City of Gilroy, 1995.

Claims to Fame. In, ePodunk, Inc., web site, http://www.epodunk.com (accessed September 13, 2004).

Cohen, Colleen Ballerino, Richard Wilk, and Beverly Stoeltje, eds. *Beauty Queens on the Global Stage: Gender, Contests, and Power*. New York: Routledge, 1996.

Conzen, Kathleen Neils. "Ethnicity as Festive Culture: Nineteenth-Century German America on Parade." In *The Invention of Ethnicity*, edited by Werner Sollors, 44–76. New York: Oxford University Press, 1989.

Conzen, Kathleen Neils, David A. Gerber, Ewa Morawska, George E. Pozzetta, and Rudolph J. Vecoli. "The Invention of Ethnicity: A Perspective from the U.S.A." *Journal of American Ethnic History* 12, no. 1 (1992): 3–41.

Coppell Farmers Market. In, Local Harvest $_{SM}$ web site, http://www.localharvest.org/ farmers-markets/M5795 (accessed January 3, 2006).

Corson, Juliet. *Miss Corson's Practical American Cookery and Household Management*. New York: Dodd, Mead & Co., 1886.

Cosgrove, Denis E. *Social Formation and Symbolic Landscape*. London: Croom Helm, 1984.

Cott, Nancy F. *The Bonds of Womanhood: "Woman's Sphere" in New England, 1780–1835*. New Haven: Yale University Press, 1997 [1977].

Coveney, John. *Food, Morals and Meaning: The Pleasure and Anxiety of Eating*. London: Routledge, 2000.

Crewe, Louise, and Michelle Lowe. "Gap on the Map? Toward a Geography of Consumption and Identity." *Environment and Planning A* 27 (1995): 1877–1898.

Crunden, Robert M. *A Brief History of American Culture*. Armonk, N.Y.: North Castle Books, 1996 [1990].

Cummins, Steven, and Sally Macintyre. "A Systematic Study of Urban Foodscape: The Price and Availability of Food in Greater Glasgow." *Urban Studies* 39, no. 11 (2002): 2115–2130.

Dal Bozzo, Jerry. *The Stinking Cookbook: The Layman's Guide to Garlic Eating, Drinking, and Stinking*. Berkeley: Celestial Arts, 1994.

Dann, Graham M. S., and Jens Kristian Steen Jacobsen. "Tourism Smellscapes." *Tourism Geographies* 5, no. 1 (2003): 3–25.

de Bres, Karen, and James Davis. "Celebrating Group and Place Identity: A Case Study of a New Regional Festival." *Tourism Geographies* 3, no. 3 (2001): 326–337.

de Wit, Cary W. "Food-Place Associations on American Product Labels." In *The Taste of American Place: A Reader on Regional and Ethnic Foods*, edited by Barbara G. Shortridge and James R. Shortridge, 101–109. Lanham: Rowman and Littlefield, 1998.

Del Negro, Giovanna P., and Harris M. Berger. "New Directions in the Study of Everyday Life: Expressive Culture and the Interpretation of Practice." In *Identity and Everyday Life: Essays in the Study of Folklore, Music, and Popular Culture*, edited by Harris M. Berger and Giovanna P. Del Negro, 3–22. Middletown: Wesleyan University Press, 2004.

Diner, Hasia R. *Hungering for America: Italians, Irish, and Jewish Foodways in the Age of Migration*. Cambridge: Harvard University Press, 2001.

Dolphijn, Rick. *Foodscapes: Toward a Deleuzian Ethics of Consumption*. Delft, The Netherlands: Eburon Publishers, 2005.

Dorst, John D. *The Written Suburb: An American Site, An Ethnographic Dilemma*. Philadelphia: University of Pennsylvania Press, 1989.

Doss, Erika. *Spirit Poles and Flying Pigs: Public Art and Cultural Democracy in American Communities*. Washington, D.C.: Smithsonian Institution Press, 1995.

Doughty, Robin W. *At Home in Texas: Early Views of the Land*. College Station: Texas A&M University Press, 1987.

Douglas, Mary. *Purity and Danger: An Analysis of Concepts of Pollution and Taboo*. New York: Praeger, 1966.

———. "Deciphering a Meal." *Daedalus. Journal of the American Academy of Arts and Sciences* 101 (1972): 61–81.

Duany, Andrés, Elizabeth Plater-Zyberk, and Jeff Speck. *Suburban Nation: The Rise of Sprawl and the Decline of the American Dream*. New York: North Point Press, 2000.

Duggan, Lou, and Jean Murph, eds. *The Citizens' Advocate Journal of Coppell History, Book I, Centennial Edition 1880–1990*. Coppell: Citizens' Advocate, 1990.

Duncan, James S., and Nancy G. Duncan. "Sense of Place as a Positional Good: Locating Bedford in Space and Time." In *Textures of Place: Exploring Humanist Geography*, edited by Paul Adams, Steven D. Hoelscher, and Karen E. Till, 41–54. Minneapolis: University of Minnesota Press, 2001.

Erlman, Veit. *Nightsong: Performance, Power, and Practice in South Africa*. Chicago: University of Chicago Press, 1996.

Escamilla, Patricia Baldwin. *Gilroy, California: A Short History*. Gilroy: Gilroy Historical Museum, 1997.

Eula, Michael J. "Failure of American Food Reformers Among Italian Immigrants in New York City, 1891–1897." *Italian Americana* (2000): 86–99.

Fabre-Vassas, Claudine. *The Singular Beast: Jews, Christians, and the Pig*. Translated by Carol Volk. New York: Columbia University Press, 1997.

Falassi, Alessandro. "Festival: Definition and Morphology." In *Time Out of Time: Essays on the Festival*, edited by Alessandro Falassi, 1–10. Albuquerque: University of New Mexico Press, 1987.

Farmer, Fannie Merritt. *The Boston Cooking-School Cook Book*. Boston: Little, Brown, 1896.

———. *The Boston Cooking-School Cook Book*. Boston: Little, Brown, 1912 [1906].

———. *The Boston Cooking-School Cook Book*. Boston: Little, Brown, 1933.

———. *The Boston Cooking-School Cook Book*. Edited by Wilma Perkins Lord. Boston: Little, Brown, 1951.

———. *The All New Fannie Farmer Boston Cooking-School Cookbook*. Edited by Wilma Perkins Lord. Boston: Little, Brown, 1959.

Featherstone, Mike. "Global Culture: An Introduction." In *Global Culture: Nationalism, Globalization and Modernity*, edited by Mike Featherstone, 1–14. London: Sage Publications, 1990.

Featherstone, Mike, and Scott Lash. "Globalization, Modernity and the Spatialization of Social Theory: An Introduction." In *Global Modernities*, edited by Mike Featherstone, Scott Lash, and Roland Robertson, 1–24. London: Sage Publications, 1995.

Federal Writers' Project. *The Italians of New York: A Survey Prepared by Workers of the Federal Writers Project, Works Progress Administration in the City of New York*. New York: Random House, 1938.

Fernandez, James W. *Persuasions and Performances: The Play of Tropes in Culture*. Bloomington: Indiana University Press, 1986.

Ferrero, Sylvia. "*Comida Sin Par*. Consumption of Mexican Food in Los Angeles: 'Foodscapes' in a Transnational Consumer Society." In *Food Nations: Selling Taste in Consumer Society*, edited by Warren Belasco and Philip Scranton, 194–219. New York: Routledge, 2002.

Flores, Richard R. *Los Pastores: History and Performance in the Mexican Shepherds' Play of South Texas*. Washington, D.C.: Smithsonian Institution Press, 1995.

Food Network. All American Festivals Episode FE1A01. In, Food Network web site, http://www.foodtv.com/food/show_fe/episode/0,1976,FOOD_9961_20517,00.html (accessed March 15, 2004).

Frazier, Ian. "Hogs Wild." *New Yorker*, December 12, 2005, 71–83.

Frenkel, Stephen, and Judy Walton. "Bavarian Leavenworth and the Symbolic Economy of a Theme Town." *Geographical Review* 90, no. 4 (2000): 559–585.

Gabaccia, Donna. *We Are What We Eat: Ethnic Food and the Making of Americans.* Cambridge: Harvard University Press, 1998.

Garrett, Dave. "Grapevine Springs Park." In *The Citizens' Advocate Journal of Coppell History, Book I, Centennial Edition 1880–1990*, 5–7. Coppell: Citizens' Advocate, 1990.

Geertz, Clifford. "Deep Play: Notes on the Balinese Cockfight." In *The Interpretation of Cultures*, edited by Clifford Geertz, 412–453. New York: Basic Books, 1973.

Gentry Foods. "Survey Shows 90% of Families Use Garlic." *Gentry Surrender*, November 1961.

Getz, Donald. "Special Events: Defining the Product." *Tourism Management* 10, no. 2 (1989): 125–137.

Gilroy Economic Development Corporation. "Gilroy EDC Celebrates Its 8th Program Year." *Gilroy Business Focus*, July 2004a, 3.

———. 2004b. Local Business, Economy. In, Gilroy Economic Development Corporation web site, www.gilroyedc.com/localbusiness.htm (accessed July 21, 2004).

Gilroy Garlic Festival Association. "Garlic Topping." *Gilroy Garlic Festival Program* (1986): 13.

Gilroy Garlic Festival Association Press Release, July 6, 2004. 2004. Penne Pasta con Pesto Is Perfect Example of Garlic Festival Evolution. In, Gilroy Garlic Festival web site, www.gilroygarlicfestival.com/pages/press.html (accessed September 1, 2004).

Gilroy Garlic Festival Committee. *The Garlic Lover's Cookbook from Gilroy, Garlic Capital of the World.* Berkeley: Celestial Arts, 1980.

———. *Garlic Lover's Greatest Hits: 20 Years of Prize-Winning Recipes from the Gilroy Garlic Festival.* Berkeley: Celestial Arts, 1998.

"Gilroy, Calif." *New York Times*, August 6, 1980, C6.

Gleason, Philip. "American Identity and Americanization." In *Harvard Encyclopedia of American Ethnic Groups*, edited by Stephen Thernstrom, 31–58. Cambridge: Belknap Press of Harvard University, 1980.

———. "Americans All: World War II and the Shaping of American Identity." *Review of Politics* 43 (1981): 483–518.

Goffman, Erving. *Frame Analysis: An Essay on the Organization of Experience.* New York: Harper & Row, 1974.

Goldman, Robert, and John Wilson. "Appearance and Essence: The Commodity Form Revealed in Perfume Advertisements." *Current Perspectives in Social Theory* 4 (1983): 119–142.

Gotham, Kevin. "Marketing Mardi Gras: Commodification, Spectacle and the Political Economy of Tourism in New Orleans." *Urban Studies* 39, no. 10 (2002): 1735–1756.

Gottdiener, Mark. *The Theming of America: Dreams, Visions and Commercial Spaces.* Boulder: Westview Press, 1997.

———. "Approaches to Consumption: Classical and Contemporary Perspectives." In *New Forms of Consumption: Consumers, Culture, and Commodification,* edited by Mark Gottdiener, 3–31. Lanham: Rowman and Littlefield, 2000a.

———. "The Consumption of Space and the Spaces of Consumption." In *New Forms of Consumption: Consumers, Culture, and Commodification* edited by Mark Gottdiener, 265–285. Lanham: Rowman and Littlefield, 2000b.

Griffith, Linda, and Fred Griffith. *Garlic, Garlic, Garlic: Exceptional Recipes from the World's Most Indispensable Ingredient.* Boston: Houghton Mifflin, 1998.

Gumina, Deanna Paoli. *The Italians of San Francisco 1850–1930 (Gli Italiani di San Francisco 1850–1930).* New York: Center for Migration Studies, 1978.

Haber, Barbara. *From Hardtack to Home Fries: An Uncommon History of American Cooks and Meals.* New York: Free Press, 2002.

Hannigan, John. *Fantasy City: Pleasure and Profit in the Postmodern Metropolis.* London: Routledge, 1998.

———. "Symposium on Branding, the Entertainment Economy and Urban Place Building: An Introduction." *International Journal of Urban and Regional Research* 27, no. 2 (2003): 352–360.

Harris, Lloyd John. *The Book of Garlic.* Berkeley: Aris Books, 1979 [1974].

———. *The Official Garlic Lovers Handbook.* Berkeley: Aris Books, 1986.

Harris, Marvin. *Cows, Pigs, Wars, and Witches: The Riddles of Culture.* New York: Random House, 1974.

———. *Good to Eat: Riddles of Food and Culture.* New York: Simon and Schuster, 1985.

Harrison, Fraser. *Strange Land: The Countryside: Myth and Reality.* London: Sidgwick & Jackson, 1982.

Harvey, David. *The Condition of Postmodernity: An Enquiry into the Origins of Cultural Change.* Oxford: Blackwell, 1989a.

———. "From Managerialism to Entrepreneurialism: The Transformation in Urban Governance in Late Capitalism." *Geografiska Annaler* 71 B, no. 1 (1989b): 3–17.

———. "From Space to Place and Back Again: Reflections on the Condition of Postmodernity." In *Mapping the Futures: Local Cultures, Global Change,* edited by Jon Bird, Barry Curtis, Tim Putnam, George Robertson, and Lisa Tickner, 3–29. London: Routledge, 1993.

———. "The New Urbanism and the Communitarian Trap." *Harvard Design Magazine,* Winter/Spring 1997, 1–3.

Haverluk, Terrence W. "Chile Peppers and Identity Construction in Pueblo, Colorado." *Journal for the Study of Food and Society* 6, no. 1 (2002): 45–59.

Hayden, Dolores. *The Power of Place: Urban Landscape as Public History.* Cambridge: MIT Press, 1995.

Heldke, Lisa. *Exotic Appetites: Ruminations of a Food Adventurer.* New York: Routledge, 2003.

Heller, Steve. "Appetite Appeal." *Social Research* 66, no. 1 (1999): 213–224.

Hellmuth, Obata + Kassabaum, Inc., and Lockwood, Andrews & Newman, Inc. "The Coppell Comprehensive Plan, City of Coppell, Texas." Coppell, 1996.

Higham, John. *Strangers in the Land: Patterns of American Nativism 1860–1925.* New Brunswick: Rutgers University Press, 1955.

Hobsbawn, Eric. "Introduction: Inventing Traditions." In *The Invention of Tradition,* edited by Eric Hobsbawn and Terence Ranger, 1–10. Cambridge: Cambridge University Press, 1983.

Hobsbawn, Eric, and Terence Ranger, eds. *The Invention of Tradition.* Cambridge: Cambridge University Press, 1983.

Hoelscher, Steven D. *Heritage on Stage: The Invention of Ethnic Place in America's Little Switzerland.* Madison: University of Wisconsin Press, 1998.

Hogan, Tim. "Pleasant Valley Promotion: The Story of Gilroy Boosterism, 1868–1907." In *Sketches of Gilroy,* edited by James C. Williams. Gilroy: Gilroy Historical Society, 1980.

Holcomb, Briavel. "Revisioning Place: De- and Re-constructing the Image of the Industrial City." In *Selling Places: The City as Cultural Capital, Past and Present,* edited by Gerry Kearns and Chris Philo, 133–144. Oxford: Pergamon Press, 1993.

Hoyt, Misty J. "Pigfest Part of Coppell History." *Coppell Gazette,* April 25, 1996, 2, 4.

HPC Publications. *Destination DFW.* Dallas: HPC Publications, 2002.

Hymes, Dell. "Competence and Performance in Linguistic Theory." In *Language Acquisition: Models and Methods,* edited by Renira Huxley and Elisabeth Ingram, 3–24. London: Academic Press, 1971.

———. "Breakthrough into Performance." In *Folklore: Performance and Communication,* edited by Dan Ben-Amos and Kenneth Goldstein. The Hague: Mouton, 1975.

Jacobson, Matthew Frye. *Whiteness of a Different Color: European Immigrants and the Alchemy of Race.* Cambridge: Harvard University Press, 1998.

Jameson, Frederic. "Nostalgia for the Present." *South Atlantic Quarterly* 88, no. 2 (1989): 517–537.

———. *Postmodernism, or the Cultural Logic of Late Capitalism.* Durham: Duke University Press, 1990.

Jankowski, Nicholas W. "Creating Community with Media: History, Theories and Scientific Investigations." In *Handbook of New Media: Social Shaping and Consequences of ICTs,* edited by Leah A. Lievrouw and Sonia Livingstone, 34–49. London: Sage Publications, 2002.

Jass, Stephanie J. "Recipes for Reform: Americanization and Foodways in Chicago Settlement Houses, 1890–1920." Ph.D. diss., Western Michigan University, 2004.

Jóhannesson, Gunnar Pór, Unnur Dís Skaptadóttir, and Karl Benediktsson. "Coping with Social Capital? The Cultural Economy of Tourism in the North." *Sociologia Ruralis* 43, no. 1 (2003): 3–16.

Judd, Dennis R., and Susan Fainstein, eds. *The Tourist City.* New Haven: Yale University Press, 1999.

Kalčik, Susan. "Ethnic Foodways in America: Symbol and Performance of Identity."
    In *Ethnic and Regional Foodways in the United States: The Performance of Group
    Identities*, edited by Linda Keller Brown and Kay Mussell, 37–65. Knoxville: University
    of Knoxville Press, 1984.
Kammen, Michael, ed. *Mystic Chords of Memory: The Transformation of Tradition in
    American Culture.* New York: Alfred A. Knopf, 1991.
Kapchan, Deborah A. "Performance." *Journal of American Folklore* (1995): 479–508.
———. *Gender on the Market: Moroccan Women and the Revoicing of Tradition.*
    Philadelphia: University of Pennsylvania Press, 1996.
Kearns, Gerry, and Chris Philo. "Culture, History, Capital: A Critical Introduction to
    the Selling of Places." In *Selling Places: The City as Cultural Capital, Past and Present*,
    edited by Gerry Kearns and Chris Philo, 1–32. Oxford: Pergamon Press, 1993a.
———, eds. *Selling Places: The City as Cultural Capital, Past and Present.* Oxford:
    Pergamon Press, 1993b.
Keen, Barbara. "Lost Food, Lost Connections." Paper presented at the Proceedings of
    the Wellington Symposium of Gastronomy, March 16–18, 2001, Wellington.
Kim, Joongsub, and Rachel Kaplan. "Physical and Psychological Factors in Sense of
    Community: New Urbanist Kentlands and Nearby Orchard Village." *Environment and
    Behavior* 36, no. 3 (2004): 313–340.
Kirshenblatt-Gimblett, Barbara. *Destination Culture: Tourism, Museums, and Heritage.*
    Berkeley: University of California Press, 1998.
Knobel, Dale T. *"America for the Americans": The Nativist Movement in the United
    States.* New York: Twayne Publishers, 1995.
Kugelmass, Jack. "Green Bagels: An Essay on Food, Nostalgia, and the Carnivalesque."
    Yivo Annual 19 (1990): 57–80.
Laderman, Carol. "Symbolic and Empirical Reality: A New Approach to the Analysis of
    Food Avoidances." *American Ethnologist* 8, no. 3 (1981): 468–493.
Lavenda, Robert H. "Festivals and the Creation of Public Culture: Whose Voice(s)?"
    In *Museums and Communities: The Politics of Public Culture*, edited by Ivan Karp,
    Christine Mullen Kraemer, and Steven D. Lavine, 76–104. Washington, D.C.:
    Smithsonian Institution Press, 1992.
———. " 'It's Not a Beauty Pageant!' Hybrid Ideology in Minnesota Community Queen
    Pageants." In *Beauty Queens on the Global Stage: Gender, Contests, and Power*, edited
    by Colleen Ballerino Cohen, Richard Wilk, and Beverly Stoeltje, 31–46. New York:
    Routledge, 1996.
———. *Corn Fests and Water Carnivals: Celebrating Community in Minnesota.*
    Washington, D.C.: Smithsonian Institution Press, 1997.
Leach, Edmund. "Anthropological Aspects of Language: Animal Categories and Verbal
    Abuse." In *New Directions in the Study of Language*, edited by E. H. Lenneberg, 23–63.
    Cambridge: MIT Press, 1964.
Lefebvre, Henri. *The Production of Space.* Oxford: Blackwell, 1991.

Levenstein, Harvey. "The American Response to Italian Food, 1880–1930." *Food and Foodways* 1 (1985): 1–24.

———. *Revolution at the Table: The Transformation of the American Diet.* Berkeley: University of California Press, 2003.

———. *Paradox of Plenty: A Social History of Eating in Modern America.* Berkeley: University of California Press, 2003 [1993].

Lewis, George H. "Celebrating Asparagus: Community and the Rationally Constructed Food Festival." *Journal of American Culture* 20, no. 4 (1997): 73–78.

———. "The Maine Lobster as Regional Icon: Competing Images over Time and Social Class." In *The Taste of American Place: A Reader on Regional and Ethnic Foods*, edited by Barbara G. Shortridge and James R. Shortridge, 65–83. Lanham: Rowman and Littlefield, 1998.

Lim, Louisa. "Ban Thwarts 'Year of the Pig' Ads in China." In *The World*, National Public Radio, 2007.

Limón, José E. "Carne, Carnales, and the Carnivalesque: Bakhtinian 'Batos,' Disorder, and Narrative Discourses." *American Ethnologist* 16, no. 3 (1989): 471–486.

Lindsey, Robert. "Garlic Town Savors the Smell of Success." *New York Times*, August 6, 1980, C1.

Linnekin, Jocelyn, and Richard Handler. "Tradition, Genuine or Spurious." *Journal of American Folklore* 97, no. 385 (1984): 273–290.

Lipsitz, George. *Time Passages: Collective Memory and American Popular Culture.* Minneapolis: University of Minnesota Press, 1990.

Lo Bello, Nino. "Breathtaking Possibilities, The World's Garlic Capital." *San Francisco Examiner and Chronicle*, September 10, 1978, 49.

Looney Ricks Kiss. "Old Coppell Master Plan Summary [brochure]." 2002.

Lowenthal, David. "Identity, Heritage, and History." In *Commemorations: The Politics of National Identity*, edited by John Gillis, 41–60. Princeton: Princeton University Press, 1994.

Lukes, Timothy J., and Gary Y. Okihiro. *Japanese Legacy: Farming and Community Life in California's Santa Clara Valley.* Cupertino: California Historical Society, 1985.

MacAloon, John J. "Introduction: Cultural Performance, Culture Theory." In *Rite, Drama, Festival, Spectacle: Rehearsals Toward a Theory of Cultural Performance*, edited by John J MacAloon, 1–15. Philadelphia: Institute for the Study of Human Issues, 1984a.

———. "Olympic Games and the Theory of Spectacle in Modern Societies." In *Rite, Drama, Festival, Spectacle: Rehearsals Toward a Theory of Cultural Performance*, edited by John J. MacAloon. Philadelphia: Institute for the Study of Human Issues, 1984b.

MacCannell, Dean. *The Tourist: A New Theory of the Leisure Class.* 2nd ed. New York: Schocken Books, 1989.

MacDougald, Duncan, Jr. "For Garlic Lovers Only." *Collier's*, January 20, 1956, 20.

Magliocco, Sabina. "Playing with Food: The Negotiation of Identity in the Ethnic Display Event by Italian Americans in Clinton, Indiana." In *The Taste of American Place: A Reader on Regional and Ethnic Foods*, edited by Barbara G. Shortridge and James R. Shortridge, 145–161. New York: Rowman and Littlefield, 1998.

———. "Garlic Festival I The Beginning." *Gilroy Dispatch*, July 3, 1979b, 2.

Manning, Frank, ed. *The Celebration of Society: Perspectives on Contemporary Cultural Performance*. Bowling Green: Bowling Green University Popular Press, 1983.

Marling, Karal Ann. *The Colossus of Roads: Myth and Symbol along the American Highway*. Minneapolis: University of Minnesota Press, 1984.

———. *Blue Ribbon: A Social and Pictorial History of the Minnesota State Fair*. Minneapolis: Minnesota Historical Society Press, 1990.

Marshall, Howard. "Meat Preservation on the Farm in Missouri's 'Little Dixie.'" *Journal of American Folklore* 92, no. 366 (1979): 400–417.

Massey, Doreen. "Questions of Locality." *Geography* 78, no. 338 (1993): 142–149.

McIntosh, Wayne, and Paul Harwood. "The Internet and America's Changing Sense of Community." *The Good Society* 11, no. 3 (2002): 25–28.

McLaughlin, Dr. A. J. [Allan]. "The American's Distrust of the Immigrant." *Popular Science Monthly*, January 1903, 230–236.

McLaughlin, Dr. Allan [A. J.]. "Italian and Other Latin Immigrants." *Popular Science Monthly*, August 1904, 341–349.

McMillan, David W. "Sense of Community." *Journal of Community Psychology* 24, no. 4 (1996): 315–325.

McMillan, David W., and David Chavis. "Sense of Community: A Definition and Theory." *Journal of Community Psychology* 14 (1986): 6–23.

Medigovich, Natalie. "Residents to Go Hog Wild over Pigfest Events." *Coppell Gazette*, April 18, 1996, 1A, 7A.

Mehren, Elizabeth. "Fame's Nothing to Sniff at in Gilroy." *The Washington Post*, August 7, 1979a, B1, B7.

———. "Gilroy—the Town That Clove to a Winner." *Los Angeles Times*, August 7, 1979b, 1,4.

———. "A Little Town Known Faaaar and Wiiiide." *The Tribune*, August 10, 1979c, D4.

Melone, Rudy. "Garlic Festival—The Beginning." In *1979 Festival Souvenir Program*, [unpaginated]. Gilroy: Gilroy Garlic Festival, 1979a.

Merton, Robert A. *Social Theory and Social Structure*. Glencoe: Free Press, 1957.

Meyer, Barbara Friedlander, and Bob Cato. *The Great Garlic Cookbook*. New York: Macmillan, 1975.

Midtgaard, Jenny. The Great Garlic Tale. In, Gilroy Garlic Festival web site, http://www.gilroygarlicfestival.com/pages/festivaltail.html (accessed March 15, 2004).

Mitchell, Don. *The Lie of the Land: Migrant Workers and the California Landscape*. Minneapolis: University of Minnesota Press, 1996.

Moore, Sally F., and Barbara G. Myerhoff. "Introduction: Secular Ritual: Forms and Meaning." In *Secular Ritual*, edited by Sally F. Moore and Barbara G. Myerhoff, 3–24. Assen/Amsterdam: Van Gorcum, 1977.

Morrison, Ellena F. "Citing Risks, Euless Cancels Arbor Daze." *Star-Telegram*, August 17, 2005, available online at http://www.dfw.com/mld/dfw/news/local/states/texas/northeast/12403489.htm (accessed August 17, 2005).

Myerhoff, Barbara G. "We Don't Wrap Herring in a Printed Page: Fusion, Fiction and Continuity in Secular Ritual." In *Secular Ritual*, edited by Sally F. Moore and Barbara G. Myerhoff, 199–224. Assen/Amsterdam: Van Gorcum, 1977.

Neely, Wayne Caldwell. *The Agricultural Fair*. New York: Columbia University Press, 1935.

Neuhaus, Jessamyn. *Manly Meals and Mom's Home Cooking: Cookbooks and Gender in Modern America*. Baltimore: Johns Hopkins University Press, 2003.

New Urbanism. [2005]. New Urbanism. In, New Urbanism web site, http://www.newurbanism.org/pages/416429/index.htm (accessed November 21, 2005.

Newman, Carol M. "What Is Gourmet?" *Art Culinaire*, no. 75 (2004): 32–71.

Nichols, Kathryn McKenzie. *Smell It Like It Is: Tales from the Garlic Capital of the World*. Santa Barbara: Fithian Press, 1991.

Nissenbaum, Stephen. *Sex, Diet, and Debility in Jacksonian America: Sylvester Graham and Health Reform*. Westport: Greenwood Press, 1980.

Noyes, Deborah. *Fire in the Placa: Catalan Festival Politics after Franco*. Philadelphia: University of Pennsylvania Press, 2003.

Oakes, Timothy. "Place and the Paradox of Modernity." *Annals of the Association of American Geographers* 87, no. 3 (1997): 509–531.

Office of Public Affairs, U.S. Department of Housing and Urban Development. "The Urban Fair: How Cities Celebrate Themselves." Washington, D.C.: U.S. Government Printing Office, 1981.

Otterloo, Anneke van. "The Riddle of Dutch Cuisine: National Taste and Global Trends." *Petits Propos Culinaires* 78 (2005): 39–51.

Ownby, Ted. "Harvest Celebration in the Rural South and the Challenge of Mass Culture, 1865–1920." In *Feats and Celebrations in North American Ethnic Communities*, edited by Ramón Gutiérrez and Geneviève Fabre. Albuquerque: University of New Mexico Press, 1995.

Paredes, Américo, and Richard Bauman, eds. *Toward New Perspectives in Folklore*. Austin: University of Texas Press for the American Folklore Society, 1972.

Pascoe, Craig S. "Barbeculture: Experiencing the South Through BBQ." Paper presented at the American Folklore Society Annual Meeting, Atlanta, Georgia, October 21, 2005.

Pedersen, Søren Buhl. "Place Branding: Giving the Region of Øresund a Competitive Edge." *Journal of Urban Technology* 11, no. 1 (2004): 77–95.

Pocock, Douglas. "The Senses in Focus." *Area* 25 (1995): 11–16.

Poe, Tracy. "The Labour and Leisure of Food Production as a Mode of Ethnic Identity Building among Italians in Chicago, 1890–1940." *Rethinking History* 5, no. 1 (2001): 131–148.

Porteous, J. Douglas. "Smellscape." *Progress in Human Geography* 9, no. 3 (1985): 356–378.

————. *Landscapes of the Mind: Worlds of Sense and Metaphor*. Toronto: University of Toronto Press, 1990.

Presbrey, Frank. *The History and Development of Advertising*. New York: Greenwood Press, 1968 [1929].

Prosterman, Leslie. *Ordinary Life, Festival Days: Aesthetics in the Midwestern County Fair*. Washington, D.C.: Smithsonian Institution Press, 1995.

Putnam, Robert D. *Bowling Alone: The Collapse and Revival of American Community*. New York: Simon and Schuster, 2000.

Radin, Paul. *The Italians of San Francisco, Their Adjustment and Acculturation*. Part 2/2 vols, *SERA: Cultural anthropology. Monograph no. 1, pt. 1–2*: n.p., 1935.

Rath, Richard Cullen. *How Early America Sounded*. Ithaca: Cornell University Press, 2003.

Rauche, Anthony T. "Festa Italiana in Hartford, Connecticut: The Pastries, the Pizza, and the People Who 'Parla Italiano.'" In *We Gather Together: Food and Festival in American Life*, edited by Theodore C. Humphrey and Lin T. Humphrey, 205–217. Ann Arbor: UMI Research Press, 1988.

Rebelloand, Kathy. "Aroma Swirls in Gilroy: Pungency Pays Off for This Old California Town." *USA Today*, July 25, 1986, 5B.

Relph, Edward C. *Place and Placelessness*. London: Pion, Ltd., 1976.

————. "Modernity and the Reclamation of Place." In *From Dwelling, Seeing, and Designing: Toward a Phenomenological Ecology*, edited by David Seamon, 25–40. Albany: State University of New York Press, 1993.

Renoux, Victoria. *For the Love of—Garlic: The Complete Guide To Garlic Cuisine*. Garden City Park: Square One Publishers, 2005.

Richter, Marice. "Coppell Hopes to Hog Attention—Community Will Kick off Pigfest next Weekend." *The Dallas Morning News*, April 21, 1996, 2T.

Riis, Jacob A. *How the Other Half Lives: Studies among the Tenements of New York*. New York: Dover Publications, 1971 [1890].

Rodaway, Paul. *Sensuous Geographies: Body, Sense and Place*. London: Routledge, 1994.

Rodriguez, Sylvia. "Ethnic Reconstruction in Contemporary Taos." *Journal of the Southwest* 32, no. 4 (1990): 541–555.

Root, Waverly, and Richard de Rochemont. *Eating in America: A History*. Hopewell, N.J.: The Ecco Press, 1995 [1976].

Rosenau, Pauline Vaillancourt. *The Competition Paradigm: America's Romance with Conflict, Contest, and Commerce*. Lanham: Rowman and Littlefield, 2003.

Rothman, Hal K. *Devil's Bargain: Tourism in the 20th Century American West*. Lawrence: University of Kansas Press, 1998.

Ryden, Kent C. *Mapping the Invisible Landscape: Folklore, Writing, and the Sense of Place*. Iowa City: University of Iowa Press, 1993.

Said, Edward W. *Orientalism*. New York: Pantheon Books, 1978.

Samuel L. Wyse Associates, and Rady and Associates Inc. *City of Coppell, Texas, Comprehensive Plan, 1972–1992*. Dallas: Samuel L. Wyse Associates, 1973.

Schultz, April R. *Ethnicity on Parade: Inventing the Norwegian-American through Celebration*. Amherst: University of Massachusetts Press, 1994.

Schwartz, Hillel. *Never Satisfied: A Cultural History of Diets, Fantasies, and Fat*. New York: Free Press, 1986.

Self-proclaimed Capitals of the World. In, Fact Index web site, http://www.factindex .com/s/se/self_proclaimed_capitals_of_the_world.html (accessed September 13, 2004).

Seremetakis, C. Nadia, ed. *The Senses Still: Perception and Memory as Material Culture in Modernity*. Boulder: Westview Press, 1994.

Shapiro, Laura. *Perfection Salad: Women and Cooking at the Turn of the Century*. New York: Farrar, Straus and Giroux, 1986.

———. *Something from the Oven: Reinventing Dinner in 1950s America*. New York: Viking, 2004.

Shortridge, Barbara G. "Ethnic Heritage Food in Lindsborg, Kansas, and New Glarus, Wisconsin." In *Culinary Tourism* edited by Lucy M. Long, 268–296. Lexington: University of Kentucky Press, 2004.

Shortridge, Barbara G., and James R. Shortridge. "Introduction: Food and American Culture." In *The Taste of American Place: A Reader on Regional and Ethnic Foods*, edited by Barbara G. Shortridge and James R. Shortridge, 1–18. Lanham: Rowman and Littlefield, 1998.

Shulman, Martha Rose. *Garlic Cookery*. New York: Thorsons Publishers, 1984.

Simnacher, Joe. "Pig Style: Festival-goers Go Hog Wild in Coppell." *The Dallas Morning News*, May 2, 1999, 39A.

Simoons, Frederick J. *Eat Not This Flesh: Food Avoidances from Prehistory to the Present*. Madison: University of Wisconsin Press, 1961.

Singer, Milton B. *Traditional India: Structure and Change*. Philadelphia: American Folklore Society, 1959.

———. *When a Great Tradition Modernizes*. New York: Praeger, 1972.

Sipos, Eric. "Pig Fest '97 This Weekend." *Coppell Gazette*, April 24, 1997, 1A, 10A.

Sklar, Kathryn Kish. *Catharine Beecher: A Study in American Domesticity*. New Haven: Yale University Press, 1973.

Sollors, Werner. *Beyond Ethnicity: Consent and Descent in American Culture*. New York: Oxford University Press, 1986.

———, ed. *The Invention of Ethnicity*. New York: Oxford University Press, 1989.

Sorkin, Michael, ed. *Variations on a Theme Park: Scenes from the New American City and the End of Public Space*. New York: Hill and Wang, 1992.

Spirn, Anne Whiston. *The Language of Landscape*. New Haven: Yale University Press, 1998.

Stacey, Michelle. *Consumed: Why Americans Love, Hate, and Fear Food*. New York: Simon and Schuster, 1994.

Stallybrass, Peter, and Allon White. *The Politics and Poetics of Transgression*. Ithaca: Cornell University Press, 1986.

Steinhardt, Anne. "There's More to Gilroy than Garlic." *San Jose Mercury News*, April 8, 1979, 26.

Stephenson, John B. "Escape to the Periphery: Commodifying Place in Rural Appalachia." *Appalachian Journal* 11 (Spring 1984): 187–200.

Stewart, Susan. *On Longing: Narratives of the Miniature, the Gigantic, the Souvenir, the Collection.* Baltimore: Johns Hopkins University Press, 1984.

Stoeltje, Beverly. "Riding and Roping and Reunion: Cowboy Festival." In *Time Out of Time: Essays on the Festival,* edited by Alessandro Falassi, 127–151. Albuquerque: University of New Mexico Press, 1987.

———. "Festival." In *International Encyclopedia of Communications,* edited by Erik Barnouw, 161–166. London: Oxford University Press, 1989.

———. "Power and Ritual Genres: American Rodeo." *Western Folklore* 52 (1993): 135–156.

Stoeltje, Beverly, and Richard Bauman. "Community Festival and the Enactment of Modernity." In *The Old Traditional Way of Life: Essays in Honor of Warren E. Roberts,* edited by Robert E. Walls and George H. Schoemaker, 159–171. Bloomington: Trickster Press, 1989.

Sutherland, Amy. *Cookoff: Recipe Fever in America.* New York: Viking, 2003.

Sutton, David E. *Remembrance of Repasts: An Anthropology of Food and Memory.* Oxford: Berg, 2001.

Symons, Michael. *One Continuous Picnic: A History of Eating in Australia.* Adelaide: Duck Press, 1982.

———. *A History of Cooks and Cooking.* Urbana: University of Illinois Press, 2000.

Tannahill, Reay. *Food in History.* New York: Three Rivers Press, 1988.

Teluja, Tad, ed. *Useable Past: Traditions and Group Expressions in North America.* Logan: Utah State University Press, 1997.

Theodoratus, Robert J. "Greek Immigrant Cuisine in America: Continuity and Change." In *Food in Perspective: Proceedings of the Third International Conference on Ethnological Food Research, Cardiff, Wales, 1977,* edited by Alexander Fenton and Trefor M. Owen, 313–323. Edinburgh, Scotland: J. Donald Publishers, 1981.

———. "The Changing Patterns of Greek Foodways in America." In *Food in Motion: The Migration of Foodstuffs and Cookery Techniques (Proceedings of the Oxford Symposium on Food and Cookery, 1983,* edited by Alan Davidson, 87–104. Leeds, England: Prospect Books, 1983.

Thrift, Nigel. "Images of Social Change." In *The Changing Social Structure,* edited by Chris Hamnett, Linda McDowell, and Philip Sarre, 12–42. London: Sage Publications, 1989.

Tognetti, Christine. "Small Idea Sparks Huge Garlic Interest." *Gilroy Dispatch,* July 2003, 25th Anniversary Keepsake Edition, commemorative section [unpaginated].

Tuan, Yi-Fu. "Place and Culture: Analeptic for Individuality and the World's Indifference." In *Mapping American Culture,* edited by Wayne Franklin and Michael Steiner, 27–49. Iowa City: University of Iowa Press, 1992.

Tumgoren, Serdar. The Top 10 Stories of 2004. In *Gilroy Dispatch*, Gilroy Dispatch web site, article dated January 3, 2005, www.gilroydispatch.com/article.asp?c=137978 (accessed March 14, 2005).

Turner, Rory, and Phillip H. McArthur. "Cultural Performances: Public Display Events and Festival." In *The Emergence of Folklore in Everyday Life: A Fieldguide and Sourcebook*, edited by George H. Schoemaker, 83–93. Bloomington: Trickster Press, 1990.

Turner, Terrence. "Transformation, Hierarchy and Transcendence: A Reformulation of Ven [sic] Gennep's Model of the Structure of Rites de Passage." In *Secular Ritual*, edited by Sally F. Moore and Barbara G. Myerhoff. Assen/Amsterdam: Van Gorcum, 1977.

Turner, Victor. *Schism and Continuity in an African Society: A Study of Ndembu Village Life*. Manchester, England: Manchester University Press, for the Rhodes-Livingstone Institute, 1957.

———. *The Ritual Process: Structure and Anti-Structure*. Ithaca: Cornell University Press, 1979 [1969].

———, ed. *Celebration: Studies in Festivity and Ritual*. Washington, D.C.: Smithsonian Institution Press, 1982.

Urry, John. *The Tourist Gaze: Leisure and Travel in Contemporary Societies*. London: Sage Publications, 1990.

U.S. Census Bureau. PHC-T-2 Ranking Tables for Metropolitan Areas, Table 3: Metropolitan Areas Ranked by Population: 2000. In, U.S. Census Bureau web site, http://www.census.gov (accessed August 16, 2005).

———. Table 66. Religious Preference, Church Membership 1980 to 2000. In, U.S. Census Bureau web site, http://www.census.gov (accessed August 23, 2005).

———. 2000a. Coppell (city), Texas. In, U.S. Census Bureau web site, http://quickfacts .census.gov/qfd/states/48/4816612.html (accessed August 16, 2005).

———. 2000b. Fact Sheet Coppell city, Texas. In, http://factfinder.census.gov (accessed August 16, 2005).

Van Esterik, Penny. "Celebrating Ethnicity: Ethnic Flavor in an Urban Festival." *Ethnic Groups* 4 (1982): 207–228.

Vashel, Maggie, and Robert Eggers. "The Good Old Days." In *When They Were Plums: A Collection of Memories*, edited by Class Members of Honors U.S. History 1985–86 Gilroy High School, 11–12. Gilroy: Gilroy High School, 1986.

Voight, Carolyn M. "You Are What You Eat: Contemplations on Civilizing the Palate with 'Gourmet.'" Master's thesis, McGill University, 1997.

Walker, Gary. Vichy, Capital of Free France compared to Gilroy, Garlic Capital of the World, 20-Sept-2003. In, Trekshare web site, http://www.trekshare.com/index .cfm?p1=48&journalid=7657 (accessed March 15, 2004).

Ward, Stephen W. *Selling Places: The Marketing and Promotion of Towns and Cities 1850–2000*. New York: Routledge, 2003.

Whorton, James C. *Crusaders for Fitness: The History of American Health Reformers*. Princeton: Princeton University Press, 1982.

Wilk, Richard R. "Food and Nationalism: The Origins of 'Belizean Food.'" In *Food Nations: Selling Taste in Consumer Societies*, edited by Warren Belasco and Philip Scranton, 67–89. New York: Routledge, 2002.

Wilson, Chris. *The Myth of Santa Fe: Creating a Regional Tradition*. Albuquerque: University of New Mexico Press, 1997.

Witt, Doris. *Black Hunger: Food and the Politics of U.S. Identity*. New York: Oxford University Press, 1999.

Wolfman, Judy. *Life on a Pig Farm*. Minneapolis: Carolrhoda Books, 2002.

Woods, Robert A. "Notes on the Italians in Boston." *Charities* (1904): 81.

Yancey, William L., Eugene P. Ericksen, and Richard N. Juliani. "Emergent Ethnicity: A Review and Reformulation." *American Sociological Review* 41, no. 3 (1976): 391–403.

Yans-McLaughlin, Virginia. *Family and Community: Italian Immigrants in Buffalo, 1830–1930*. Ithaca: Cornell University Press, 1977.

Young, Charles H., ed. *Grapevine Area History*. Edited by Grapevine Historical Society. Dallas: Taylor Publishing Company, 1979.

Zukin, Sharon. *Landscapes of Power: From Detroit to Disney World*. Berkeley: University of California Press, 1991.

———. *The Cultures of Cities*. Cambridge: Blackwell, 1995.

INDEX

—